COLBY JUNIOR COLLEGE

FRIENDS OF THE LIBRARY

MACKLIN'S
MONUMENTAL BRASSES

MACKLIN'S
Monumental Brasses

REVISED BY

JOHN PAGE-PHILLIPS

FREDERICK A. PRAEGER, *Publishers*
New York · Washington

BOOKS THAT MATTER

Published in the United States of America in 1969
by Frederick A. Praeger, Inc., Publishers
111 Fourth Avenue, New York, N.Y. 10003
Monumental Brasses by Herbert Macklin was first published in 1890
Revised editions appeared in 1913 (6th) and 1953 (7th)
This edition is extensively revised and rewritten
©1969 by George Allen & Unwin Ltd.

NB
1840
M3

Library of Congress Catalog Card Number: 74-84096

Printed in Great Britain

ACKNOWLEDGEMENTS

I am indebted to the Monumental Brass Society and to many people for help in rewriting this book, in particular to Adrian Baird, Claude Blair, G. H. S. Bushnell, H. K. Cameron, Madeleine Ginsberg, J. A. Goodall, J. Roger Greenwood, F. A. Greenhill, J. H. Hopkins, N. H. MacMichael, Malcolm Norris, Jane Plante, S. E. Rigold, Meg Rutherford for artwork, and my wife for much encouragement and help.

Jacket/cover: *Taking rubbings (left foreground) in the new church at Delft. Detail of a 17th cent. painting by Hendrik van Vliet. Collection of Lord Northbrook.* See p. 108.

Binding (Library Edition) : Unicorn from the brass of Thomas Chaucer, 1434, who is supposed to be a son of Geoffrey Chaucer, poet, Ewelme, Oxfordshire.

CONTENTS

ACKNOWLEDGEMENTS   *page* 7
ILLUSTRATIONS   11
INTRODUCTION   13
1 BRASS AND BRASSES FROM THE CONTINENT   15
   The Manufacture of Brass Sheet   15
   Franco-Flemish Tomb Manufacture   16

2 THE FIRST BRASSES ENGRAVED IN ENGLAND   21

3 THE LAST FRANCO-FLEMISH IMPORTS   29

4 BRASSES FROM FLANDERS   32

5 LONDON SCHOOLS OF BRASSES AFTER 1350   37

6 PROVINCIAL SCHOOLS OF BRASSES   45

7 FASHIONS IN DRESS   47
   Ecclesiastical Dress   48
      Mass Vestments   48
      Processional Vestments   53
      Monastic Dress   54
         Abbots
         Priors
         Monks
         Abbesses and Nuns
   Academic Dress   56
   Legal Dress   56
      Judges
      Sergeants-at-law
   Civilian Dress   58
      Shoes
   Men in Armour   61
   Feminine Dress   74
      Jewellery   78
   Chrysoms and Shrouds   81

8 LOST BRASSES AND PALIMPSESTS   83
   Lost Brasses   83
   Palimpsests   88

      Palimpsest Links   93
 9 THE CARE OF BRASSES   96

10 INSCRIPTIONS   97
      Shape of letter and Position   97
      Numerals   99
      Languages   99
      Facts and Sentiments Expressed   100

      Reading Inscriptions   101

11 HERALDRY   103

12 SAINTS   106

13 BRASS RUBBING   108

      BIBLIOGRAPHY   117
      COUNTY LISTS OF BRASSES   125
      INDEX   181

ILLUSTRATIONS

1   Franco-Flemish Brasses: Indents in Dun-
    drennan Abbey and Durham Cathedral   *page* 18
2   The Earliest English Brasses: Purbeck indent,
    ladies of *c.* 1320 and the earliest brass in
    England   22
3   Franco Flemish Brasses: From Higham Fer-
    rers, Northants, Islington and Rothwell,
    Northants   30
4   Flemish Brasses: Friezes from Flemish slabs
    and details from Flemish brasses in Yorkshire   34
5   Flemish Brass: Thomas Pownder, 1525   35
6   London Workshops: Different styles of en-
    graving   38
7   London Workshops: William Cure's work-
    shop   41
8   Ecclesiastical Dress: William de Grenfeld and
    William Ermyn   50
9   Ecclesiastical and Academic Dress: Richard
    Harward, a monk, a priest, a Bachelor of Art,
    a Master of Art and a Doctor of Divinity   55
10 Legal Dress: Sir John Cassey and his wife   57
11 Civilian Dress: Different gowns and hoods   60
12 Men in Armour: At the time of Edward II and
    Edward III   62
13 Men in Armour: At the time of Edward III and
    Henry IV   64
14 Men in Armour: At the time of Henry V and
    Henry VI   66
15 Men in Armour: At the time of Edward IV
    and Henry VII   68
16 Men in Armour: At the time of Edward VI
    and Elizabeth I   70

17 Men in Armour: At the time of Charles I   *page* 72

18 Feminine Dress: Head-dresses   75

19 Feminine Dress: Head-dresses   77

20 Jewellery   79

21 Lost Brasses: Weathercock from York Minster
and Lantern clock *c.* 1693   85

22 Lost Brasses: Gerard Visch de la Chapelle
identified by the arms on his dog   87

23 Palimpsests: At Yealmpton, Devon and Ewell,
Surrey   89

24 Palimpsests: Rejected versions and palimpsest links   92

25 Inscriptions: The development of lettering
in England and Flanders   98

26 Brass Rubbing: Iconoclastic destruction of
1566, compared with painting of children
grave rubbing in 1656   109

27 Brass Rubbing: Illustration of techniques   111

28 Present Distribution of pre-1700 Brasses   126

INTRODUCTION

The Rev. Herbert Macklin died in 1917, and his original book *Monumental Brasses* has passed through many editions since it first appeared in 1890. Although over the years, some revisions were made, the main text was kept intact. Charles Oman, formerly keeper of the Department of Metalwork at the Victoria and Albert Museum, was the last to edit this book in 1953, and in 1960.

Monumental Brasses was the first cheap handbook to appear on the subject, and even though others appeared on the scene later, it has retained its popularity for over seventy-five years. However so many new facts have come to light over the half-century since Macklin's death that in order to bring this new edition up to date the text has had to be drastically changed and re-written.

Origins

The origins of brasses are now better understood, although further research is by no means precluded. Macklin derived them from incised slabs and Limoges enamels. The first brasses were certainly a development from incised slab designs, making use of brass sheet from the continent, but Limoges enamels appear to have been more a parallel art form only occasionally used for 'monumental' purposes, in the twelfth century.

Late Brasses

Brasses are thought to have reached a peak in the decorated period of the fourteenth century, and more attention has been paid to earlier brasses than to late ones. The merits of late brasses of the seventeenth and eighteenth and even nineteenth centuries are now beginning to attract more attention. Nineteenth-century writers did not pay any attention to brasses so near their own times.

Styles and Workshops

The classification of brasses by styles and workshops is a modern approach to the subject. It seems helpful to be able to distinguish London from provincial work, and to see brasses through the eyes of the workshops, not simply arranged in geographical groups or by costume or with all the emphasis on the persons commemorated. A serious study of any other art form has emphasis on style, and it seems natural that this should be so for brasses. The foreign school that Macklin associated with Lubeck has since proved to be Flemish. The earlier and now very fragmentary Franco-Flemish series from the Tournai area is only now beginning to be known. This is due to palimpsest discoveries, the petrological examination of slabs and a greater knowledge of continental slabs.

Costume

Macklin devoted most space to describing the costume found on brasses—ecclesiastical, military and civilian. The names of items of dress, especially on military figures, do not tally with modern knowledge of the subject, and some names, therefore, have had to be changed. A note on shoes and jewellery has been added.

Palimpsest and County Lists

Many new palimpsests have been discovered but have been refixed so that they cannot be seen. Those that can be inspected are listed. The county lists of brasses have been completely revised, so that they are now the most up-to-date lists available. London has grown in size and eaten into neighbouring counties. To assist in identifying churches in London, the saints' dedication or the address of the church is given, and the churches are listed in a geographical instead of an alphabetical order.

Brass Rubbing

Methods and materials for brass rubbing have changed and there is a trend to rub positives rather than traditional black negatives that will no doubt continue. A note on the care of brasses and their slabs has been added.

I

Brass and Brasses from the Continent

THE MANUFACTURE OF BRASS SHEET

The making of brass in all its stages was one of the most complicated chemical manufacturing processes of medieval times and was not carried out in England until the late sixteenth century.

The story of monumental brasses begins on the continent where brass was one of many metal products developed in the area between Dinant on the Meuse and Cologne on the Rhine in the late twelfth or early thirteenth centuries. It was here that the necessary raw materials were brought together, copper mined from the Hartz mountains at Gozlar and carried by wagon and barge,[1] and calamine found more locally at Aachen. Albertus Magnus in his *Book of Minerals*[2] written in the thirteenth century described the process carried out on copper 'in Paris and Cologne and other places where I have been' to convert it to brass by means of powdered stone called calamine.

Medieval brass (latten) was an alloy of copper (at least 65 per cent) and zinc and the way it was made then is now called a cementation process. Calamine ore (i.e. zinc carbonate) was ground up and mixed with charcoal and small pieces of copper. Placed in a crucible these were heated sufficiently to distill out the zinc but not strongly enough to melt the copper. The zinc being volatile permeated the pieces of copper and formed brass. With increased heat the brass was melted and poured into moulds. While it was

[1] A long route. Perhaps copper was also mined nearer at hand?
[2] Translated by D. Wyckoff, O.U.P., 1967.

fairly simple to smelt the ores of copper or tin to produce a cake of metal, with zinc this was impossible since it had a much lower boiling point and 'smelted' away into the atmosphere leaving nothing in the hearth. Zinc in the form of metal was unknown in Europe until the sixteenth century.[1]

The moulds for making sheet brass for monumental brasses were probably shallow stone matrices into which the metal was poured to a depth of three to five millimetres. Subsequent hammering and polishing could reduce the thickness.

The earliest brass surviving in Europe is at Verden, near Bremen, West Germany to Bishop Yso Wilpe who died in 1231. The main part of the brass is a rectangular sheet about six feet long with many casting flaws. Judging from the size it was a special casting. It seems significant that it is beside a river flowing from the copper bearing Hartz mountains. In the Tournai area where demand for brass to decorate tomb slabs developed, a smaller sheet casting size evolved, perhaps governed by the weight or size that a man can conveniently handle, some three feet by two feet. Such sheets could be carried off from the foundries to the tomb workshops in France, Flanders, or England (chap. 2).

In the sixteenth century, Protestant England began to develop a policy of self sufficiency, especially for strategic raw materials such as brass, which was needed for ordnance, and while a certain amount of remelting and recasting of brass had gone on previously, it was only from this time that the search for raw materials and the complicated process of brass manufacture began in England.

FRANCO-FLEMISH TOMB MANUFACTURE

Since the first brass sheets used for English brasses were brought across the Channel it is logical to seek the origins of brasses not in England but on the Continent. There, brass sheet appears to have been called for by the makers of incised slabs in order to make a more varied and interesting (more expensive) inlay design.

Incised slabs were a type of monument that had increased in popularity in Western Europe from the twelfth century, and in the hinterland between France and Flanders, around Tournai, the masons found various ways of

---

[1] For more details see 'The metals used in monumental brasses' by H. K. Cameron, Ph.D., *M.B.S. Trans.* VIII, 109.

making such monotone slabs more attractive. By the mid thirteenth century they had developed a way of incising a figure on the slab and recessing white marble or other light-coloured inlays to show flesh. (E.g. Perone de Lerinne 1247. Creeny's *Incised Slabs*, p. 6.)

The first sheets of brass to be added to such slabs in Tournai may have been brought from the metal-working Dinant/Cologne area, but brass founders were established at an early date in Tournai. Among some 200 people there in 1305 listed to receive legacies from Jehan Bierenghiers were '*Sebelain de Bondues ki fait le laiton*' and '*Matiu le fondeur de laiton*'.[1]

With the invention of brass, metal figures could be added to the black marble. An abbot *c.* 1310 in the abbey of St Bavon, Ghent (Creeny's *Incised Slabs*, p. 31), was of white inlay and brass set in an intricately incised slab, with a brass fillet marginal inscription. A Tournai contract of 1311 engaged Jacques Couves to make such a slab for Canon Jean du Mur, archdeacon of Ghent, specifying a brass figure with alabaster inlays for face, hands and alb.[2]

The makers of these often elaborate and weightly slabs were confronted with considerable handling problems. But as brass inlay developed they never seem to have contemplated sending the engraved metal to a distant church to be set in local stone. Their product was the slab, and it was sent out with all the incising, and inlaid materials, complete. For large figures the sheets of brass were joined on the back with soldering bands. On matrices the deeper recesses for such bands can often be seen.

Very many tomb slabs made in the Tournai area seem to have been made of marble from Chercq or Antoing, a very short distance by river. One incised slab *c.* 1270 showing a priest with a tonsure, in civil dress, his feet on a dog, and a straight gable canopy above his head, was actually found at Antoing—it had never left the quarry. It is now in the Tournai museum.[3] The discovery of this tombstone ties up this style of figure and canopy with Tournai, and shows where some slabs were completed.

Tournai marble (blue stone, 'touch') varied in colour from black to light grey, and was quarried throughout the medieval period. A contract of 1536 for a Flemish brass for Sir William Sandys (d. 1540) (see *M.B.S Trans.* IX, 354–61) specified '*pierre d'Antoing*'. The brass has long disappeared

---

[1] Adolphe Hocquet. *Le Rayonnement de l'Art tournaisien aux XII et XIV siècles.*
[2] *Ibid.* p. 25.
[3] Illus. in R. M. Edleston's, *Supplement to Creeny*, pt II pl XXVII p. 79.

1 *Detail of Franco-Flemish indent in Dundrennan Abbey, Scotland, showing man in armour who had white inlay for face and hands,* c. *1320.*

2 *Franco-Flemish indent in Durham Cathedral to Bishop Louis de Beaumont 1333. According to H.E. Field* (M.B.S. Trans. *II, 291) a man unfit for the office of Bishop, who, unequal to his predecessors while living, planned to outshine them in death by ordering the largest and most elaborate brass in the country. Size about* $15\frac{1}{2} \times 9\frac{1}{2}$ *ft.*

but remains of Antoing marble belonging to the monument can still be seen in a ruined chapel in Basingstoke (Hants) town cemetary.

The variety and magnificence of the early slabs evidently appealed to people in England, and their success is seen in the way the masons sold their skill not only locally but across the Channel.[1] With their size and weight it is significant that they are found mainly in churches near the coast, along the south and eastern seaboards and as far north as Scotland. Since they are so ancient very few examples of the metal parts survive, but the slabs have often remained functional as paving, and can still be discovered, cut down, turned over or worn smooth by the passage of feet. The texture of the marble and the shapes of the matrices are clues to origins and date. There are examples in Scotland at Dundrennan Abbey (detail illustrated p. 18) (two knights and ladies c. 1320) St Johns' Perth (civilian and wife c. 1360) and Whithorn Priory, Wigtownshire (mitred figure c. 1360). In England the finest is an indent in Durham Cathedral to Bishop Louis de Beaumont, 1333 (illustrated p. 18). Other indents are at Winchelsea, Thornton Abbey, Lincs. (in the open air) and several in Boston, Lincs. The finest tomb with the brass still surviving is unquestionably at Higham Ferrers. Northants (illustrated p. 30). Lawrence de St Maur (Seymour) 1337 stands in mass vestments within an elaborate canopy. The brass of John de Grofhurst c. 1340 (relaid in 1867) at Horsmonden, Kent shows a figure, similarly clad, that may belong to the Franco-Flemish series.

To summarise the characteristics of these imported brasses, they were full length figures, sometimes with white inlay for flesh (Dundrennan Abbey) with narrower border inscription fillets and straight-sided or ogee arched gable canopies. A rose window might be placed under the gable with censing angels on or above. There were many variations, with more elaborate canopies with flying buttresses and saints. Designs became more elaborate as time passed and could always be more lavish for a special person.

As well as deriving brasses from incised slabs—which is quite clearly correct—some writers have also derived them from Limoges enamels, and pointed to such enamel plaques as that commemorating Geoffrey Planta-ganet, 1155–1180, in the Le Mans museum. This is small, from the side of

---

[1] The import of Tournai marble tombs can be traced back well before the import of brasses. Tournai marble tombs in Salisbury Cathedral (Bishop Roger of Sarum) Ely Cathedral (St Michael holding a soul) and Southover, Lewes, (Gundrada, wife of William de Warenne, Count of Warenne in Normandy) are all c. 1150.

a long 'casket' tomb.[1] There were life-size enamelled copper tombs in France at places such as the Abbey of Fontaine Daniel, Mayenne, and the Abbey of Evron, Mayenne. However these are all much earlier (twelfth century) than the brasses we have been discussing and were not entirely flat monuments. They do not seem to lead on to brasses where the only use of enamelling may have been to show heraldry on a few ailettes and shields. Two men in armour *c.* 1325 at the Abbey of Ourscamp, Oise[3] may be French examples where shields and ailettes (shown as indents on the drawing) were enamelled copper. These parts only seem to have held metal and the rest of the figures seem to have been incised. Limoges enamels although used for monuments in the mid twelfth century became more applied to three dimensional objects such as caskets, reliquaries, and candlesticks. Limoges monuments were always rare and the main occupation of the enamellers was the production of domestic and church utensils.

[1] R. de Gaignières, vol 14 pp. 190, 191.
[2] *Ibid.* vol. 14 pp. 192, 200, 205.
[3] *Ibid.*vol. 13 p. 84.

2

The First Brasses Engraved in England

EARLY DESIGNS

As we have already shown, brass was a foreign product and many early brasses in England from *c.* 1320 were foreign, set in foreign marble. However we can find earlier brasses (or matrices) in England that show English designs from *c.* 1275. These can be derived from the English incised or low relief slabs of the thirteenth century whose design characteristics were long slender crosses, with or without a simple Lombardic inscription. Sometimes a symbol such as a sword or chalice indicated the occupation of the deceased. These slabs were usually coffin lids, and as such, were coffin-shaped— wider at the head than the foot.

The earliest of all the brasses in the country, with brass surviving, are two coffin-shaped slabs each with part of a brass cross and Lombardic inscription to the two children of William de Valence (Henry III's half brother), Margaret, 1276, and John 1277, in Westminster Abbey. The floor of this part of the Abbey had been set with glass mosaic by the Cosmati family who had come over from Rome in 1259. Where the children were buried their slabs broke up part of this flooring, but pieces of mosaic were used on one of the slabs between the cross and the inscription, perhaps to blend it in with the rest of the floor (illustration p. 22). It seems likely that the slab with the mosaic and centre line position in the floor was the first burial, and should therefore be attributed to Margaret.[1]

---

[1] In the Royal Commission of Historical Monuments volume for Westminster Abbey it is attributed to John. (Information supplied by Mr N. H. MacMichael, Keeper of the Muniments.)

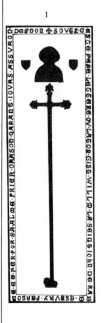

1

2

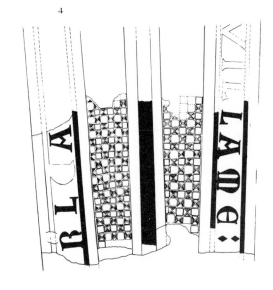

3

4

1 *Purbeck indent* c. *1325 to Wm. de St John, Ramsbury, Wilts, with inscription mentioning letters of laton.*

2 & 3 *Ladies probably from cross brasses* c. *1320.* (2) *Pitstone, Bucks, 12 in. high. Dug up in churchyard, 1935.* (3) *Sedgefield, Durham. 11 in. high.* (2) *perhaps from the head of a cross and* (3) *from the foot.*

4 *The earliest brass (with metal surviving) in England. Coffin shaped Purbeck slab to Margaret, dau. of Wm. de Valence, 1276. Cross and letters of brass with white, red and gold glass mosaic between.*
Westminster Abbey, London.

When Henry V's chapel was built a step was placed across their coffin slabs so that only a portion can be seen (and that is kept permanently covered).

A coffin slab of similar date, *c.* 1275, once held eighty letters (no cross or other decoration) at Hook Norton, Oxon. Their poor alignment suggests that the mason who chipped out their matrices was illiterate.[1]

At Dean, Beds., we can see the largest collection of actual brass letters *c.* 1300; fourteen letters and four stops, which separate words like colons. They have been preserved in a coffin-shaped slab, and were buried above floor level in the wall of the church, until uncovered in 1934. Faint guidelines which helped the mason to align the letters can still be seen.

An examination of loose letters in the Cambridge Archaeological and Ethnological Museum and in Westminster Abbey shows that they were cut from sheet metal. This was certainly manufactured and probably cast on the Continent. The letters were only held by bitumen—no rivets existed in England at this date—and were easily loosened and lost. A fragment of a slab *c.* 1280, at Santarem, Portugal. (*M.B.S. Trans.* IX, 39–42) is an example of an exported Franco-Flemish incised slab that held separate inlay brass letters (parts of eleven still remaining) round the margin. This is precious and undeniable evidence that the first separate brass letters used for inscriptions in England were inspired by Continental examples.

The Santarem letters appear to have been held only by small brass dowels while the English letters were held only by bitumen. A Purbeck slab in Ramsbury, Wilts., shows a half effigy above a cross *c.* 1325. Round the slab runs an inscription '*SOUTZ CESTE PERE LETTERE OV LATON GIST WILLM LA SEINT JOHN. . . .*' (under this stone lettered with laton lies William de St John) but not a single brass letter remains.

Late thirteenth-century English brasses with brass Lombardic letters, and perhaps crosses, made use of little metal. In the period *c.* 1300–25 it seems that heads or half effigies, almost life size, were incorporated into the design, either above the cross, as at Ramsbury, or in the cross head (Richard de Hakebourne 1322, Merton College, Oxford). An indent in Salisbury Cathedral *c.* 1320, shows a bishop's half effigy superimposed on a cross, and a long crozier.[2]

By *c.* 1310 we find two developments, one is the full length brass figure which, as it were, blots out the cross completely, and the other is the setting

[1] *M.B.S. Trans.* VIII, 205.
[2] Perhaps Bishop Mortival 1330; not a mid thirteenth-century bishop as suggested by E. Kite.

of diminutive figures either in the cross head or at the base of the cross. It seems probable that the earliest examples of diminutive figures are at Pitstone, Bucks. (a standing lady) dug up in the churchyard in 1935, and at Sedgefield, Durham (a kneeling lady) both *c.* 1315.

Another development which affects cross brasses and full length brass figures alike is the introduction of canopies. These reflect the architecture of the period and surround the figures rather like a frame round a picture. A cross indent at Wotton-under-Edge, Glos., *c.* 1320, shows a kneeling figure of R. de Wotton, rector, under a little canopy at the foot of the cross. The shaft of the cross is a label bearing his prayer '*Sis michi virgo pia dux et lux sancta mrie*',[1] with a seated Virgin in the middle of the cross head. Often the stem of a cross led up to a bracket supporting, instead of a cross head, a canopy over a small figure. Sometimes this was the deceased, and sometimes the Virgin and Child. (Indent in Lincoln Cathedral *c.* 1370 *M.B.S. Portfolio*, vol. IV, pl. 23) or the Trinity, with the deceased kneeling below. The canopy, even on a bracket brass could enclose both bracket and stem (Clifton Campville, Staffs. *c.* 1360 *M.B.S. Portfolio* vol. V, pl. 61) just as it could enclose a full length figure (Trotton, Sussex, *c.* 1310).

THE EARLIEST MILITARY FIGURES AND THEIR DATES

The dates given to early military figures need careful re-checking. Confusion can arise where a son had brasses made for himself and his father at the same time, so that dates of death can differ by a generation from the date of engraving. (E.g. Setvans brasses at Chartham and Canterbury Cathedral, both in Kent, could be to father and son.) Sometimes the date of a brass has been guessed and aligned with the wrong name in a family tree (Stoke d'Abernon, where eldest sons bore the same Christian names?). It seems that, in this sort of way, several of the large early knights have been dated too early—so far as the dates of engraving are concerned.

The following grouping is tentatively suggested:

c. 1300
Surrey, Stoke d'Abernon, Sir John Daubernon.
Cambs., Trumpington, Sir Roger de Trumpington.
Staffs., Clifton Campville, part of a large cross-legged knight on back of a 1360 brass.
Suffolk, Pettaugh, fragment of surcoat on back of a brass *c.* 1530.

[1] 'Pious Virgin, Holy Mary, be my guide and light.'

c. 1310

Lincs., Croft, half effigy.

c. 1320

Lincs., Buslingthorpe, Sir Rich. de Boselyngthorpe, half effigy.

Kent, Chartham, Sir Robt. de Setvans 1306.

Suffolk, Acton, Sir Robt. de Bures 1331 (see *M.B.S. Trans.* X, 144).

Suffolk, Gorleston, Sir —— de Bacon.

Essex, Pebmarsh, Sir Wm. Fitzralph 1323.

c. 1330

Kent, Minster in Sheppey, Sir John de Northwoode (?) A lady. Both French work.

Cambs., Westley Waterless, Sir John de Creke and wife.

Bucks., Edlesborough, 1540, and Crowan, Cornwall, *c.* 1550, palimp. frags. possibly of same man in surcoat showing area near shoulder and a foot.

Surrey, Stoke d'Abernon, Sir John Daubernoun, 1327.

c. 1350

Norfolk, Elsing, Sir Hugh Hastings, 1347.

Essex, Wimbish, Sir John de Wautone 1347 and w. in head of cross.

Essex, Bowers Gifford, Sir John Gifford 1348 (re-laid).

INDENTS OF MILITARY BRASSES
(all examples of full length figures)

c. 1310

Notts, Hawton, Sir Robt. de Cumpton, 1308.

Oxon, Aston Rowant, Sir Hugh le Blount, 1314.

c. 1320

Cambs., Whaddon, Thos d'Eschallers and w. 1306 (*M.B.S. Trans.* VIII, 349).

Kent, Canterbury Cathedral, (not an indent but a silhouette on the wall where the brass had been fixed. See *Archaeologia Cantiana*, LXV, 138). Possibly Sir Wm. de Septvans 1323 who perhaps ordered the brass for his father, d. 1306, at Chartham in *c.* 1320.

Norfolk, Emneth, Sir Adam de Hakebech.

Lincs., Norton Disney, Sir Wm. d'Iseni.

Suffolk, Stoke by Nayland, Sir John de Peytone.

WORKSHOPS

The list of indents could be extended. They help to give a truer picture of the production of military figures.

To summarise—up to and including the *c.* 1310 group, we have full-length brass figures all set in Purbeck marble, and almost certainly made in London. Some slabs are coffin-shaped and some rectangular; there are separate Lombardic letters on all.

If the use of enamel on the copper shield at Stoke d'Abernon seems to show French influence the designs of this and the *c.* 1310 group are English, set in Purbeck slabs. They appear to be the work of several artists and at least two workshops, perhaps distinguished by their respective use of lighter or darker Purbeck. (*M.B.S. Trans.* X, 285.)

The *c.* 1320 group marks the change to brass fillet inscriptions, some slabs showing separate letters and some the fillets.

The draughtsmanship of the *c.* 1330 group (excluding the Minster in Sheppey brasses) with long thin figures, is finer than the earlier group and appears to be the work of one artist. A double canopy has disappeared from the Westley Waterless brass, but its shape can be imagined from a palimpsest at Norbury, Derbyshire, and the type of marginal inscription—Lombardic letters on a narrow brass fillet. Great interest has been shown in the stamped mark on the Westley Waterless brass, showing an inverted 'N', two stars [*sic*] and a mallet, near the lady's feet. They were thought to be an engravers mark, but the engraving partly obliterates the stamp, suggesting that it must have been made earlier.

The Minister in Sheppey figures (these are two separate brasses) are by a different artist, and have been relaid. They are probably French, judging from the lady's dress and low-slung shield on the man. (Compare these details on a French incised slab to Sir Pierre de Chantemelle, 1352, and wife, in the Cluny Museum, Paris.)

The *c.* 1350 group, all attributable to one artist, are three of the most beautiful English brasses and are typical of the Decorated style. The Elsing and Wimbish figures rest more weight on one foot so that the body sways gracefully. This same stance can be seen in stained glass and manuscripts of the period, and suggests that the brasses were the work of Westminster or Court craftsmen. At Elsing the canopy is remarkably similar in design to the canopy above Aymer de Valence's tomb, 1324, in Westminster Abbey.[1] St George on horseback under the gable at Elsing compares with Aymer on horseback, the brackets at Elsing which once supported figures above the gable can be seen at Westminster where they once supported angels holding candlesticks.

THE EARLIEST ECCLESIASTICAL FIGURES AND THEIR DATES

To gain a fuller picture of native brass production in the period 1300–50 we should remember the great toll of ecclesiastical brasses at the Dissolution.

[1] Illustration in A. Gardner, *English Medieval Sculpture*, pl. 358, 1951 Ed.

Many of the full-length figures with lions at their feet were bishops, abbots and priests. The evidence of palimpsests and indents, as well as surviving brasses, is gathered below and shows a group of full-length figures *c.* 1310, that must have formed as impressive an array as the knights. Wm. de Grenefeld (illustration p. 50) survives in part to show this magnificence. Other surviving ecclesiastical brasses are only heads or half effigies.

LISTS OF ECCLESIASTICS UP TO THE BLACK DEATH, GROUPED BY DATES OF ENGRAVING

BRASSES (where any metal part of the effigy survives).
c. 1310
Yorks., York Minster, Wm. de Grenefeld, 1314, archbishop, in mass vests.
c. 1320
Cambs., Burwell, 1542, palimp. frag. of face and amice, broken into four pieces and dalmatic with maniple and orphreys. All *c.* 1320.
Devon, Stoke-in-Teignhead, priest in mass vests. Once in cross.
Kent, Ashford, head of priest.
Kent, Woodchurch, Nichol de Gore, half eff. of priest in cross.
Norfolk, Norwich, St John the Baptist, Maddermarket, 1558, palimp. frags. of abbot in mass vests.
Norfolk, Ingham, 1466, palimp. frag. of bishop or abbot showing gloved hand and maniple.
Oxford, Merton Coll., Rich. de Hakebourne 1322, head of priest in cross.
Oxon., Chinnor, head of priest in cross.
c. 1330
Bucks., Twyford, 1550, palimp. frag. of priest in mass vests.
Northants, Charwelton, *c.* 1520, palimp. frag. of priest in mass vests.
c. 1340
Essex, Corringham, half eff. of priest.
Herts. Wyddiall, 1546, palimp. frag. of bishop or abbot with vexillum.
Northants, Gt Brington, 1344, half eff. of priest in mass vest. on bracket.
Kent, Kemsing, 1347, half eff. of priest.

INDENTS (all examples are full length figures).
c. 1300
Cambs., Bottisham, Sir Elyas de Bekingham, 1298, judge in mass vests.
Cambs., Ely Cathedral, Bishop Wm. de Luda, 1298.
c. 1310
Dorset, Milton Abbey, Abbot Walter de Sydling, tonsured figure in mass vests. on animal.

Dorset, Bindon Abbey, Abbot Rich. de Maners, tonsured figure in mass vests on animal.

Somerset, Wells Cathedral, Bishop Walter de Heselshaw 1308.

Suffolk, Oulton, Adam de Bacon, in mass vests. on animal. Brass stolen 1857.

Herts., St Albans Abbey, Abbot John Berkhamstede 1302.

Wales, Llanfaes, Anglesey, Lower half of archdeacon of Anglesey, on lion.

c. 1320

Herefordshire, Hereford Cathedral, Bishop St Thos. de Cantilupe, 1282 canonized 1320, and shrine completed 1349. Indent of fillet inscr. suggests brass engr. not earlier than *c.* 1325.

Norfolk, Harpley, John de Gurnay, d. 1332 in mass vests. Tomb earlier.

Kent, Hever, priest in mass vests.

Kent, Saltwood, priest in mass vests.

c. 1330

Northants, Peterborough Cathedral, Abbot Godfrey de Croyland, 1329, in mass vest.

Norfolk, Redenhall, Wm. de Neuport in mass vests.

Herts, St Albans Abbey, Abbot Rich. Wallingford, 1335.

THE EARLIEST LADIES
(full length figures)

The earliest life-size figure is at Trotton, Sussex, Lady Margt. de Camoys, *c.* 1310, whose dress was sprinkled with small heraldic shields which are now lost. These may have been made of coloured glass placed on white composition backgrounds. The figure of Dame Jone de Kobeham, Cobham, Kent, is of similar date, although she died before 1298.

Indents of full-length figures of ladies can be seen at Weekley, Northants, Dame Anneys wife of Sir Mauger le Vavasour, *c.* 1310, and Tewkesbury Abbey, Glos., Lady Maud de Burgh, 1315.

Palimpsest fragments of ladies engraved *c.* 1330, have been found at Norbury, Derbyshire, 1538, probably showing one of the wives of Sir Theobaud de Verdun, 1316, who was buried in Croxden Abbey (*cf.* the lady at Westley Waterless, Cambs.) and parts of another lady behind brasses at Little Walsingham, Norfolk, *c.* 1540, and a lost inscr. to Charlis Clayden 1545. (*M.B.S. Trans.* X, 206, and IX, 198.)

3
The Last Franco-Flemish Imports

The Black Death which reached England in 1348 is thought to have killed as much as half the population. There was an acute shortage of labour and villages and churches in some areas were allowed to fall derelict. A brass from such a church may be the knight used to make the bracket brass *c.* 1360 at Clifton Campville, Staffs.

Imports of Franco-Flemish brasses seem to have dwindled and continuity with the earlier series is partly lost. Draughtsmanship is poor and totally eclipsed by purely Flemish-style brasses, made perhaps in the area of Ghent or Bruges (see chap. 4). In England too, judging from the evidence that remains, continuity with earlier brasses is lost. The small mutilated knight at Bodiam, Sussex, *c.* 1360, and a London fishmonger at Taplow, Bucks. *c.* 1350, are the only evidence of good London work.

The brass at Rothwell, Northants, 1361, appears to be an import; Wm. de Rothewelle, wearing surplice and almuce, rests his head on a cushion supported by angels (illustration p. 30). These have been thought to show Flemish influence but are more closely derived from the large censing angels of earlier Franco-Flemish slabs. The design is poorly drawn and entirely lacks the competence of contemporary Flemish brasses. A Tournai slab was imported for Sir John Matravers, Dorset, 1364, in Lytchett Matravers, Dorset. It is heralidic with a Matravers fret and marginal inscription set in narrow brass fillets.

Proof of other imports of Franco-Flemish brasses lies in palimpsests behind brasses made mainly between 1520 and 1560, using monastic spoil. At St Mary Islington, London, 1540, and Isleworth, Middx., 1544,

2 *Franco-Flemish fragment* c. *1350 on the back of a brass to Robt. Fowler and w. 1540 St Mary Islington, London, N.1. 11 in. wide.*

3 *Detail of Wm. de Rothewelle 1361 Archdeacon of Essex, Rothwell, Northants. Probably Franco-Flemish.*

1 *The finest Franco-Flemish brass remaining in England. Laurence de St Maur, rector, 1337, Higham Ferrers, Northants. 6 ft. 4 in. × 2 ft. 9 in.*

are parts of a Franco-Flemish brass (probably the same brass but this cannot yet be proved) *c.* 1350 (illustration p. 30). Characteristics are a rose window and a large censing angel on a gable roof. The Isleworth fragment shows a saint in a canopy identified as St Simon because his clause of the Creed is inscribed on a tablet that he holds. The name of a saint above this fragment is given in Lombardic capitals, 'BARTELOMEVS', an untypical feature, but useful because Lombardic letters suggest a date before *c.* 1360.

To summarize, therefore, information about Franco-Flemish brasses has remained scanty because they were sent over to England up to *c.* 1370, and very few of these brasses survive. Their origins have seldom been recognized as there is so little with which to compare them in France. However, a number of these brasses and incised slabs survived in France up to the time of the Revolution, in 1791, and were sketched before then for Roger de Gagnières (1642–1715). The drawings which he presented to Louis XIV in 1711 are now divided between the Bibliothèque Nationale, Paris, and the Bodleian Library, Oxford. Further, a great number of indents and incised slabs still remain in the area. The Franco-Flemish series has been overlooked because it differed less in style and design from English brasses. Attention has been drawn away by Flemish brasses which differ far more and are consequently more easily recognized as foreign.

4
Brasses from Flanders

As the fourteenth century progressed the traffic in copper from the Hartz mountains was oriented more and more towards Flanders and England. Copper was also mined in Scandinavia and shipped to Bruges. Finished metal articles were sent to England, and the Hanseatic league developed an intense traffic between Flanders and England, Germany, Scandinavia, France, and Spain. Flemish brasses set in Tournai marble slabs were one of the many cargoes carried on ships like that partly shown on the back of a Flemish brass at Topcliffe, Yorks. (see illustration). The international spread of Flemish brasses, undoubtedly as a result of the league's network,

Part of a kogge or trading ship used by Hansa merchants, discovered on the back of a 1391 Flemish brass at Topcliffe, Yorks. Perhaps part of a ship owner's brass. The only actual kogge so far discovered is at Bremen.

(some were made for its merchants) is proved by examples found in Norway, Poland, Finland, Germany, Denmark, Holland, Spain, Portugal, Madeira and Italy (a metal icon or tryptich). The earliest on the Continent may be that in Denmark, to King Eric Menved and Queen Ingeborg who both died in 1319. The general similarities between the faces of the king (restored 1883) and queen (face original) which were of marble inlay, and the presence of censing angels on the flying buttresses (very similar to the censing angels on Franco-Flemish slabs) show that the Flemish school was influenced by, or even developed from, the Franco-Flemish school. Flemish brasses must have been made not far from the others, possibly in Ghent or Bruges, and both used the same sources for marble. Antoing, Tournai, Ghent and Antwerp all lie on the river Scheldt, and Bruges was a short distance further by sea.

Flemish brasses can be found in England at the following places:

Kings Lynn, Norfolk, 1349 and 1364. (Sizes 9 feet 10 inches × 5 feet 8 inches and 8 feet 11 inches × 5 feet 1 inch.)
St Albans Abbey, Herts., Abbot Delamere, 1396, abbot for 47 years, ordered brasses for himself and his predecessor, Abbot Mentmore c.1360. Only Delamere's survives, size 9 feet 3 inches × 4 feet 4 inches, relaid.
Wensley, Yorks, c. 1360.
North Mymms, Herts., 1361 (now mural).
Aveley, Essex, 1370 (small).
Newark, Notts., c. 1375 (size 9 feet 4 inches × 5 feet 7 inches).
Topcliffe, Yorks, 1391 (now mural).
All Saints, Newcastle-on-Tyne, Northumberland, 1429 (now mural behind glass).
The Museum, Ipswich, Suffolk, 1525.
Fulham, Middx., 1529.
All Hallows, Barking, London, 1533.

These brasses are mostly dedicated to rich merchants who would have had connection with Flanders, or Flemings who died in England, or rich clergy. Some are very large in area such as those at Kings Lynn, St Albans, and Newark, and were some of the most luxurious forms of monument. The style of engraving has been much admired for its intricate detail and sure draughtsmanship. But as time passed the repetitive detail lacked freshness and originality. The fourteenth-century diaper patterns were more or less repeated in the fifteenth century. Fresh inspiration came from paintings in the sixteenth century, perhaps even from paintings by the husband of

1 & 4 *Friezes from the margins of Flemish slabs* (1) *in brass, Adam de Walsokne, 1349, St Margaret's, Kings Lynn, Norfolk, and* (4) *in Tournai marble, now part of an altar tomb in Ripon Cathedral, Yorks.*

2 & 3 *Details from Flemish brasses in Yorkshire* (2) *at Wensley, and* (3) *at Topcliffe. The 'violin' lips are peculiar to the Flemish style.*

Thomas Pownder, 1525, with his wife Emme. Merchants mark and arms of Ipswich and Merchant Adventurers. Ipswich museum, Suffolk. Once in St Mary Quay, Ipswich.

Margaret Hornebolt (her brass is at Fulham). The similarities between paintings and brasses in Flanders can be seen on pp. 87 and 89.

Flemish brasses are most commonly distinguished from English brasses by the criterion that on Flemish examples the metal covers the whole slab while English examples are cut out figures in stone backgrounds. This is not, however, altogether true. Flemish cut-out figures can be seen at Wensley and North Mymms, in England, and Wm. Wenemaer is a fine example in Ghent museum in Belgium. The North Mymms figure must have originally stood on a slender stem to give it the familiar 'bracket' design, but the original slab no longer remains.

Many other Flemish brasses were imported, and some proof of this is given by palimpsests from brasses laid down before 1560, for example an inscription *c.* 1480, at Sall, Norfolk, with Flemish work, *c.* 1400, on the back. A black Tournai slab, now forming an altar tomb-top in Ripon Cathedral, has the remains of a frieze showing a lion in a landscape and a small kneeling figure (illustration p. 34), similar to the frieze below Margaret Walsokne's feet at Kings Lynn. Possibly the slab was covered mainly with brass plates.

After about 1560, as explained in chapter 8, many English brasses were made by engraving the reverse sides of Flemish brasses that had once been in Flemish churches. The existence of a number of these palimpsests have been recorded, but many more still wait to be discovered.

5

London Schools of Brasses
after 1350

Few English brasses have survived from the period 1350–65 and it is possible that, due to the effects of the Black Death, few were in fact made. Altogether, about a third to a half the population was wiped out. However, imports of completed brasses from Flanders during this period (see chap. 4) show that brasses continued, if only as a form of monument for the rich.

The larger number of surviving English-made brasses from 1360 to around 1400 shows that imports of virgin brass sheet must have increased rapidly, and that in the early fifteenth century these sheets were being made into brasses not only for clergy and knights, but for a wider market which included the middle classes who were now more affluent.

A brass could to some extent be made to suit a man's purse. Figures could be life-size or much smaller, full or half length. But the main part, the slab, with all its transport problems, was a considerable basic item of cost. It is as well to remember that many small figures or parts of brasses now separated from their matrices were originally parts of large slabs.

During the fourteenth century English masons became more efficient at fixing brasses in slabs and by about 1320 they were beginning to use, as well as bitumen, brass dowels set in lead, to keep the pieces in place. Small pieces of brass could thereby be secured as effectively as large undoweled figures which had relied mainly on their weight to hold them in place (e.g. Fitzralph, Pebmarsh, Essex). Demand for brasses to be placed in churches far from London led to brass sheet being taken to provincial centres, and subsequently provincial schools of brasses were established, notably in Norwich and York. (See chap. 6.)

The very different ways of engraving the mail of aventails separates two London engravers (C. J. P. Kent's styles A & B) (1) Sir Nich. Burnell, 1382, Acton Burnell, Salop and (2) Sir Wm. de Bryene, 1395, Seal, Kent.

3 *The different ways of engraving tasse hinges and neck or wrist frills in London c. 1525–87, distinguish four main styles, named after the first example listed under each.*

1525–54 Stafford Style	1548–54 Fermour Style	1554–74 Lytkott Style	1573–87 Daston Style

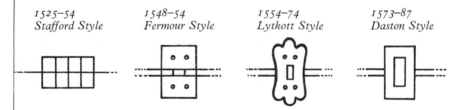

| Blatherwycke, Northants, 1548. Charwelton, Northants, 1541. Ellesborough, Bucks, 1544. Harlington, Middx, 1545. Islington, London, N.1, 1546. | Somerton, Oxon, 1552. Easton Neston, Northants, 1552 and others listed page 94. | Swallowfield, Berks, 1554. Thames Ditton, Surrey, 1559, etc. | Broadway, Worcs, 1572. Hasely, Warwicks, 1573, etc. |

Interest in styles or workshops of brass engraving is a fairly recent development. Malcolm Norris writing in 1965[1] emphasizes this approach. Previously the only study on the subject had been an essay on styles of military brasses between *c.* 1360 and *c.* 1485.[2] One of the obstacles to more thorough studies has been the mass of material to be examined—some 7,500 brasses still survive in the British Isles (engraved not later than 1700). Although many people recognize some of the styles, no comprehensive classification and description has yet been published.

Characteristics of a style (artist, engraver or workshop) often lie in a small detail such as the method of showing mail. Links of mail are not only small but tedious to engrave, and different shorthand was adopted by different artists to convey the same original. The illustration shows two quite different ways in which aventails of knights were engraved. Such a comparison is only possible for the period during which the aventail remained in fashion. Fashion changes are an added difficulty in the search for styles. However, taking the aventail as a starting point, it is possible not only to distinguish different schools of engravers in the military figures, but because some of the knights are engraved beside their wives, to distinguish ladies, and even some civilians since, (for example) Symond de Felbrig (in civilian clothes) and his wife, and their son, wearing an aventail (Kent's style B) all form one brass *c.* 1380.

Analysis of brasses along these lines brings us to the conclusion that before the end of the fourteenth century there were two or three distinctive styles emanating from London, probably from two workshops. Although there is no documentary evidence to that effect, it seems that the workshops must have come under the wing of some London Guild or Mystery, but it is not clear which of them would have been concerned with brasses in the early fifteenth century. The Mystery of Latoners, flourishing at this time, was by its name the most obvious, but little is known about it. Perhaps the Latoners were eventually absorbed by the Marblers, for in the sixteenth century its wardens had to inspect not only 'stone-werk of marbyll' but 'laton werke or coper werk belongyng or perteynyng to the same Crafte . . .' In turn the Marblers were absorbed by the Masons in 1584, and it is notable that Edward Marshall 1598–1675, who made brasses, was master mason to the Crown. The lack of documentary evidence covering these early periods

[1] *Brass Rubbing,* chap. 3.
[2] 'Monumental Brasses—A new classification of military effigies,' *British Archeological Association,* XXII, 1959.

is frustrating and the only way to separate the styles is to look very carefully at the brasses themselves.

The shapes of letters on inscriptions can be compared with reasonable ease. In the sixteenth century in particular, inscriptions can be recognized like individual handwriting. Sometimes different hands combined with one style of figure, showing that some degree of specialization had been reached. One man might have concentrated on cutting inscriptions, one on heraldic shields and another on figures. Much sixteenth-century lettering is untidy and compares unfavourably with Continental Flemish inscriptions of similar date. One London script that stands out as slightly more attractive can be seen at Strethall, Essex, 1508 (raised letters), at the Society of Antiquaries, London, 1518, at Bigby, Lincs., c. 1520, and at Moreton, Dorset, 1523 (raised letters). The script can be spotted by a central bar through 'J's and 'H's and a curl at the end of the 'h's which goes in the opposite direction on 'y's.

A distinct and attractive London figure style can be found on a number of brasses dated between 1548 and 1554. Points of comparison are rings on fingers, girdle pomanders or pendants, tasset hinges, frills and a general attention to small detail which is lacking on preceding styles. It has been called the 'Fermour' style and is typified by brasses at Easton Neston, Northants, and Somerton, Oxon., to the brothers Richard and William Fermour, both of whom died in 1552. Both have the same figure style and script. A preceding figure style typified at Blatherwyck and Charwelton, Northants. (the 'Stafford' style) has several different scripts, and this seems to point to the fact that more than one engraver worked on such inscriptions. Palimpsest links (for an explanation of links see p. 93) confirm this.

Additional information about these two styles was supplied when it was discovered that a 'Stafford'-style brass at Edlesborough, Bucks., 1540, and a 'Fermour'-style brass at Crowan Cornwall, c. 1550 had linking backs, as did those at Charwelton, Northants., 1541 (Stafford) and Braunton, Devon, 1548 (Fermour), which proved conclusively that both the 'Fermour' and the 'Stafford' styles came from the same workshop. This would have been in London, and several of the palimpsest inscriptions can be traced to destroyed London churches.

The simplest way to pigeon-hole 'Stafford', 'Fermour' and two succeeding London figure styles is to compare tasset hinges and neck frills. Although tassets are confined to men in armour, frills are common to both

William Cure's workshop in Southwark may have been responsible for both sculptured tombs and brasses showing this arrangement of kneeling figures. The sculptured tomb is to Sir Michael Blount and his father whom he succeeded as Lieutenant of the Tower of London, St Peter ad Vincula, Tower of London (photo by permission of the Tower Authorities), and the brass (inscr. omitted) is to Wm. Dunche, 1597, engr. c. 1580, Little Wittenham, Berks.

sexes. The illustration shows how differently they are interpreted in each style, and the name of each style is the name of the man commemorated at the first church listed.

With the 'Daston' style we reach a period when the names of some tomb sculptors are known[1] and it is possible to hazard a guess that William Cure of Southwark had a hand in their manufacture. He seems to have pioneered wall monuments with sculptured kneeling figures and prayer desks[2] and possibly supplied brasses of this pattern as well. Cure's workshop was perhaps of greater importance than Johnson's (see below) but its products are far less documented. Cure's son Cornelius worked with his father and became Master Mason to the Crown in 1596, but died in 1607.

In 1568, a company called the Mineral and Battery Works was formed in England to seek out and mine calamine and subsequently to beat ingots of brass into thin sheets. This is possibly the first evidence of sheet manufacture in England. Thin hammer beaten sheets are found forming parts of some Fermour style brasses c. 1550, but these would have been 'reprocessed' by melting and being hammered thin from the brasses taken from dissolved religious houses.[3]

A large number of brasses were being made towards the end of the sixteenth century and the next style can be linked with the workshop of Gerard Johnson, in the parish of St Saviour's Southwark, alongside the Thames. Drawings of two brasses proposed by Johnson for the Gage family have miraculously survived among the family's archives at Firle Place, Sussex, together with the finished brasses in West Firle. Mrs Esdaile,[4] commenting on the drawings wrote that they 'identify the artist responsible for some of the finest brasses and effigies of the period'. Some of Johnson's tombs held no brass and consisted of elaborately carved English alabaster with imported black and red marbles from Tournai and Normandy. His workshop erected alabaster tombs (no brass parts) in Bottesford, Leics., costs of which are recorded in the Belvoir Household Accounts, and also garden ornaments—two fountains for the Privy Garden at Hampton Court[5]

[1] Margaret Whinney, *Sculpture in Britain 1530–1830*.

[2] Probably Sir Rich. Alington 1561, Rolls Chapel, Public Record Office, and Sir Rich. Blount 1574, St Peter ad Vincula, Tower of London.

[3] The Fermour style brass at St Mellion 1551 has a marginal inscription all of hammer beaten brass, only 2mm. thick.

[4] *M.B.S. Trans*, VIII, 44.

[5] P.R.O.E. 351–3226.

in 1591–92 and a figure of Neptune for the garden at Hatfield in 1611, the year he died. His workshop also made a brass sundial which was signed R. Treswell and dated 1582 (now lost), the back of which was part of the same Flemish brass used to make a brass in Tor Mohun, Devon (Wilmot Cary, 1581) and another in Paston, Norfolk. Stylistically these brasses can be linked with many others such as those at Cumnor, Berks., 1577; Littlebury, Essex, 1578; Yateley, Hants., 1578; Lydd, Kent, 1578; Woodford by Thrapston, Northants, 1580; Lee St Margaret, Kent, 1582; Steventon, Berks., 1584 and St Werburgh, Bristol, 1586. Johnson probably did not have time to design all the brasses that come under the heading of the 'Johnson style', and certainly a number are of poor quality. He was always keen to give the flat brass figures something of his three dimensional alabaster effigies by much use of cross-hatching or shading. On traditional black or negative heelball rubbings this shows up badly, and the designs are seen far more clearly on positive rubbings.

Johnson had emigrated from Holland in 1567, married an English girl and settled in Southwark. As an alien he could not work in the City. He was assisted by his sons Nicholas and Gerard, who carried on his business after his death.

Another Southwark sculptor who made brasses and like 'R. Treswell' may have been associated with the Johnson workshop, was Epiphany Evesham. Born in 1570, he made a brass sundial in 1589, preserved in the Hereford museum, and a brass dedicated to Edmund West at Marsworth, Bucks, in 1618. He had worked in Paris from 1601 to 1614 and the brass, with curious incised marble figures on the sides of the tomb chest, shows foreign influence.

Nicholas Stone, c. 1587–1647, a generation younger than Johnson, made both brasses and sculptured tombs. Although apprenticed in Southwark he was working in Long Acre in 1613. He collaborated with Nicholas Johnson in 1615, and was Master Mason to the Crown. Some of his account books have survived and prove that he made an inscription in St Mary's Warwick 1636, and an inscription with brass relief effigies in St Decumans, Somerset in 1645.[1]

---

[1] The account book itemizes the costs of the Warwick brass—the black marble slab £6, squaring and smoothing £1, three plates of brass £1 12s cutting the inscription and letting them into the stone and riveting £1 10s and finally gilding the plates and picking the letters out with black £1 8s.

Edward Marshall 1598–1675, another Master Mason to the Crown, was not apprenticed in Southwark but made some of the finest late brasses. He signed the brass at East Sutton, Kent to Sir Ed. Filmer, (illustration p. 72) 1629, and wife. On stylistic grounds he almost certainly made the brasses to Archbishop Harsnett, 1631, at Chigwell, Essex, Dorothy Saunders, 1632, at Stoke by Nayland, Suffolk, and Eliz. Culpeper, 1633, at Ardingley, Sussex.

With him one can say that the medieval tradition of brass engraving burnt itself out. There was no serious attempt to revive it until the nineteenth century, when Gawthorpe and Sons offered their machine surfaced 'culm brass (registered)' plate complete with 'Albascript (registered)' lettering. There is now some interest in nineteenth-century brasses, where figures are shown, and some are worthy products of their age, such as that of Frances Stubbs at Aylesbury, Bucks, 1877.

Two nineteenth-century writers on brasses, Haines and Creeny, are commemorated on brasses, respectively in the south choir aisle of Gloucester Cathedral and under the tower in All Saints, Norwich, in sad need of restoration.

6

Provincial Schools of Brasses

By the fifteenth century, brasses had clearly become a desirable form of monument, not only for people with London or court connections, but for people living in remoter regions. Provincial masons or men with other skills sometimes turned their hands to making brasses. Examples at Brandsburton, Yorks 1397, Harpham, Yorks 1418 and Spilsby, Lincs, c. 1410 are very fine, but in general such monuments tended to be less grand and less up-to-date in the fashions shown. However, the mere fact that they are provincial does not mean that they are without artistic merit or interest.

A group of brasses c. 1400–90 can be distinguished in Yorkshire and were perhaps made in York. The men in armour wear their helmets (e.g. Richard Ask, 1460, at Aughton) and stand with long pointed sabatons on lions that gaze upwards. London styles usually show lions full face or in profile and helmets used as pillows. The school probably started in the fourteenth century but earlier, locally made brasses such as that to Sir John de St Quintin (head lost) and wife in Brandsburton and the earlier knight, Wm. de Aldeburgh, at Aldborough near Boroughbridge, c. 1365, are large and very different in design. A particularly curious feature in the Aldborough figure is that the face is in base-relief.[1] The Yorkshire school made a number of very simple brasses consisting of inscriptions only, or inscriptions and chalices for priests.

---

[1] The only other example of such treatment in England is the face of a man wearing an amice, dated c. 1320 on the back of canopy work at Burwell, Cambs., 1542.

45

In about 1600, some brasses were again being made in Yorkshire, inspired in design by portrait painting. They show three-quarter length figures, such as Robt. Askwith 1597, St Crux, York and Jas. Cotrel 1595, York Minster.

By far the most prolific provincial school flourished in Norfolk from c. 1460–1550. Its products can be recognized by local distribution and by several figure and inscription styles that are at times rustic and primitive compared with London work. One difference in design found on some Norfolk school brasses is that children are sometimes placed in the folds of their mother's dress rather than as quite separate groups below. Women sometimes wear a type of mob cap not seen on London brasses (illustration p. 77). As in the Yorkshire school, many brasses are very simple and consist of inscriptions only, or inscriptions with chalices for priests. One Norfolk script is attractive and easily identified, for example at Halvergate, 1543 and Honingham, 1544. Certain other provincial schools less prolific in output existed and a study of slabs would help in their identification.

Some country brasses were probably made by local masons, bell-founders or goldsmiths. An empty slab to Thomas Newcombe (d. 1520) which includes indents of three bells, in All Saints, Leicester, shows that he was a bell-founder and the brass was probably bell-founder's work. Two brasses in St Stephens Norwich were probably made by the bell-founder and goldsmith family of Brasyer c. 1513 for members of their family. The draughtsmanship is not quite up to the standard of the Norfolk school brasses. A raised inscription to Tobie Norris, bellfounder, at Stamford St George, Lincs, 1626, was almost certainly cast by his foundry.

Due to its fine detail, it may be that Sir Lionel Dymoke's brass (1519) at Horncastle, Lincs, is goldsmiths work, and more certainly by the same criterion, is the fine engraving on the reverse of a palimpsest inscription, c. 1500 at Great Berkhampstead, Herts. To give some idea of the fine detail, the capital 'O' at the start of this inscription encloses St Jerome in cardinal's robes. The brass was to Thos. Humfre, a London goldsmith.

In the 1560s certainly one, and probably two brasses were made in Scotland by a goldsmith called James Gray, one to James Stewart, Earl of Moray, Regent of Scotland (assassinated at Linlithgow in 1570) consisting of a rectangular plate in St Giles Edinburgh, and one (by Gray on grounds of style) to Alexander Cockburn (1563) from a ruined chapel at Ormiston, East Lothian, now in the National Museum of Antiquities of Scotland, Edinburgh.

7

Fashions in Dress

There are several sources beside monuments which show the changes that have taken place in fashion since the fourteenth century—seals, manuscripts, stained glass, sculptures and paintings. Some of these, by being three-dimensional or coloured, or even by showing people handling clothes, convey more of the shape and cut than brasses, which nearly always show a frontal view. But brasses cannot be overlooked by anyone who studies costume, since they present a continuous, dated series over four centuries.

In general the date of death on a brass is roughly the date of engraving and of the fashion shown, although there was some pressure to depict an earlier fashion on the brass of an old person. For example Ann Polsted's brass at Thames Ditton was set up by her daughter in 1582 when the latter was already 73, and depicts her in the dress of *c.* 1540. Sometimes a brass was made for a man while he was alive, so that by the time he died the fashion on his effigy was outmoded. But a date of death, if it was ever added to such a brass, can usually be seen to be a later addition.

Just as the engraver of a brass produced a standard face, so he produced a standard dress to show the profession and status of the deceased. The standard changed with fashion. Figure brasses can be looked on as the fashion plates of the period, not inspiring people to wear such clothes (like true nineteenth-century fashion plates) but showing everyday dress as worn at the time. Sometimes a note of individuality is detectable on some brasses, but in any one workshop there seems to have been a norm from which there was only slight deviation. The figures are similar and yet each one is different. Perhaps the long beard on Sir William Tendring at Stoke by Nayland, Suffolk was requested, but it could simply have been the artist's way of showing any old man. He died in 1408 and beards had been fashionable in the late fourteenth century. Details such as special badges, or heraldic mantles formed part of the individual's status image.

When a brass was ordered for a man while he was still alive he may well have lent clothes or armour to be copied. The first 'fashion plate' drawing that Gerard Johnson sent to Firle to show the proposed brass to John Gage and his two wives was not only sent back with orders that the ladies dresses should be ungirt (less fashionable) but one of his wife's caps was sent to London 'in a boxe bowed and dressed as it should stand upon their heads'.[1] The desired changes were made as the brass itself at West Firle, Sussex, proves (illustration p. 77).

In each of the following sections a different type of dress is described. This separation of priests from knights, judges and so on is logical and convenient, but there was plenty of cross-influence which such an arrangement tends to hide. For example in the fourteenth century priests, civilians and ladies all wore tight sleeves with rows of buttons to the wrist, and towards the end of the same century a narrow waist was shown on both civilians and knights. Military dress tended to follow the contours of civilian fashion, with changes in armament to meet changing weapons. Legal, academical and widow's dress mostly ossified from fashions found on early brasses. But of all types of dress, ecclesiastical was the most ancient and fossilized, showing only slight modifications until, as far as English brasses are concerned, the upheaval of the Reformation.

ECCLESIASTICAL DRESS

Mass Vestments
Chasubles, like judges wigs, are quite unlike garments worn today, but both evolved from ordinary civilian fashion, the one from Roman dress long before the existence of brasses and the other from powdered wigs of the early eighteenth century. Ecclesiastical vestments have changed at quite a different pace from civilian costume.

The clothes of a priest at the altar have the effect of separating him

[1] *M.B.S. Trans.*, VIII, 43.

from his congregation and raising him above them to be a more worthy mediator with God and administrator of His Sacraments. Mass vestments add authority and dignity to a priest in the same way that robes and wig give presence to a judge.

The time and skill devoted to making some vestments was enormous, and during the late thirteenth and early fourteenth century up to the time of the Black Death, England was famous in Western Europe for its *'opus angli-canum'*,[1] embroidery in silver or silver gilt threads laid on a ground material and drawn through it in little loops, which were attached at the back with linen thread. The background was carried out in similar silver or silver gilt thread worked in underside couching with animals, diaper patterns, etc. Seed pearls and precious stones were added, but most of this sort of work was carried out by professional embroiderers. Brasses hardly begin to show the splendour of these early vestments, but a few actual garments such as the Syon and Jesse copes, survive from the early fourteenth century in museums and in a few cathedrals and churches.[2] Surviving brasses to ecclesiastics before the Black Death are few (see list p. 26) and tend to be only fragments, heads or half effigies. Wm. de Grenefeld (see p. 50) and Lawrence de St Maur, Higham Ferrers show mass vestments with little embroidery.

Just as some of these ecclesiastical brasses survive in the form of palimpsest fragments, so parts of these early vestments survive in the binding of books such as the Felbrigge Pslater in the British Museum, on cushions, or as altar frontals or parts of other vestments. Very many were completely destroyed at the time of the Reformation. Dr William Fulke, Master of Pembroke Hall, Cambridge, writing in about 1580 mentioned people's beds 'garnished with old copes'. Vestments made rich hangings for four-poster beds. Henry Ashton, vicar of Hitchin, Herts, in Queen Mary's reign complained that a chalice that he might be using was serving as a tankard in Susan Aunsell's alehouse at Kimpton, and a black velvet cope was now on the back of her tapster.[3]

After the Black Death, and probably as a result of it, fine *opus anglica-num* was no longer made. No embroidered vestments from the second half of the fourteenth century survive complete. A great change came with the

---

[1] See A. F. Kendrick, *English Needlework* 2nd ed. 1967, chap. 3.

[2] Notable vestments are in the Victoria and Albert Museum, London, Schatzkammer, Vienna (vestments of the Golden Fleece) and the Museum fur Kunsthandwerk, Vienna.

[3] Reginald Hine, *History of Hitchin*, vol. I, p. 98.

ECCLESIASTICAL DRESS

William de Grenefeld, Archbishop of York and Lord Chancellor 1315. York Minster. Effigy (4 ft. 2 in. remaining) from fringe of pallium down, lost, but based on 'Suckling' drawing in Brit. Mus. Canopy lost. Worn Purbeck slab.

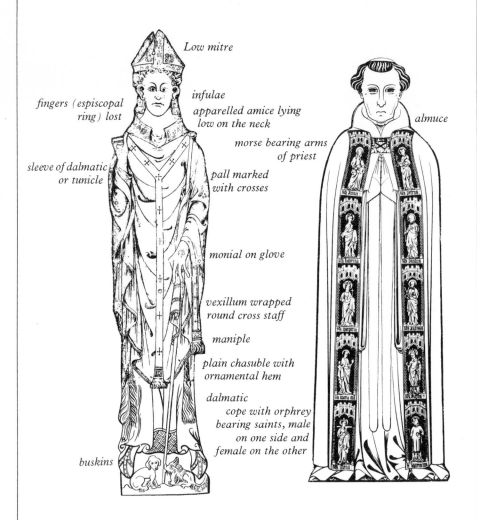

Low mitre

fingers (espiscopal
ring) lost

infulae

apparelled amice lying
low on the neck

almuce

morse bearing arms
of priest

sleeve of dalmatic
or tunicle

pall marked
with crosses

monial on glove

vexillum wrapped
round cross staff

maniple

plain chasuble with
ornamental hem

dalmatic

cope with orphrey
bearing saints, male
on one side and
female on the other

buskins

William Ermyn, rector, 1401, wearing cope with named saints. Castle Ashby, Northants. Length 5 ft. 3 in.

import of Italian brocades and velvets in the early fifteenth century. Italian merchants came to England, bought English wool, and sold woven fabrics. To these were attached the orphreys (see the patterned fabric on Simon Bache's cope, 1414, Knebworth, Herts) but the fine designs of the earlier work were not achieved. Underside couching was abandoned, and on later copes brocade patterns can be seen at places such as Beeford, 1472.

A number of later fifteenth-century brasses of priests in chasubles show a pillar orphrey on the front (Arundel 1445, Carshalton, 1493). Usually, the decoration on the back was more elaborate and 'T'-shaped, perhaps with a crucifixion scene. It is significant that as a priest celebrated the Mass he had his back to his congregation for much of the time and the back of his chasuble was more lavishly embroidered than the front.

Single or pairs of saints were often embroidered on the orphreys of copes or chasubles. When in pairs, they were sometimes male on one side and female on the other; the orphrey of a cope on a brass at Castle Ashby, 1401, compares with an early fifteenth-century chasuble in the Victoria and Albert Museum, in showing this arrangement.

Many original vestments survive from the first half of the sixteenth century and prove that rebuses or initials referring to the deceased, such as the 'I B' on John Baker's orphrey, Arundel, 1445, were actually made, and were not purely an idea for a brass memorial. From the late fifteenth century onwards, Flemish embroidery took the lead and influenced the embroidery designs of English vestments. Some of the orphreys appear to have been woven rather than embroidered (e.g. Croyden, 1512).

With the Reformation all this splendour was lost and post-Reformation clergy depicted on brasses wear gowns. Edward Nayler 'a faithfull and painefull minister of God's word', kneels in his gown with his wife and children (Bigby, Lincs., 1632).

In the following paragraphs the clothes worn by priests at the altar —mass vestments—are listed in the order in which they were put on. The extra vestments which distinguish bishops, mitred abbots, and archbishops, are described in the ultimate section.

Amice. A rectangle of linen with an embroidered panel fixed along one side in such a way that, when placed round the neck and folded outwards, it formed an ornamental collar. The ornamental border (*apparel*) was often decorated with silver and silver gilt thread, and jewels, perhaps matching the apparel on the alb and other parts. Early fourteenth-century amices tended to be low and loose on the neck, and this may be due to the custom of using it as a head covering during the early part of the Mass. Later amices became tighter and rose towards the chin, following the lines of civilian dress.

Alb. A linen vestment reaching to the feet and decorated with six apparels—chest and back, the front and back of the lower hem and the cuffs. Early brasses show the apparels completely encircling the wrists, but later ones show them only covering the upper part. The alb was held at the waist by a girdle or belt. Angels were usually represented in albs.

Stole. A long and often richly embroidered band passing round the neck and hanging down in front. It was crossed over the chest and held in place by the girdle of the alb. Bishops usually wore the stole straight, and only deacons draped it over the left shoulder. Its fringed ends appeared beneath the chasuble. On early brasses the ends widen out, but later stoles continue the same width throughout their length. Their exact origin is not known, but they date from the early Christian period.

Maniple. Like the end of a stole, but looped over the sleeve of the left arm. Its origins are obscure, but it may be descended from the mappula or napkin carried to meals by Roman citizens.

Chasuble. Originally a circular garment with a hole in the centre for the head, the chasuble became cut away at the sides to allow more freedom for the arms. Early brasses show a supple garment as compared with later examples which bear stiffer embroidery.

The chasuble was sometimes ornamented in front with a 'Y'-shaped *orphrey* (applied embroidery, like an apparel) which, in the fifteenth century ceased to divide at the top and became a simple pillar.

The vestments described above were worn by the priest at the altar and in them he was commonly buried. On brasses he is often shown dressed in the vestments and holding a chalice and wafer, for pewter or tin chalices were normally buried with priests. Brasses of chasubled priests are common and usually small in size.

Bishops and mitred abbots also wore:

Tunicle and Dalmatic. Two garments with sleeves, worn under the chasuble and above the stole, and reaching down to the knee, where they were fringed. The tunicle was the sub-deacon's vestment and the dalmatic the deacon's, and since the bishop wore the vestments of all the lower orders, he wore both.

Mitre and Infulae. Probably derived from a cap that was tied under the chin by two straps of material, but by the thirteenth century it had become a low-pointed sideways-cleft hat with two silk strips (infulae) hanging down behind the ears. Later mitres became taller and crocketed. The late twelfth-century *opus anglicanum* mitre, said to have belonged to St Thomas of Canterbury, can be seen in the Victoria and Albert Museum.

Sandals, Gloves and Ring. Sandals (buskins) were embroidered with stripes, gloves were decorated with enamelled plates or jewels on the backs of the hand (monials) and the Pontifical Ring fitted over the glove on to a finger of the right hand. On brasses the thumb and first two fingers are usually shown raised in blessing (revealing the end of the sleeve of the dalmatic or tunicle below).

Crozier and Vexillum. The left hand normally held a crozier, which resembled the general shape of a shepherd's crook. The crook section might be finely worked ivory or metal. A scarf (vexillum) with a tasseled end, hung down or twisted round the staff. It probably prevented the shaft from becoming tarnished.

Archbishops used the same vestments as bishops, with the addition of:

Pall. A 'T' or 'Y'-shaped circle of white lambswool, decorated with crosses, and with pendant ends in front and behind, worn over the chasuble. (Not to be confused with a 'Y'-shaped orphrey on a chasuble.) It was given by the Pope to each archbishop when he visited Rome to receive his authority, and was buried with him.

Cross staff. A cross head is usually shown rather than a crook, the head sometimes being plain or a crucifix.

Processional Vestments

Cassock and surplice. The modern choir boy's dress needs no description, but in the fourteenth century the cassock (undertunic) generally black, was fur lined for warmth, the fur sometimes showing at the cuffs on brasses. The surplice was a loose linen vestment with long hanging sleeves, usually shorter than the cassock, but on early brasses sometimes of equal length. The surplice developed from the alb to fit over the fur-lined cassock.

Almuce. A fur hood with long pendant ends (not to be confused with stole ends), used to keep the head warm in draughty churches that often had shuttered rather than glazed windows. The grey almuce is sometimes shown on brasses by lead inlay. Examples of priests in almuces are common, and the garment was worn with or without the cope. No brass shows it over the head, but it is arranged like this on two fourteenth-century sculptured effigies of canons at Bitton, Glos.[1]

Cope. A semi circular cloak-like outer garment with a broad orphrey along the edge, fastened at the neck by a clasp (morse). It resembled fourteenth century civilian cloaks, some of which were presented to churches to be converted into copes.

Post-Reformation Ecclesiastics dressed in civilian or academic clothes, e.g. Chevening, Kent, 1596, Ely Cathedral, 1614, and Battle, Sussex, 1615.

Monastic Dress

Monastic brasses have suffered very severely because of their mass destruction or removal from monasteries under the dissolution of Henry VIII. A few survive but a growing number are coming to light in the form of palimpsests.

Abbots. Although the abbots shown on brasses usually wear vestments, an abbot of the Augustinian or Black Canons can be seen in a long black choral cope, over an almuce, at Dorchester, Oxon, *c.* 1510.

Priors. Thomas Nelond, 1433, was prior at Lewes, and his brass must have been moved to Cowfold, Sussex when his Cluniac monastery was dissolved in 1538. He wears a cowl over his cassock and is the largest and perhaps the finest brass in Sussex. Part of a prior *c.* 1500 is on the back of a brass in Piddlehinton, Dorset (1562) and may be a Dominican who would have worn a white habit.

Monks were supposed to be poor, so few brasses to them survive and perhaps few were made. They wore habits and hoods. A gown with long hanging sleeves was worn over this, only by Benedictines (e.g. St Albans, *c.* 1470, where Robert Beauner holds a bleeding heart in his hands). A very strange brass to an anchorite, *c.* 1460 (illustration p. 55), was discovered on the back of a brass in St John de Sepulchre, Norwich, dated *c.* 1535. He dressed as a monk in habit and hood, and peers through stout iron bars. The engraving is local Norfolk work and the anchorite must have been walled up in some Norfolk church or monastery.[2]

Abbesses and Nuns dressed like widows who wore wimples and veil head-dresses. Only two brasses to abbesses survive, one at Elstow, Beds, to

[1] F. A. Greenhill, 'A Note on the Almuce' *M.B.S. Trans.,* IX, 208.
[2] For an account of such people see R. M. Clay, *Hermits and Anchorites of England,* 1914.

pileus

almuce with cape
and tassels

cassock with
furred cuffs

surplice with
full sleeves

Almuce, surplice
and cassock. Rich.
Harward 1493. St
Cross. Winchester,
Hants.

tonsure

Monk's habit. An
anchorite c. 1460 on
the rev. of a civilian
and w. c. 1535.
Both sides Norfolk
school.

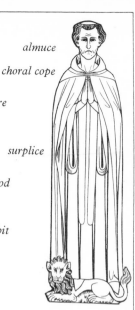

almuce

choral cope

surplice

hood

habit

Priest in choral cope
c. 1370. Watton,
Herts.

hood

gown with
close sleeves

fur-lined tabard
with pointed sleeves

cassock
(undertunic)

Bachelors of Art,
Medicine and Can-
non Law wore hood
and tabard.

hood

Masters of Art wore
a cappa clausa with
two arm slits.

hood

cappa clausa with
double and single
arm slits

Doctors of Divinity
and Canon Law
wore a cappa clausa
with single arm slit.

a Benedictine and one to a Brigitine at Denham, Bucks. Widows often became nuns, and an inscription at Appleton, Berks, 1518, tells how 'Dorathe his wyfe whiche aft his dethe toke relygyon in ye monastary of Syon'.

Academic Dress
Academic dress evolved from fourteenth-century costume. In particular, the academic hood developed from the chaperon, which went out of use for the man in the street *c.* 1450. The brass to Thos. Baker (All Souls, Oxford, 1510) shows the hood and gown of an undergraduate—the only brass depicting this humble status.

Proceeding up the scale a Bachelor of Art, Medicine or Canon Law wore a hood and tabard, a long fairly close-sleeved or sleeveless garment. Before the Reformation, he wore no head-dress (Geoffrey Hargreve, B.A., New College, Oxford, 1447), but in Tudor times there was a trend towards less cumbersome dress, and gowns were worn in place of the tabard.

A Master of Art wore a hood, skull cap and cappa clausa, a long garment worn over a cassock (undertunic), fur-lined with two arm slits. (John Kyllingworth, 1445, Merton College, Oxford.) In the sixteenth century it became open all down the front.

Doctors of Divinity and Canon Law wore a cappa clausa that only had one central slit for the hands to emerge. (Dr Hautryve, 1441, New College, Oxford.) Doctors of Medicine on brasses are all post-Reformation and wear false sleeved gowns (e.g. New College). Doctors of Law wore a pileus, a cap generally showing a point on the top of the head, such as John Lowther, 1427, New College.

There is considerable confusion in naming the various items of academic dress, but the clearest distinction of senior rank is the single central slit on the cappa clausa.

Inventories show that variously coloured garments were worn until the mid fifteenth century and that colour was less important than cut, however during that century different colours became associated with different faculties. Brasses are unhelpful with colours; one should probably picture Thomas Hylle, 1468, Doctor of Divinity, New College, Oxford, wearing scarlet.

LEGAL DRESS

Judges
The most characteristic garment worn by Judges was the armelausa, a

coif

armelausa fastened
on right shoulder

long gown (supertunica)

Judges wore the armelausa and coif. Sir John Cassey, 1400,
chief baron of the exchequer. Dog named Terri at his wife's
feet. Marg. inscr. omitted, but figure of John Bapt.
(stolen c. 1860) included. Deerhurst, Glos. Length of
judge 3 ft.

loose mantle fastened on the right shoulder (Deerhurst, 1400) lined with miniver and worn over a long gown (supertunica). Its origins probably lie in early medieval mantles secured with a brooch on the shoulder and worn into the thirteenth century. For judges it survived until the seventeenth century and can be seen on brasses at St Mary Redcliffe, Bristol, 1439, Dagenham, Essex, 1479, and Milton, Cambs, 1553. In the fifteenth century its colour became established as scarlet. A coif was worn on the head. In Charles II's time large black or brown wigs became a male fashion, powdered white or grey after 1705. Present day judges' wigs are survivals of that fashion.

Sergeants-at-law
Sergeants-at-law also lack colour on brasses (e.g. Thos. Rolf 1440, Gosfield, Essex, and John Brook, 1522, St Mary Redcliffe, Bristol) since, as well as coifs and hoods, they wore parti-coloured gowns, for example blue and green or blue and grey, a civilian colour scheme of the fourteenth century.[1] By the mid sixteenth century parti colours gave way to scarlet.

A few brasses show barristers-at-law, some in armour and some in gowns. John Edward, (1461, Rodmarton, Glos.) wears a high cap edged with fur, which is probably part of his official costume. The most recent example is Robert Shiers 1668 (Great Bookham, Surrey) in civilian costume holding a book. Only judges and sergeants-at-law emerge with definite legal costume.

CIVILIAN DRESS

Men in the thirteenth century often wore beards, but in the fourteenth they were clean shaven and hair was kept short. However, beards on some brasses would seem to typify old age rather than current hair fashion. Bishops and priests remained clean shaven until the seventeenth century, but various changes took place among civilians. A drooping moustache and beard was common towards the end of the fourteenth century, but beards disappeared in the first quarter of the fifteenth century and hair was kept short until around 1480. From c. 1460–70 a pudding-basin cut can be seen, and the back of the head was shaved up to ear level. Hair became quite long on civilians and priests c. 1490, and in the early sixteenth century there was a bobbed style, with straight hair cut level across the forehead. Beards were

[1] Walter Pescod, 1398, Boston, Lincs, appears to be wearing a parti-coloured gown.

in vogue *c.* 1540 (Henry VIII) and these became pointed with small moustaches in Elizabethan times. Beards remained until Van Dyck, and hair was gradually worn longer.

Head coverings worn by men in the fourteenth century were soft hats, sometimes with plumes, and hoods, (chaperons) rather like the shape of aventail and helmet combined, only with the top extended into a liripipe which could hang down the back or be wound round the neck like a scarf. A fragment from a fourteenth-century Flemish palimpsest in Margate, Kent (Rev. of inscr. to Thos. Fliitt, 1582) shows a hood being used like a net to catch a butterfly (illustration p. 60). The same scene can be found on manuscripts of the period.[1] At the end of the century the 'aventail' part of the hood was rolled up and tucked in to form a curiously shaped hat. By the mid fifteenth century the hood form was lost and the shape was that of a cap with a scarf attached to either side. (See the brass to a notary where this type of hat is resting on his shoulder, St Mary-le-Tower, *c.* 1475, Ipswich, Suffolk.) Although men did not necessarily have the habit of taking their hats off when entering a church in medieval times, very few effigies of ordinary civilians show hats being worn, and one cannot but conclude that there was an ideal of bare heads in the presence of God—at all events in the prolonged presence. Unfortunately brasses show none of the extravagant male hats, inspired by Milan, that were worn at the end of the fifteenth century.[2] Such hats can best be seen on tapestries, they were large, worn at various angles, with a variety of accessories, and continued in use to the end of the sixteenth century. In the seventeenth century they acquired much wider brims and their crowns became stiffer and more raised.

Moving further down the body, the main garment worn in the second half of the fourteenth century was a waisted pourpoint and (shown on the first civilian brasses) a gown, at first long and loose, and then girt at the waist with tight sleeves and a high neck line. In the late fourteenth century bag sleeves developed often with narrow furred cuffs and a hem line half way to the knee. Towards the end of the fifteenth century a purse and a rosary often hung from the belt. The bronze or laten cross pieces from which the pouch

---

[1] e.g. *Franco-Flemish Book of Hours.* Walters Art Gallery, Baltimore. MS. 88 fo. 19. Early fourteenth century, and N. French Psalter & Hours, Bibliotheque Nationale, Paris. MS Latin 13260 fo. 1 Second half fourteenth century. Both illustrated pl. LXXI in Lilian M. C. Randall, *Images in the Margins of Gothic Manuscripts.*

[2] The word 'milliner' or lady's hat maker has its derivation at this period, but the pattern of hat only survives on Yeoman of the Guard.

1 *Bag-sleeved gowns were worn by civilians in the early 15th cent. Nicholas Canteys, 1431. Margate, Kent. (Most men were clean shaven at this time.) Length 34 in.*

2 *A longer gown with tighter sleeves evolved. A notary with ink and pen case and hat on shoulder. c. 1475. St Mary Tower, Ipswich, Suffolk. Length 44 in.*

3 *A 16th century gown. Mariner with a ship's whistle. Inscr. and w. omitted. John Deynes, 1527. Length 22 in.*

The top of the hood extended into a liripipe, shown clearly on the back of a brass. Margate, Kent, 1582. In a series of scenes of the 'ages of man' this shows a youth trying to catch a butterfly in his hood. Flemish, c. 1400.

of the purse was hung, and the metal buckles and belt ends can often be seen in museums.

By the time of Henry VIII, a long, fur-lined gown was worn, opening in front, the opening edged with fur and held by a belt. It is perhaps worth noting that at this period men seemed to display themselves more than women. Male doublets were designed to emphasize broad massive shoulders and stockings showed off calf muscles. By Elizabeth's reign the belt had gone and doublet and hose could be glimpsed down the front. The most obvious change in Stuart times was that the hose became more like riding breeches, and tucked into knee-length boots.

Shoes

Although as a rule women's shoes were virtually hidden beneath long dresses and so were not much swayed by fashion, men's shoes were more visible and brasses show them in detail. In the fourteenth century shoes were flat and pointed, made of hide, and towards the end of the century the points were extended, stuffed and curled up. The points were called 'crackowes' after Cracow in Poland whence the fashion probably came. Pointed toes remained following the natural point of the foot (instep lacing can be seen on some brasses, e.g. Margate, Kent, 1431). The points became slightly exaggerated in the mid fifteenth century, but disappeared with blunt Tudor toes. The width of the toes gradually lessened as the sixteenth century progressed, to become rounded, and in Elizabeth's reign cork heels were introduced for both sexes. In the early seventeenth century the toe became blunted.

Boots for riding were made throughout the period but became very fashionable for walking in the early seventeenth century. They had wide tops which could be pulled up to reach the hose. Shoes of the time often had elaborate roses and flamboyant garters at the knees.

It is perhaps worth noting that the shapes of right and left shoes were not differentiated until *c.* 1860, and that top lacing only became fashionable at about the same time.

MEN IN ARMOUR

Brasses are well known for showing how fashions in armour changed down the centuries. Examples can be found at regular intervals from the late

MEN IN ARMOUR

EDWARD II   EDWARD III

bascinet

hood as part of hauberk
becomes an aventail

guige holding shield

metal rerebrace but lions'
masks probably leather

sword hung at two points
(lacing or rings) at angle

cuirie
hauberk
aketon

poleyn probably leather

long surcoat becomes
shorter in front

addition of metal
plates to chausses

prick spurs

rowels

sabatons

*Sir Robt. de Bures, 1331,
engr. c. 1320. Acton, Suffolk. Length 78 in.*

*Sir John de Creke, c. 1330.
Westley Waterless,
Cambs. Length 64 in.*

thirteenth century to the mid seventeenth century. But although brasses provide a long and fairly closely-dated series, they lack certain interesting details, and some types of armour are not even represented. Their main disadvantage is that the men face you on parade and you cannot walk round and inspect them at the back. To learn in any detail how pieces of armour were attached to the body we must look at sculptured tombs, manuscripts and in particular at surviving pieces of armour. Museums with important collections of medieval or renaissance armour include

ENGLAND	London, Wallace Collection
	London, Tower of London
	Glasgow, Museum and Art Gallery
	Edinburgh, Royal Scottish Museum
EUROPE	Berlin, Museum für deutsche Geschichte (E. Germany)
	Vienna, Kunsthistorichen Museum
	Paris, Musée de l'Armée
	Madrid, Real Armeriá
	Dresden, Historiches Museum (E. Germany)
	Brussels, Musée Royale d'Armes et d'Armures, Porte de Hal
	Stockholm, National Historical Museum
	Copenhagen, Danish National Museum
	Churburg (Castell Coira) Nr. Sluderno N. Italy.
USA	New York, Metropolitan Museum of Art
	Cleveland, Ohio Museum of Art
	Worcester, Mass., The John Woodman Higgins Armoury

In one way brasses showing armour are misleading because the largest and most detailed figures were the earliest (early fourteenth century) whereas from an armour point of view the best suits were produced much later, c. 1450–1550, a period coinciding with some of the poorest brass engraving. The best period in armour is demonstrated by surviving military suits scattered in collections throughout Europe and America. By c. 1450 armour had become highly developed and expensive, and although in the troubled fifteenth century most men could probably muster defensive clothing, the pieces must often have been old and out-of-date. Some men depicted on brasses as wearing armour may never have worn it, or at least may never have worn armour of the design shown. It is probable that whatever armour they had worn, neither they nor their executors would have felt the desire or the need to find fault with tomb engraving. The design was largely left to the

EDWARD III

HENRY IV

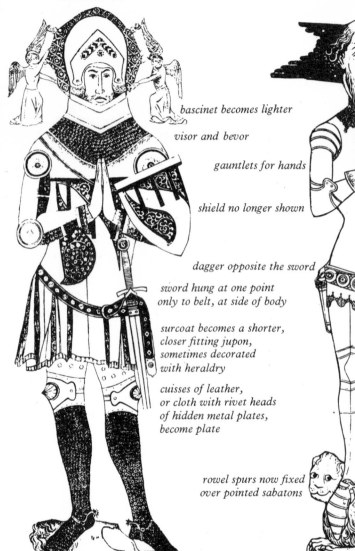

bascinet becomes lighter

visor and bevor

gauntlets for hands

shield no longer shown

dagger opposite the sword

*sword hung at one point
only to belt, at side of body*

*surcoat becomes a shorter,
closer fitting jupon,
sometimes decorated
with heraldry*

*cuisses of leather,
or cloth with rivet heads
of hidden metal plates,
become plate*

*rowel spurs now fixed
over pointed sabatons*

*Sir Hugh Hastings, d. 1347,
Elsing, Norfolk.*

*Sir William Tendring, d. 1408,
Stoke-by-Nayland, Suffolk.*

workshop, and there is no reason to doubt that London workshops showed the approximate fashion current at the time of engraving. In this respect it is worth pointing out that the general shape of armour followed that of civilian fashion. The cyclas of the early fourteenth century paralleled flowing cloaks, the tight jupon at the end of the fourteenth century is like the waisted pourpoint, and in Elizabethan times the peascod breastplate and large pauldrons paralleled the shape of the doublet with its puffed shoulders and plunging centre line. Although early, finely engraved brasses do not coincide with perfection in armour, they are of great interest from the armour point of view since a few remain, whereas practically no actual pieces of armour have survived. Brasses like those listed on p. 24 where, in some cases only fragments survive are of value, especially when they can be imagined complete and in the round by looking at sculptures of knights as well (e.g. Temple Church, London).

Writers on armour have used words from various languages to name the various component parts. A will of 1389 (Westminster Abbey Muniments 253558) written in Latin, concerning Walter Laycestr' used not only Latin, but French and English words to describe pieces of armour that he wished to leave to John Draper. Writers have tried to search back in old documents for the names that were actually used. As a general principle it seems best to use English wherever possible. A number of books on brasses give French words (e.g. *genouillière* for poleyn) or words mistranslated from the French (e.g. *tuile* for tasse) where shorter English words seem preferable. This move to sort out the vocabulary of armour dates mainly from 1929,[1] so that most books on brasses are now out of date in this respect. In listing the various pieces of armour used at different dates some alternative names will be given.

The dates at which the earliest military figures were engraved, as mentioned in chapter 2, need careful rechecking. There has been a tendency to make some of these brasses earlier, but the new grouping makes a closer sequence, *c.* 1300–50.

Armour before the Black Death, 1348

Aketon (wambais, gambeson). A simple garment with or without sleeves, quilted to deaden blows. It was mainly used under armour, although the common soldier wore it with nothing on top.

---

[1] See, *The Armoury of the Castle of Churburg*, London, 1929.

HENRY V

HENRY VI

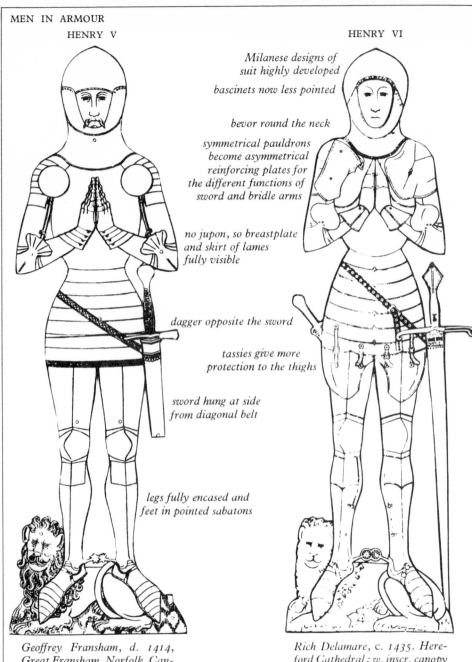

Milanese designs of
suit highly developed

bascinets now less pointed

bevor round the neck

symmetrical pauldrons
become asymmetrical
reinforcing plates for
the different functions of
sword and bridle arms

no jupon, so breastplate
and skirt of lames
fully visible

dagger opposite the sword

tassies give more
protection to the thighs

sword hung at side
from diagonal belt

legs fully encased and
feet in pointed sabatons

Geoffrey Fransham, d. 1414,
Great Fransham, Norfolk. Can-
opy marg. inscr. and shs. omitted.
London school C. J. P. Kent's
Series B. Length 60 in.

Rich Delamare, c. 1435. Here-
ford Cathedral; w. inscr. canopy
and shs. omitted. London school
C. J. P. Kent Series D.
Length 70 in.

Hauberk (byrnie). A skirt of mail that reached nearly to the knees, split in front and behind for sitting on horseback. A hood of mail was an integral part of it (later to become a separate garment) and the sleeves were long enough to cover the hands. Slits in the palms enabled the hands to be freed (e.g. Chartham). Mail stockings were worn reaching over the knees.

The engraving of mail on brasses merits special notice since the various ways that different engravers used to represent it have led writers to think that there were different types of mail. The evidence of surviving pieces of mail is that in Europe it was all of one kind—interlinked rings, each ring holding four neighbouring rings. This formed a very complicated and tedious design for the engravers of brasses, who as a result, adopted different kinds of shorthand to represent it. At Chartham a complicated pattern was begun on the dexter foot, and never carried through. The different short-hands are useful clues to the identity of the various workshops (see chapter 5).

Cuirie (coat of plates). A leather garment worn over the hauberk and under the surcoat reinforced with metal plates (Westley Waterless). Apart from one brass this only shows on a few sculptured tombs dated up to the mid fourteenth century (e.g. knight in Pershore Abbey, Worcs).

Surcoat. Worn over the hauberk, it fell loosely to the knees, divided front and back for ease on horseback. Later it became shorter in front, (*cf.* the two D'Abernon brasses) and was sometimes decorated heraldically. Its origins may lie in the long dresses worn in Mohammedan areas since it dates back to the twelfth century (first crusade *c.* 1100 AD).

Ailettes. Tied to the shoulders by laces, these may have been made of leather, and could have given protection to the shoulders like the Japanese sode. No actual ailettes survive. Some writers believe them to have been purely decorative; at Chartham and Buslingthorpe they are shown sticking up behind the shoulders, those at Chartham bearing heraldic decoration. The angle at which they are shown is possibly artists' licence, in real life they were more on, than behind the shoulders.

Spurs. Prick spurs, each with a single point, would appear to have wounded rather than encouraged a horse and could have caught in clothing. Rowels (revolving spiked wheels) began to appear *c.* 1260. The method of engraving rowels on brasses has caused confusion. The cut-away background between the spikes of the rowel can look like a protective hood. There is no evidence that hoods were worn and the background metal was necessary simply to give strength to an otherwise fragile brass shape.

EDWARD IV

HENRY VII

Crested helmet used as pillow

stop ribs to prevent weapons slipping to the throat

Tudor portcullis badge

lance rest

top heavy armour becomes lighter

mitten gauntlets

foretasses and hindtasses

lames on skirt become narrower and show mail

sword moves from centre to side of body

pointed sabatons become blunt toed

Ralph St Leger, d. 1470, Ulcombe, Kent.

John Payne, d. 1496, Hutton, Somerset.

Helm. When fighting, a large helm was worn on the head, which could be attached by a chain to the body so that if knocked off while the soldier was on horseback, he could recover it without dismounting (e.g. Trumpington). Padding under the helm was provided by an arming cap under the mail.

Swordbelt and sword. The method of hanging the sword changed from a double to a single hooked or sewn attachment early in the fourteenth century (compare Trumpington and Elsing). The sword itself was straight and long bladed, more for cutting than thrusting. As plate armour developed, the design was adapted to thrusting towards the end of the fourteenth century.

Shield. This was straight (Stoke D'Abernon) or slightly curved (Acton) at the top, with two curved sides meeting at a point at the bottom, known as 'heater shaped'. It could be slung from the right shoulder by means of a strap (guige), but as plate armour developed so the shield became unnecessary. Although brasses do not show shields after *c.* 1350, they were probably carried in battle until the early fifteenth century.

Cuir Bouilli was leather hardened by soaking in heated wax. It is not always possible to tell on brasses when certain parts are representing leather or plate armour. Leather was light, could be made remarkably tough, and could carry complicated decoration (e.g. Chartham).

Developments in the fourteenth century. The weapon against which plate armour was primarily needed was the arrow. There was a demand throughout Western Europe for more and more plate, and mail only showed round the neck, and at elbows and knees. A greater weight of armour was compensated by better protection. The surcoat became a shorter, lighter, sleeveless garment called a jupon, sometimes decorated heraldically. English longbows had been largely responsible for victory at Crecy 1346, and arrows remained the main weapon until outpaced by French canon, towards 1450.

Armour c. 1410

Bascinet. Large helms were replaced by lighter pointed bascinets, to which the aventail was stapled and laced. Towards 1430 the helmet became lower and rounder.

Aventail. Mail covering the neck and shoulders, replaced *c.* 1420 by a steel beaver.

Breastplate. A single piece of plate stretching from the neck to just below the waist, and after *c.* 1400 usually worn with a backplate. The jupon disappeared *c.* 1420 so that the armour was fully visible.

EDWARD VI

ELIZABETH I

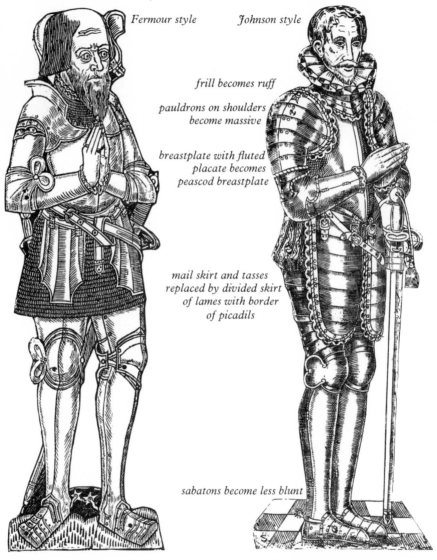

Fermour style

Johnson style

frill becomes ruff

*pauldrons on shoulders
become massive*

*breastplate with fluted
placate becomes
peascod breastplate*

*mail skirt and tasses
replaced by divided skirt
of lames with border
of picadils*

sabatons become less blunt

*Peter Coryton, Esq, d. 1551, St
Mellion, Cornwall.*

*Sir Edward Gage, knt, d. 1569,
eng. 1595, West Firle, Sussex.*

Lance rest. A simple hook attached to the breastplate. Lances (only shown at Stoke D'Abernon) were commonly made of ash, about 13 feet long. A ring of metal (grate or grapper) was fastened to the shaft and during a fight, was placed over the lance rest. On impact the lance rest (arrest) helped to spread the shock. Originally a simple arrest, in the fifteenth century it was also used as a support.

Rerebrace. Plates protecting the upper arm and shoulder.

Vambrace. Plates covering both forearm and elbow (couter). The division between the rerebrace and vambrace is not always clear, as the couter is sometimes attached to the rerebrace and sometimes to the vambrace.

Cuisses. Plates for each thigh and knee (poleyn).

Jamber (greave). Plates enclosing the leg below the knee.

Gauntlets. They were developed from leather gloves covered with strips of metal; after *c.* 1340 articulated plates were made, under which a glove was stitched.

Sabatons. Shoes formed of strips of metal riveted to leather and kept in position by a band under the foot, as on modern ski pants, their development followed that of gauntlets. The very long pointed sabatons (aping civil dress) could be removed when not on horseback.

Dagger. A narrow-bladed dagger was hung opposite the sword and brought into action when the enemy had fallen. It could be thrust between the plates of armour to administer the '*coup de grâce*'.

Armour c. 1460

Towards *c.* 1460 plate armour achieved a peak of functional beauty. Great attention was paid to designing a suit so that it afforded not only protection but flexibility. The thickness of the plates varied according to their function, and the sword arm and bridle arm were differently protected.

Armour was imported from the continent and the best suits of this period were from North Italy and South Germany. A London workshop making brasses (Kent series D) based its patterns on contemporary Milanese suits. Slightly later London brasses *c.* 1470, with heavy exaggerated shoulders (pauldrons) and thin waists seem unreal, but may not be unfaithful records of real suits.

Kettlehat (chapewe). A brimmed helmet was used even in the thirteenth century, but found favour at about this date, sometimes with a greater

CHARLES I

Half suits of armour

shoulders still
heavily protected

peascod shape
less pronounced

sword with
knuckle guard

skirt of lames
more rectangular

leather boots with
heels and spurs

Sir Ed. Filmer, d. 1629, East
Sutton, Kent. Engraved by Ed.
Marshall.

John Pen, 1641, Penn, Bucks.

projection at the back of the neck, in which case it was called a sallet. These helmets were more practical for fighting and resemble the 'tin hats' of modern times.

Crests. On brasses these often stick out flamboyantly at the side because the helmet is being used as a pillow. Made of moulded and painted leather, they were worn in particular at tournaments, and were part of a man's heraldry.

Early Tudor Armour
The standard of brass engraving was at its lowest ebb in early Tudor times and the suits of men in armour on brasses of this period are not of great value for study. Some new features can however be seen:

· *Sabatons.* The pointed sabaton became blunt toed, more suitable for fighting on the ground.

Placate. A plate or plates covering the stomach and lower part of the breastplate. The placate became smaller to show more of the mail skirt below.

Fore Tasse. First used *c.* 1450 these became common in the sixteenth century. They were narrow plates riveted to leather straps and hung by buckles to the breastplate, giving protection to the thighs on top of the mail skirt. Hind tasses hung down at the back.

Elizabethan Armour
The changes from *c.* 1550 (see 'Fermour' style examples which were carefully engraved) to Elizabethan armour reflected the changes in the contours of civilian dress. The breastplate followed the peascod shaped pourpoint (Mr Punch) and shoulders were covered by large pauldrons. Armour was designed to combat hand fire-arms and thicker, less elegant, convex surfaces were produced. Fine quality armour was 'proved', and bullet marks on actual pieces of armour are sometimes evidence of this.

The hemming of armour (and civilian clothes) with material trimmings can be seen (picadils). The area of London called Piccadilly may be a survival of this name, either by being the edge or hem of London at that time, or where pickadils were made and sold. Functionally they prevented the armour from chafing.

The Making of Plate Armour
Compared with the construction of laten plates for brasses, the making of

plate for armour required far more hammering, which was done by hand and by water-powered hammers. By the mid sixteenth century, at least on the Continent, some rolled plate was being produced. The plate not only had to be beaten to varying thicknesses and shapes, but then had to be polished, perhaps etched and gilded, and have hinges, buckles and linings attached. Henry VIII who imported Dutch and German craftsmen to make his own armour (1515) had a workshop with 'hammermen', 'millmen' (polishers) and 'locksmiths' (who fitted hinges etc.) at Greenwich.

Bibliography
Claude Blair, *European Armour,* Batsford, London, 1958.
Vesey Norman, *Arms and Armour,* Weidenfeld and Nicholson, London, 1964. (Includes some illustrations of brasses.)
R. E. Oakeshott, *Archaeology of Weapons,* Lutterworth Press, London, 1960. (Some details of brasses.)
Bengt Tǫhordemann, *Armour from the Battle of Wisby,* 1361, 2 vols, Stockholm, 1939.

FEMININE DRESS

Usually ladies are shown with their husbands, but one of the earliest is a large single figure (5ft. 2in.) to Margaret de Camoys in Trotton, Sussex engraved *c.* 1315. She may be on her own because of her scandalous conduct before her husband died.[1] In any event, she and another large single figure *c.* 1320 in Cobham, Kent, (possibly related to Robt. de Setvans, Chartham, Kent) show the fashion of the period.

Both women are shown wearing long gowns with linen veils and wimples under the chin, so that the visible part of the face is triangular. In fact at this time the whole body was covered except for face, hands and feet.

Towards the end of the fourteenth century, women at court began to display themselves ostentatiously in various ways. Elaborate hair styles were one method which we can trace to 1650 as there are good examples on brasses. The first has been called the nebuly, a reticulated or framed head-dress, in which a close cap was worn with a very frilly or crimped border to the face. It cannot really be understood from brasses alone since without exception examples show ladies full face, but many sculptured tombs (e.g. at East Harling, *c.* 1370) reveal the close cap behind.

[1] See H. R. Morse, M.D., *The Monumental Effigies of Sussex,* 2nd ed., p. 178.

Hair gathered outwards and then upwards into horns.
2 *Arundel, Sussex, engraved c. 1430.* 3 *Ash-next-Sandwich, Kent, 1455.*

4 *Herne, Kent, 1470.*

5 *Blickling, Norfolk, 1485.*

1 *'Nebuly' hair net of many frills. Anon. c. 1390. Holme Pierrepont, Notts, discovered under church floor in 1960. Length 4 ft.*

(4) *Material draped behind the horns, and* (5) *splayed out on a wire frame—the butterfly headdress.*

By the end of the fourteenth century the hair was arranged so that it covered the ears in rolled square frames. The 'crespine' hair style was the first notable change of the fifteenth century and caught the hair in a jewelled net, bunched over the ears and then arranged outwards in cauls. In the horned, mitred or heart shaped head-dress *c.* 1440 these cauls were pointed up above a headband (illustration p. 75).

The 'butterfly' head-dress of *c.* 1460–70 extended the horns with a light wire framework and a kerchief. False hair was sometimes used. This is only a slight change, but the side view of the head, shown on many brasses, makes it look very different. Judging from the very high brushed back appearance it is possible that ladies plucked their foreheads.[1] By 1500 the frame work was cut down to the pedimental head-dress—the face is framed in a Tudor arch. Side flaps hung below the ears, but after 1525 the flaps were cut off or folded back at ear level.

In the 1540s the Paris cap, distinguished by a jewelled band over the head with points towards each cheek, appeared, and remained in fashion until nearly the end of the century. A 'lappet' that fell behind, even to waist level, can be seen disappearing behind heads. Around 1600 this lappet was stiffer and folded so that it lay on the head, shading the forehead. Some of the *prie dieu* groups (e.g. Constantine, Cornwall, 1616) show this arrangement in profile. It sometimes took the form of a stiffened hood, arched over the head, the ends falling loosely behind either to waist or ground level. Some brasses show the fashion for brushed up hair displays, as at Marden, Herefordshire, 1614.

At the end of the century wide brimmed hats were common and by 1630 a head scarf trailing below the waist, is often depicted.

The wimpled face of the early fourteenth century lasted until the Dissolution for widows and nuns, the wimple latterly becoming a piece of crimped material under or over the chin, helping to hide the wearer from view.

The other means women used to display themselves were tight lacing and décolletage. By 1350, womens dresses were tighter with sleeves tightly buttoned from elbow to wrist, and the dress became divided into a bodice and a full skirt. The curious cote hardi over dress with cutaway sides *c.* 1350–70, was a draughty method of displaying the lady rather than

---

[1] This was the period when the steeple head-dress was fashionable in France and Burgundy, but no brass or sculptured tomb shows that it ever reached England.

1 *A mob cap found only on Norfolk school brasses. Beeston Regis, Norfolk, 1527.*

2 *'Pedimental' headdress. Bramley, Hants, 1529.*

3 *The side flaps were eventually folded up. St Mellion, Cornwall, 1551.*

4 *A Paris cap. A very late example specified by John Gage for his wife, 1595 (see p. 48). West Firle, Sussex.*

6 *Brushed up hair displays encouraged the use of earrings. Marden, Herefordshire, 1614.*

5 *A wide brimmed hat, c. 1590. Soc. Ant. London.*

keeping her warm. Sometimes the garment was not cut away but worn tightly round the waist. By 1430 the waistline had ascended to a 'Regency' level just below the breasts, where it stayed until *c.* 1470, but subsequently the natural waist line came once more in evidence and décolletage, which was moderate at the beginning of the century, became somewhat more daring.

A reaction away from waisted garments set in at the end of the fifteenth century and dresses fell rather loosely from neck to foot, hiding the lady from view. By the middle of the sixteenth century, however, puffed and slashed shoulders began to appear and also frills at wrists and neck. There was some shaping to the bosom and sleeves were tighter. Perhaps the most amazing development was the use of starch on the neck frills which grew larger into ruffs. Both sexes surrendered immediately to the novelty of this new neckline. The shapes of clothes hardly hinted at the shape of the body, for shoulders were puffed and the head was isolated by a wide ruff[1] and farthingales spread and padded the hips so that ladies walked in swaying tents. James Laver[2] described late Elizabethan fashions as 'surely among the ugliest that have ever been invented' but one cannot but admire the vast display, as a lady drifted about in such clothes like a galleon. Full-length portraits of ladies show some of the colour and glitter of jewels, so lacking on brasses. After 1615, hip pads disappeared and dresses fell loosely almost to ground level. Turned back cuffs appeared and the ruff became smaller until by *c.* 1640 it became a widely turned down collar, either plain or edged with lace.

Jewellery

Rings are not often shown on brasses because the scale of drawing is too small or the engraving too sweeping for such tiny objects. When rings and other jewellery do appear on brasses they are sometimes conspicuous for their size, such as the necklaces on some ladies wearing butterfly head-dresses (e.g. Blickling, Norfolk).

In the fourteenth century romantic rings and brooches were popular. Actual rings survive with clasped hands or inscriptions, one with a large amethyst found near Cardiff says *'PAR GRANT AMOUR'* ('in great love'). Lombardic letters were used as love brooches, the letter being the initial of the beloved. An 'E' survives in the Hirsch collection in Basle

---

[1] 'These cartwheels of the divels charet of pride', Philip Stubbes.
[2] 'Fashions from Brass Rubbings', *Sphere*, Nov. 8, 1957.

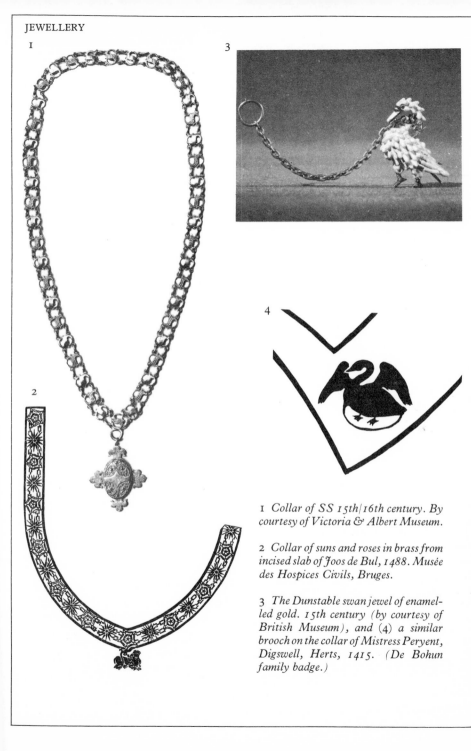

1 *Collar of SS 15th/16th century. By courtesy of Victoria & Albert Museum.*

2 *Collar of suns and roses in brass from incised slab of Joos de Bul, 1488. Musée des Hospices Civils, Bruges.*

3 *The Dunstable swan jewel of enamelled gold. 15th century (by courtesy of British Museum), and (4) a similar brooch on the collar of Mistress Peryent, Digswell, Herts, 1415. (De Bohun family badge.)*

which hinges apart to reveal an inscription. The collar of SS which dates from the fourteenth century and appears on a number of brasses on both men and women between 1405 and 1501 shows the use of letter design. The earliest representation is at Spratton, Nortants, *c.* 1370, on the alabaster effigy of Sir John Swynford. The meaning of SS is not certain but may be short for 'Souvereyne', for Henry IV's motto as Earl of Derby, or *'Soveigne vous de moy'* (forget me not).[1]

Whatever its meaning or original purpose the SS collar became associated with members of the Royal Household, and one can see an original of the fifteenth or sixteenth century in the Victoria and Albert Museum (illustration p. 79). On the accession of Edward IV a collar of alternate suns and roses was worn (examples on brasses 1465–*c.* 1490), but the SS collar survived also. The finest example (illustration p. 79) of this in brass is preserved in the Musée des Hospices Civils in the Rue des Chartreuses in Bruges, from the incised slab (still in the Hospice) to Joos de Bul, 1488. The collar was probably given to him by Edward IV in return for hospitality when he had fled to the city in 1471.[2]

A number of badge brooches are shown on brasses and represent family or political allegiance. The Dunstable swan jewel showing a crowned swan (illustration p. 79), bought by the British Museum in 1966, is an actual example of the de Bohun badge, shown in Alianor de Bohun's canopy in Westminster Abbey (1399) and on Mistress Peryent's collar at Digswell, Herts, 1415 (illustration p. 79). The Beaufort portcullis can be seen on John Payne, 1496, Hutton, Somerset (illustration p. 68). The enamelling of gold developed in France in the fourteenth century and the Dunstable swan jewel in this medium, is fifteenth century, either English or French.

Stones used in jewellery were held in claws or high collets which followed the shape of the stone. From the mid fifteenth century they were faceted, table cut and sometimes backed with foil to add sparkle.

It is interesting to quote the valuation of Benevuto Cellini (1500–71) for gem stones of similar size. A ruby was the most valued, 800 scudi, compared with an emerald (400) a diamond (100) and sapphire (10).

Towards 1500, rosary beads were popular and can be seen on brasses

---

[1] A payment in one of Henry's accounts for 1396–97 was 'for the weight of a collar made, together with esses, of flowers of seveigne vous de moy hanging and enamelled weighing eight ounces'.

[2] See *M.B.S. Trans.,* VI, 320.

hanging from the belts of men (e.g. Boughton Malherbe, Kent, 1499) and some women. The will of Thomas Iden of Stoke, Kent, 1511, asked for a stone to be placed over him and his wife 'wt the pictor of a man and a woman and the pictor of a little man child holdyng her by the beades' (R. H. D'Elboux 'Testamentary Brasses' in *Antiquaries*, vol. XXIX, 1949, p. 183). Such beads were made of box wood, ivory or metal. Hat badges, with the arms and initials of the owner were popular at the same time.

Jewellery often had a combined religious and secular nature. Thus musk balls (pomanders) found on brasses towards the end of the fifteenth century were sometimes contained in devotional jewels. Several Fermour-style brasses *c.* 1550, show pomanders with the Sacred Heart or Monogram (see for example, Easton Neston, Northants, 1552).

In Elizabethan times magnificent chains and pendants were worn, made of gold, pearls, precious stones and glass. The brushed-up hair style encouraged the display of ear rings (Marden, Herefordshire 1614) (illustration p. 77).

CHRYSOMS AND SHROUDS

Chrysoms
After a baby was baptised it was given a chrysom, i.e. a length of linen or other fabric which was wound over the underclothes, and worn for the next month until the mother came to be 'churched' or purified by the priest (the Purification of Women). She then handed it back. During that month the baby itself was referred to as a 'chrysom' and if it died during that time was buried in the chrysom garment. There is a chrysom child on a brass at Stoke D'Abernon 1516, and several others elsewhere. Babies in swaddling clothes

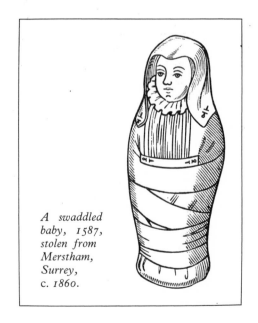

A swaddled baby, 1587, stolen from Merstham, Surrey, c. 1860.

occur on several brasses. The most charming little figure was stolen from Merstham, Surrey, *c.* 1860 (renewed 1911). It wore a little plaited bib, held in place with pins (see illustration).

Shrouds

The custom of engraving people in shrouds is shown on brasses between 1431 (Sheldwich, Kent) and 1714 (Bibury, Glos.). It was most common from 1480–1520.[1] The deceased was depicted wrapped in a shroud or winding sheet that was tied above the head and below the feet. The body was glimpsed, either with flesh still intact, in a state of emaciation, or even crawling with worms (Oddington, Oxon.). Some later examples show a grinning skeleton (Weybridge, Surrey). The anatomy of the skeletons is quaint.

In the late seventeenth century, actual shrouds had to be made solely of sheep's wool to encourage the wool trade. Their depiction on brasses was an extreme method of showing man's mortality. This design is found on sculptured tombs and brasses not only in England but also on the Continent. Flemish, London and Norwich schools all engraved shrouds.

On eighteenth-century inscription brasses this feeling of '*memento mori*' was present in the form of lightly engraved skulls, crossbones, scythes and hour glasses.

[1] The earliest brass showing a shroud is dated 1389 to Wouter Copman in Bruges Cathedral, Belgium.

8

Lost Brasses and Palimpsests

Losses of brasses have been enormous down the centuries—events of history have swept thousands away; the Black Death in 1348, the Dissolution of the Monasteries, the Reformation of the sixteenth century, the Civil War and Commonwealth, the Great Fire of London in 1666, even the Second World War have all contributed to their disappearance.

Natural hazards too, have taken their toll. The earliest brasses had no rivets to hold them in place. Many brasses were placed in the floors of churches where they were trodden and kicked underfoot, and new monuments were sometimes built over old brasses. Churches fell into disrepair, roofs and spires toppled, naves and chancels were extended or rebuilt so that brasses were moved or thrown away. Slabs were often cut down and used merely as paving stones or building blocks.

There are so many empty slabs and records of brasses now lost, that one can estimate very roughly that the number of brasses made up to the date 1700 amounted to something like 100,000, although only 7,500 of these remain today.

When brasses or plate were officially taken out of a church they were usually sold at so much per pound (11d per pound from Thame Church, Oxon., in 1550) and the transaction recorded in the churchwardens' accounts. The men who bought such metal were probably middlemen who in turn sold it to metal workers. Very often at this stage the metal was broken up and melted down. A brass in Okeover, Staffs, is now in fifty-five pieces. In this case, it was recovered from a thief, who in about 1857 had already prepared it for the melting pot. Some metal workers were glad to purchase the old brasses still in the form of sheet metal because sheet metal was what they wanted; so just occasionally a part of a brass has been preserved in some other context, for example as the back of a sundial, (now lost) in Bristol in 1851,[1] clock face (illustration p. 85) or cut into a weathercock such as that made for a turret of York Minster (illustration p. 85). One brass was discovered in use as a fireback in a farmhouse, another as a footscraper outside a house in Royston, Herts. The Society of Antiquaries in London, possesses a set square cut from an inscription plate. The eventual purchasers of these brasses, with the exception of the clock maker, must have been builders or stone masons.

In the sixteenth century 'masons' were also still making monumental brasses and the lost sundial (a rubbing of which exists in the Society of Antiquaries, London) was cut from a Flemish brass, more of which lies hidden on the back of a brass dated *c.* 1582 at Paston, Norfolk. In other words, in about 1582 a mason used the back of an old brass to make a new brass and a sundial.

This curious form of cannibalism, brasses eating brasses, took place in the tomb workshops of both London and Norfolk, and the practice became more prevalent with the Dissolution of the Monasteries. Alien monasteries were dissolved in 1523, smaller and eventually larger religious houses around 1537, and chantries and chapels in 1545. High and low pestered the government for monastic goods and property and the Court of Augmentations was set up to channel the goods in an orderly way. A spate of monastic goods passed through its hands between 1541 and 1543, followed by a spate of land sales in 1544 and 1545. Thousands of brasses must have been moved and very many melted down. Sometimes these were not altogether destroyed but cut up, and new brasses engraved on their backs. Many palimpsest brasses date from this period, and these will be described in the next section.

By about 1560 this source of metal must have been drying up and the tomb makers had once more to look to the Continent for supplies of sheet metal. But, instead of new sheet, they were able to use old Flemish brasses torn from slabs as a result of conflict between the Catholics and the Netherland Protestants—mostly Calvinists. Religious persecution not only brought

[1] *M.B.S. Trans.*, IV, 313.

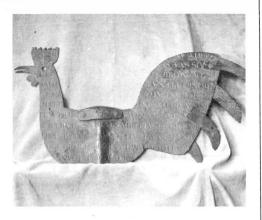

1 *Weathercock from a turret of York Minster (now in vestry), cut from an inscr. to John Moore, 1597. (Inscr. once set in floor of the Lady Chapel. MBS. Trans. V, 49.)*

2 *Latern clock by Thos. Knifeton c. 1693, the face of which was cut from a Latin inscr. c. 1610. Courtesy of Society of Antiquaries, London.*

MARMORE CA
A FVIT:
MPLEVERAT
VIT: •
GNORA MATE
VTE DVAS
TIDEMO·PVF

brasses to England, but Protestant refugees, including Gerald Johnson (see p. 42) who was soon to design many English brasses. It is interesting to read of the many Dutch influences on English culture at this time, from architecture to music.[1]

Many churches in Flanders were wrecked for purely iconoclastic reasons, and in particular brasses from places near the coast reached England. The sundial was part of a Flemish brass, from exactly where we do not yet know, but a Flemish raised letter inscription now divided behind brasses at Harlow, Essex, 1575, St Peter-in-the-East, Oxford, 1574, and Isleham, Cambs, 1574, has come from the neighbourhood of Bergen-op-Zoom, on the Dutch coast. The inscription mentions the creek at 'Crom-fliet' which is nearby, and was perhaps torn up by the 'Sea Beggars'. The sort of behaviour leading to such vandalism by raiding parties is described in *Camden's Annals* for 1580.

'After the English forces had scaled the walls of Mechlin, they rifled the citizens' goods with all insolvency of pillage but raged also even against the Churches, holy things, and tombs, offering violence to the dead. For we saw (which I am ashamed to speak) many tomb stones sent over from thence into England and openly set to sale as arguments of their impiety.'

Two pieces of the back of a brass at Thorpe, Surrey, (obverse 1578) can be traced from the heraldry to Bruges. The heraldry belonged to Richard Visch de la Chapelle, cantor of St Donat's.[2] A picture painted by Gerard David survives in the National Gallery London; it was painted for Richard, and shows him kneeling as the donor in the foreground. As on the brass, the means of identification is a heraldic shield, in this case painted on the collar of his dog. The picture shows the Marriage of St Catherine, (illustration p. 87) and has almost certainly come from this same chapel.

Anti-Catholic feeling developed in England in the late sixteenth and

---

[1] See, for example, D. W. Davies, *Dutch Influences on English Culture 1558–1625*, Cornell University Press.

[2] *S.A.C.*, XXXIII, 3, and XL, 113.

Richard Visch de la Chapelle identified by the arms of his dog, originally in the same chapel as his brass (now a palimpsest illus. p. 92). He wears a lawn surplice and furred almuce. A detail from 'The Marriage of St Catherine' by Gerard David. Illus. by permission of the National Gallery, London.

seventeenth centuries and led to the destruction and mutilation of many brasses. 'Popist' sentiments in inscriptions and representations of Trinities, crosses, and saints were removed.[1] In 1643 a man was paid sixteen shillings 'to erace the superstitious letters from brasses' in All Hallows, Barking, London. The result can be seen on the Evyngar brass.

In the era including the eighteenth century, brasses were accorded little appreciation and were thrown out with little worry, especially if they seemed mutilated. The restorers of churches often got rid of brasses and their slabs when they repaved churches and cathedrals (e.g. Lincoln, 1782). Destruction of brasses in the nineteenth century was often due to the fashion for covering church floors with glazed tiles, and by the introduction of a heating system, whereby long trenches were dug up the aisles to take the heating pipes. A brass of a man in armour, *c.* 1365, was discovered in the furnace room of Freshwater Church, Isle of Wight, some years after restorations in 1876. The slab was found in the churchyard.

Brasses are now appreciated and valued far more, but this in itself can be a hazard to their survival. They present a greater temptation to thieves and are sometimes stolen for their value as antiques. The palimpsest figure of Richard Thorneton, 1544, was stolen from Great Greenford Church, Middx. between 1916 and 1920. In 1954 it appeared in a London antique shop and was sold to a private customer. At the time of its purchase, its origins were not known, but it is naturally hoped that the owner will one day return it to Great Greenford.

PALIMPSESTS

The word palimpsest was first invented to describe a page of manuscript where the original text had been rubbed or scratched away, and to save vellum, had been used again. It is a combination of two Greek words Παλιν (*palin* = again) and Ψηστος (*psēstos* = rubbed).

Palimpsest, used in connection with brasses, however, more often means that the sheet of metal has been turned over and re-used on the back —not on the same side as the original. This was an economy and saved buying new brass sheet.

There are various types of palimpsest:

---

[1] See H. F. Owen Evans, 'Malicious Damage to Brasses', *M.B.S. Trans.*, X, 186–91.

1 *Palimpsest at Yealmpton, Devon, 1580 (22 in. long) and another at Denham, nr. Eye, Suffolk, 1574, forming parts of one rectangular brass from a monastery on the continent. Jacob Wegeschede, c. 1500, kneels in front of the seated Virgin, with St James of Compostella behind him.*

2 *Doodles on the back of a brass at Ewell, Surrey, 1577. The very shallow engraving has been made bolder for this illustration. (17½ in. long.)*

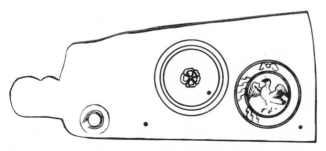

(a) The back shows nothing but experimental 'doodles' (illustration p. 89) or a first or un-finished attempt at some design (illustration p. 92). The front and back are therefore of about the same date. Ocassionally blank spaces on earlier brasses have been 'doodled' on (e.g. St Olave, Hart St. 1566, London).

(b) The back shows earlier work which has come from a dissolved or despoiled church or monastery in England. If the earlier side is dated before *c.* 1560 (even if the engraving is Flemish) one can expect it to have come from an English site. If the work is after *c.* 1560 and Flemish, one can expect it to have come from the Continent.

(c) The older brass has not been turned over but has been re-used (appropriated) with or without any extra engraving. For example at Bromham, Beds, a brass of 1435 has taken on the date 1535 merely by receiving a new inscription. At Chalfont St Peter, the figure of a priest *c.* 1440 has had lines of shading added, his toes blunted, and an inscription added, to turn him into Robt. Hanson, 1545. This type of palimpsest was most commonly made in the 1540s when the market was flooded with old brasses.

Examples of categories *(a)*, *(b)* and *(c)* are listed on p. 94.

The re-use of stonework is more easily detected in the period *c.* 1520–60 since a number of slabs were re-used without being turned over. A slab with an incised cross was used in Braunton, Devon in the year 1548, and a slab that had held a man and lady of *c.* 1480 (dated by the outline of a butterfly head-dress) was re-used at Easton Neston, Northants, 1552. At Hainton, Lincs, a mural brass of 1553 has been set in the wall above an appropriated altar tomb. The asymetrical adaptation of the carving and meaningless initials in the stone prove that it was not originally intended to accompany the brass.

The value of palimpsests can be summarized as follows:

Those of paragraph *(a)* above give us a glimpse of the human aspect of the workshops, and thus we see the rejected work, or the doodling of an idle or experimental moment.

Those in *(b)* and *(c)* show parts of earlier brasses and here we are able to recover parts of many monuments destroyed at the dissolution in England or a little later by events in Flanders. Some of these date back to the early fourteenth century and are of vital importance since they add to the little evidence we have to indicate the style and quality of perhaps the most magnificent period of all for brass engraving.

Occasionally, some of the fragments can be joined to other fragments (see palimpsest links section) so that a partial reconstruction can be made. Sometimes heraldry or inscriptions enable the brass to be traced to its church of origin, either in England or in Flanders. One aspect of palimpsest links is their value in linking the brasses on their backs (the fronts as seen in the churches) to one workshop (see pp. 93–94).

The main problem of palimpsests is that the earlier side is nearly always hidden, riveted, covered in bitumen and bedded in the matrix of the slab. The vast majority cannot be seen or rubbed. However, evidence to date shows that very many English brasses made between 1520 and 1580 are palimpsest. Such brasses bear signs such as their thickness, filled-in rivet holes, or several joined pieces of metal to suggest that they are palimpsest. From time to time a piece of brass works loose, when the earlier side can be cleaned and examined. If there is any engraving it can then be rubbed, and perhaps a cast taken, before refixing. Because of the importance of preventing loose pieces of brass from getting lost, and the value of recording palimpsests, the Monumental Brass Society, (c/o Society of Antiquaries, Burlington House, Piccadilly, London, W.1.) is always interested to hear when pieces of brass come loose. Advice and help in refixing is available from the Society.

Antiquarian interest in palimpsests began in the eighteenth century. One part of a brass at Walton on Thames (see illustration p. 92) was known in 1775 and at Norton Disney an earlier Flemish inscription was known in 1782 (palimpsest type (b)). By 1864, about 25 palimpsests had been reported, if not adequately recorded. The pioneer of methodical palimpsest recording was Mill Stephenson, who illustrated and described discoveries made up to 1900 in Vol. IV of the *Transactions of the Monumental Brass Society*. His work was continued by Mr R. H. Pearson when the M.B.S., dormant since the First World War, was eventually revived in 1930. By about 1942, 330 brasses had been discovered to be palimpsest and the figure in 1968 is about 385. The number of *separate* palimpsest fragments (one brass might have been made from many old pieces) is over twice that number.

Palimpsests have become a new if obscure addition to the general study of brasses. To see them one must consult books and old rubbings in the brass rubbing collections of museums. The best-known collections are at the Society of Antiquaries, London, Archaeological and Ethnological Museum, Cambridge, and at the Victoria and Albert Museum, London.

1 *back*   2 *front*

1 *Rejected version on the back of (2) at Walton-on-Thames, Surrey, 1587. Tho. Selwyn was keeper of St Mary Oatlands Park and this scene records a feat he performed in front of Queen Eliz. I. 8 in. × 7½ in. wide, on hinge.*

3 *Part of inscr. at Gunby, Lincs, 1552, used twice before, first c. 1440 'die mensis', second (4) c. 1500 'hys' and third (3) 1552 by cutting away to leave raised letters 'charyte to'.*

Palimpsest links which form part of a life-size monastic figure, c. 1430, wearing a cloak and drawstring pendant of the Order of St John of Jerusalem.

6 & 7 *Harlington, Middx, 1545, (8, 9, 11, 12 & 13), Ellesborough, Bucks, 1544, (10), Lambourne, Essex, 1546. (18¾ in. long.)*

5 *Palimpsest at Thorpe, Surrey, 1578, showing feet and shield of Richard Visch de la Chapelle from St Catherine's chapel in St Donat's, Bruges (see p. 87).*

3 *front*

4 *back*

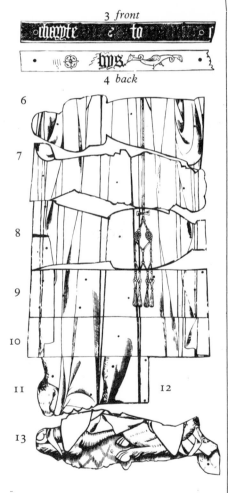

Some palimpsest fragments may not be parts of earlier brasses, but metal icons. The 'Durer'-like crucifixion *c.* 1540 discovered at Easton Neston 1552 is large in scale for a brass (illustrated in *M.B.S. Trans.*, IX, 54).

PALIMPSEST LINKS

Whenever a new palimpsest discovery is made a search begins, since more of the earlier brass may have been discovered in some other church, behind another brass made at about the same time. In several instances a number of pieces have been fitted together like a huge jigsaw puzzle. So eight fragments from Harlington, Middx, 1545, Lambourne, Essex, 1546, and Ellesborough, Bucks, 1544 almost complete the lower half of a large monastic figure *c.* 1430 wearing a cross pendant at the end of mantle drawstrings and almost certainly identified with the order of St John of Jerusalem, (see illustration p. 92). There are many other links mostly behind 'Fermour'-style brasses, and the search for them is one of the obvious fascinations of the study of palimpsests.

The list below shows the network of links that have been made behind 'Stafford' and 'Fermour'-style brasses. Research on these lines is continuing.

SCRIPT A
1540	London, N.1. Islington, St Mary (P)
1540	Bucks., Edlesborough (P)
1544	Middx., Isleworth (P)

etc.

SCRIPT B
1541	Northants., Charwelton (P)
1544	Bucks., Ellesborough (P)
1545	Middx., Harlington (P)
1546	London, N.1. Islington St Mary (P)
1546	Essex, Lambourne (P)

etc.

SCRIPT C
1548	Devon, Braunton, (P)
c. 1550	Cambs., Dry Drayton
c. 1550	Cornwall, Crowan, (P)

c. 1550	Group of lost chil. probably from Quarrendon, Bucks. (P)
1550	Cambs., Isleham, Inscr. only
1550	Bucks., Twyford, (P)
1550	Yorks., Sessay, (P)
1551	Bucks.,Dinton, (P)
1551	Cornwall, St Mellion, (P)
1551	Cumberland, Greystoke, (P)
1551	Hants, Winchester St Cross Inscr. only
1551	Notts., Ossington, (P)
1552	Hants., Stoke Charity, Inscr. only (P)
1552	Cambs., Horseheath
1552	Kent, Beckenham
1552	Northants., Easton Neston, (P)
1552	Oxon., Somerton, (P)
1553	Bucks., Halton, (P)
1553	Bucks., Great Hampden, (P)
1553	Cambs., Kirtling
1553	Cambs., Milton, (P)
1553	Kent, Penshurst
1553	Kent, Shorne, a lost inscr. (P)
1553	Lincs., Hainton, ((P) stonework)
1553	Northants., Ashby St. Legers.
1553	Middx., Littleton, Inscr. only
1554	Bucks., Chilton, Inscr. only
1554	Salop., Ludford (P)

LIST OF VISIBLE PALIMPSESTS

A few palimpsests have been hinged or framed in such a way that both sides can be seen (even if it is not possible to take rubbings), these are listed under each category of palimpsest:

(a) Workshop doodles or rejected work
Bucks., Chalfont St Giles, 1523, Inscr. 1521.
Middx., Cowley, 1502. Inscr. 1497.
Surrey, Walton-on-Thames, 1587. Rejected stag hunt scene, *c.* 1587.
(b) Earlier English work. An asterisk signifies that the palimpsest is of special interest. Note that most examples are behind brasses from c. 1520–60.
Berks., Binfield, 1558. Inscr. *c.* 1400.
Berks., St Laur., Reading, 1538. Fixed to wall of N. chancel in brass frames. Part of brass to Sir John Popham buried in the Charterhouse, London, 1463.
Bucks., Denham, 1545, *c.* 1440.
Bucks., Haddenham, 1539, *c.* 1420.

Cheshire, Holy Trinity, Chester, 1545, Leg of man in armour wearing the Order of the Garter c. 1520.

*Devon, Luppitt, c. 1440. Framed behind glass. Lady c. 1400.

Devon, Braunton, 1548, man in armour c. 1370.

Dorset, Piddlehinton, 1562. Electrotype of abbot or prior c. 1500.

Essex, Fryerning, 1563. Pieces of c. 1460 and 1500.

*Herts., Great Berkhamstead, 1558. Inscr. c. 1500. Fine goldsmith's work.

Kent, Faversham, c. 1550. Shields hinged to pillar in N. Aisle. c. 1460.

Kent, Hever, c. 1540. Cross with pt. of inscr. c. 1520 on back.

Kent, Orpington, 1522. Pts. of inscr. 1516 and c. 1520 in revolving brackets behind glass (possibly rejected work).

*Lincs., Great Bowden, 1403. Framed behind glass. Flemish civilian in canopy c. 1370.

London, E.C.3, All Hallows, Barking, 1556. Head of lady c. 1430.

London, S.E.5, Camberwell St Giles, 1538. Inscr. c. 1480 and appr. arm c. 1465: 1582, Flemish frags. c. 1500.

Middx., Harefield, c. 1537. Electrotypes of civilians c. 1460, shrouds c. 1490, priest in mass vests. c. 1390, etc.

Oxon, Shipton-under-Wychwood, 1548. Inscr. c. 1510.

*Staffs, Clifton Campville, 1360. Electrotype in vestry of man in arm. c. 1300. A rare early figure.

Surrey, Cobham, c. 1560. Priest in mass vests. c. 1510 in glass case.

Westmoreland, Morland, 1562. Inscr. 1520.

(c) Earlier Flemish Work from the Continent behind brasses from c. 1560–85.

*Kent, Biddenden, 1572. Electrotype of some fine Flemish pieces, c. 1360 and c. 1525.

Kent, Erith, 1574. Behind glass in hinged frame. Part of a Flemish brass c. 1485 showing heraldic sh. (more is at Isleham, Cambs., 1574 and Isleworth, Middx., 1575).

Devon, Yealmpton, 1580. Pt. of Flemish brass, more at Denham (Nr. Eye), Suffolk, c. 1500.

*Kent, Margate, 1582. Pt. of border of Flemish brass c. 1400 showing ages of man (illustration p. 60).

Lancs., Rufford, 1443 (engr. later), electrotype showing pt. of Flemish brass c. 1525, more of which is at Bradfield, Essex, 1577 and Thames Ditton, Surrey, 1580.

Lincs., Norton Disney, 1578. Flemish inscr. 1518 from Middleburg, Holland.

Somerset, Fivehead, c. 1565. Pts. of Flemish brass to a lady c. 1365 with Spanish marg. inscr. More pieces at Chalfont St Giles, Bucks. c. 1560, Dinton, Bucks., 1551 and Pottesgrove, Beds. 1563.

Suffolk, Hadleigh, c. 1574. Head and shoulders of civilian, Flemish c. 1500.

Suffolk, Halesworth, 1581. Pt. of civilian, Flemish c. 1510.

Warwicks., Haseley, 1573. Pt. of civ. Flemish c. 1510.

Wilts., West Lavington, c. 1571. Flemish inscr. 1518 from Middleburg, Holland.

9

The Care of Brasses

No slab should be moved unless there is evidence that it is not in its original place. A brass should remain in its slab. Any loose pieces should be refixed as soon as possible if necessary with skilled advice which is freely available from the Monumental Brass Society. When a brass on the floor is in an exposed position it should be covered with a nonabrasive material such as felt. Coconut matting is abrasive and rubber underlay contains chemicals which may attack the metal. A brass should never be polished since this will soon wear away the engraving. If it is dirty or corroded it can be cleaned with paraffin or petrol and then wiped dry.

The slabs tend to flake unless kept well polished. Purbeck, Bethersden and other stones can be washed clean with alkali-free soap (e.g. baby soap) and distilled water. After the slab is completely dry it can be polished with a mixture of melted white beeswax with a little turpentine added to make a good paste. If the surface is very scratched a mixture of soft soap and powdered whiting can be rubbed in to get a new surface gloss. This mixture should not be rubbed over the metal parts.

The above advice has been extracted from a leaflet called 'The Care of Monumental Brasses and Ledger Slabs in Churches'.[1]

[1] Published by the Church Information Office, Church House, Westminster, S.W.1, for the Central Council for the Care of Churches and the M.B.S.

10

Inscriptions

Inscriptions on brasses varied from century to century not only in letter shapes and positioning on the slab but in the facts and sentiments expressed.

SHAPE OF LETTER AND POSITION

Lombardic (Uncial, Longobardic, Lombardic-Uncial) Up to *c.* 1360.
Letters were broad, well-formed, and legible, each a separate piece of brass, set into its own matrix, but now mostly lost. By about 1310 the lettering began to be cut on narrow brass fillets, and set near the edge of the slab, but these too have mostly been lost. Fillets were not only easier to engrave but could be fixed more easily to the slab. Lombardic letters were used until *c.* 1360. On Flemish brasses the Lombardic letters were not separate pieces of brass but part of the general groundwork of joined and engraved plates.

Black letter (Old English) *c.* 1360–*c.* 1590
At first letters were rounded, easily read, and clearly derived from the Lombardic shapes, *c.* 1360–1410, then letters became more upright, and were largely composed of straight lines often making inscriptions very difficult to read, *c.* 1400–1460. From *c.* 1460 to *c.* 1590 black letters were more rounded and legible but less neat and even, and had many individual characteristics. This is a distinct help in recognizing different workshops or engravers. (See chapter 5.) From *c.* 1470 to *c.* 1530 the lettering was sometimes raised (the background was cut away instead of the letter shapes) which was more laborious, but more decorative.

97

The development of lettering in England (left column) and Flanders (right column) from the 14th to the 17th century.

1 Lombardic cut-out letters from Dean, Beds, c. 1300
2 Early black letters, Brightwell Baldwin, c. 1370.
3 Black letters, New College, Oxford, 1451.
4 Black letters, Norfolk school, 1509 (rev. of Walsingham, Norfolk, 1539).
5 Black letters, Norfolk school, Walsingham, Norfolk, 1539.
6 Roman capitals, c. 1600 (rev. of Fingringhoe, Essex, c. 1600).
7 Rough script, Shepherdswell, Kent, 1660.
8 Lombardic incised letters, c. 1360 (rev. of Topcliffe, Yorks, 1391).
9 Black letters, c. 1380 (rev. of Adderley, Salop, 1560).
10 Black letters, c. 1520 (rev. of Terling, Essex, 1584).
11 Roman capitals, c. 1550 (rev. of Stokesby, Norfolk, 1570).

Inscriptions were placed round the margin of the slab, or beneath the feet of the figures from *c.* 1350 onwards. Foot inscriptions tended to become lengthy. Invocatory prayers were sometimes added, issuing from the mouths of the figures on scrolls, *c.* 1450–1535. Flemish brasses went through similar changes, but were often neater and more elaborately engraved.

Roman lettering Mainly from *c.* 1590
Roman lower-case inscriptions and capital letter inscriptions were adopted by the Southwark workshops *c.* 1590, but a few examples are earlier (e.g. Hever, Kent, 1538).

Copperplate
Typical of small eighteenth-century brasses, copperplate is easy to read provided that the shallow engraving has not been polished away. The size of letters has become much smaller. Some of these inscriptions, decorated at the top and bottom with emblems of mortality like a winged hourglass, grave-digging tools or a scythe, were made by men who engraved clock faces. A plate signed R. Banister to Bridget Thomas 1723, in Crewkerne, Somerset is not only the shape of a grandfather clock's face, but has one lightly scratched on the reverse side. Charles Sherborn, of Gutter Lane, London E.C.2, who made a plate at Kenilworth, Warwicks, 1753, and Carhampton, Somerset, *c.* 1763, also engraved bookplates. Such brasses were often attached to churchyard tombstones.

NUMERALS

Roman numerals were used until the sixteenth century, but Arabic numerals began to appear *c.* 1450 (Northleach, Glos, 1447 and Ware, Herts, 1454).

LANGUAGES

Norman French, found on the earliest brasses was the language used at Court. It survived until *c.* 1420, but Latin was used during that period for ecclesiastics and went on being used for ecclesiastics with some exceptions in later centuries. English first appeared at the end of the fourteenth century, although an undated inscription at Brightwell Baldwin, Oxon, in early black letters may be dated *c.* 1370. Around 1410 it is possible to find any of these languages being used, even all three in one inscription (e.g. palimpsest at Aldershot, Hants, 1583). Occasionally Greek and Hebrew are found. (Greek, Latin and English at Swanton Abbot, Norfolk, 1641.)

FACTS AND SENTIMENTS EXPRESSED

It is not only the letter shapes of early inscriptions which merit study, the actual sentiments expressed are interesting in themselves. Indents of letters in a heavy slab at Albury Surrey, *c.* 1330 read, *'WILLELMUM TERNUM DE WESTONE SUSCIPE CHRISTE LUMEN AD ETERNUM QUEM DEPRIMIT HIC LAPIS ISTE'*. ('Accept O Christ, William the third of Weston, to eternal light, whom this stone weighs down'.)

The contents of inscriptions at different periods varied considerably. The saying of prayers for the deceased was of growing importance until the Dissolution. (Toft Trees, Norfolk, *c.* 1325) *'WS KE ICI PASSEZ PUR LALME THOMAS DE MELHAM PRYEZ'*. ('You who pass here pray for the soul of Thomas de Melham'.) It was felt that souls could be preserved from some of the tortures so vividly shown on Doom paintings by regular prayer offered up on their behalf; so wealthy men built churches and chantry chapels and gave land to provide money to pay for priests, who would pray for them when they were dead. The words 'pray for the soul' and 'On whose soul may God have mercy, Amen' occur again and again. In order to persuade the passer-by that he should say a prayer for the deceased a pardon of a given number of days was sometimes offered—40 days for Sir Robt de Bures at Acton and an incredible 26,000 years and 16 days for Roger Leigh 1506, Macclesfield, Cheshire.

Inscriptions on tombs were often worded to remind passers-by that they too were sure to die, and the phrase, either in Latin or English that 'as I am so you will be' was common in the fifteenth century. Such words might be illustrated by a macabre and anatomically quaint representation of the deceased lying as a skeleton or cadaver in a shroud. (See the section on shrouds p. 82).

Sometimes figures were shown with special labels issuing from their mouths asking for Divine help 'Jesu mercy, Lady helpe'. The labels might stretch towards a Trinity to which their prayers were directed.

INSCRIPTIONS

After the Reformation there was a noticeable change in feeling, indeed phrases such as 'pray for the soul' and 'on whose soul may the Lord have mercy' were scratched from old brasses (e.g. Cople, Beds, 1550).

Inscriptions then began to show that the monuments were not marking souls waiting for heaven so much as ancestors from whom passers-by might be descended—they had become genealogical records for the benefit of the living. Men were named and given their trades or professions (as before) but the fathers of the wives were also named. It was at this time that people began to have family portraits painted—they even influenced the design of some brasses (e.g. Jas Cotrel, 1595, York Minster). Pride in the very size of the family became apparent. At Lenham, Kent, 1642, an inscription states that the grandmother of the deceased had when she died 367 children, 16 of her own body, 114 grand children, 228 in the third generation and 9 in the fourth.

In the late sixteenth century and in the seventeenth, a note of eulogizing began—carefully chosen balanced compliments which seem too good to have been entirely true. So, at Washfield, Devon, 1605 the widow of Philip Steyning possessed: 'Birth, beauty, personage, good grace, court breeding, gravitye, chast love, trueth, virtue, constant faith, and sincere piety.' Ann Emptage 1622, depicted at St Nicholas, Wade was 'towards God religious to her husband loving and comfortable, over all his children (having no issue of her own body) tender and carefull'.

Puns and poetry in English or Latin were common throughout the period of brasses. Just as the heraldry sometimes punned on a man's name, so we find *'More super virides montes'* on a brass to Thomas Greenhill 1634, Beddington, Surrey, and a little engraving of a harp after the name Harper, on a marginal inscription at Swardeston, Derbyshire (1473). Much of the verse on inscriptions is of poor quality. The largest number of lines on the smallest area of brass must surely be 96 lines of minute Roman letters on a plate 20in. $\times$ 14$\frac{1}{2}$in. at North Cadbury, Somerset, to Lady Magdalen Hastings, 1596.

READING INSCRIPTIONS

Let it be said at the start that some inscriptions are at best hard to understand. However, very many use the same form of words, especially at the beginning and end. These stock phrases are found in Norman French, English, Latin and Flemish, so that when once they are known, hundreds of inscriptions come very near to complete translation. Certain stock phrases in Norman French inscriptions differ slightly from those on later brasses, and are given first.

'*Vous ki passez par ici pries pur lame de* . . . (name), (number) *jours de pardoun avera.*' (Literal translation) 'You who pass by here say prayers for the soul of (name) and you will have 'x' days of pardon.'

It became customary in the fourteenth century to add dates of death and the formula changes to:

Ici gist			
	name,	*qui morust*	
Hic jacet	profession and	*qui obiit*	date
Here lies (buried)	wife	who died on	
Hier (vooren) light (begraven)		*die overleet den*	

Dieu de sa alme eit merci. Amen
Cuius anime (animabus) propicieter Deus. Amen.
On whose soul(s) may the Lord have mercy. Amen
Bidt got voer die ziele(n)

One of the main problems is that words are often abbreviated, especially the phrase at the end. At Oulton, Suffolk, 1478, it has been shortened to '*q⁰r aïabz ppiciet dê amē*'. But if one knows the phrase it is still very easy to read, and seven marks in the form of lines, squiggles or small letters show exactly where the words have been abbreviated.

Practice is the key to success, and the best training is to look at many inscriptions and to become familiar with the letter shapes, like getting used to someones difficult handwriting—there is no special short cut.[1]

NOTE S in the long s form ſ is different from f.

ff means F.

i and y are often interchanged.

v and u are often interchanged.

---

[1] Obscure Latin words can be looked up in *A Medieval Latin Word List*, O.U.P., and old Flemish in *Middel-Nederlansch Hardwoordenboek* (translated into modern Dutch).

11

Heraldry

Heraldry appears on very many brasses and adds a pleasing touch of colour to the brown metal. Small shields of arms were often set near the corners of slabs. They bore the arms of the deceased persons and are useful in identifying them when inscriptions have been lost. In order to identify and describe such shields accurately some heraldic knowledge should be acquired.

The terms *dexter* (right hand) and *sinister* (left hand) are used to specify shields on a slab, and should be used also to describe the component parts of a shield itself. The dexter side is on the right hand of the effigy and therefore on your left hand as you face the brass.

When a shield is divided down the middle *(party per pale)*, with a separate coat of arms on either side, a married couple is implied, the husband's arms being on the dexter side, and the wife's on the sinister. The former is then said to *impale* the latter. If the wife is an heiress, the coats are not impaled, but an *inescutcheon,* or small shield, bearing the wife's arms, is placed upon the centre of those of the husband. Where there are two wives, the husband's arms, on the dexter side, impale the two wives' on the sinister, one above the other.

When a shield is divided into four parts, it is said to be quartered, and the quarters are numbered—the upper pair, dexter and sinister, first and second, and the lower pair respectively, third and fourth. When a man quarters two coats only, the first and fourth (identical) are the arms of his father, and the second and third those of his mother, or some more remote ancestress.

In heraldry two metals are used, namely gold and silver (yellow and white) respectively *or* and *argent*. Colours or tinctures are more numerous, but the two most common are blue and red, *azure* and *gules*. The others are black, green and purple—*sable, vert,* and *purpure*. With respect to metals and tinctures, it is a rule that a metal is never put upon a metal, nor a colour upon a colour. A method of expressing the metals and colours with dots and lines was invented in 1640. In medieval and Tudor times the shields were shown thus: the surface of the brass was cut away, and the cavities filled with pigments mixed with resin, of which in the vast majority of examples, little or no trace remains. Gold was treated differently, and forms the key to the armorial bearings of nearly all brasses. In this case the surface of the brass was not cut away, but was gilded or left plain. Thus on a black heelball rubbing, the parts which appear black are almost always *or*. *Argent* was sometimes represented by lead inlay. Later, the charges were simply engraved (no pigment) and in the eighteenth century, hatching lines are sometimes found.

Besides tinctures, two kinds of fur were in constant use. *Ermine*, white with black spots, with the variants *ermines,* sable with white spots, and *erminois*, of which the ground was *or*—the most easily recognized. *Vair*, a blue and white fur, was represented by alternate pieces dovetailed together.

For the names of charges and other technical information, the reader is referred to one of the many illustrated books on heraldry (see bibliography).

Coats-of-arms are not, however, confined to separate shields. They appear also in various parts of the canopies, as finials, or in the spandrels, or hung from the shafts; they are sometimes placed half-way down the sides of border fillets, or on either side of the foot inscriptions; they are blazoned on banners (Felbrigg, Norfolk; Ashford, Kent), and on pennons (Stoke d'Abernon, Surrey); they appear on the war-shields of early knights, and on ailettes (Trumpington, Cambs); they are embroidered on the dress of both knights and their ladies. A good example to be seen on a surcoat is at Chartham, Kent, where Sir Robert de Setvans, d. 1307, has his surcoat *semée* (i.e. sown or sprinkled) with winnowing fans. The shorter surcoat or jupon was sometimes charged with armorial bearings. (Aldborough, Yorks, *c.* 1360; Southacre, Norfolk, 1384; Baginton, Warwick, 1407.)

Tabards-of-arms came into use *c.* 1450 and continued until the reign of Elizabeth. Since then they have been worn only by heralds on great public occasions. They were short coats of silk, worn over armour. The arms of the wearer were embroidered on the front and on the back and were repeated on each sleeve. (Childrey Berks, 1444; Broxbourne, Herts, 1473; Hunstanton, Norfolk, 1506; Cardington, Beds; *c.* 1540.)

Several methods were used to blazon ladies' dresses. One of the earliest was to embroider the lady's own arms on her kirtle, and her husband's arms on her mantle. (Long Melford, Suffolk; *c.* 1480; Cardington, Beds, *c.* 1540.) Another was to blazon only the mantle, placing the husband's arms on the dexter side and the lady's on the sinister. (Enfield, Middlesex, *c.* 1470; Beckenham, Kent, 1552.) Sometimes, and especially on late brasses, the husband's arms were omitted, and the lady's embroidered alone on her mantle. But this is sometimes because we see only one side of the mantle as the lady kneels. (Impington, Cambs, 1505; Wrotham, Kent, 1525.)

Crests were frequently placed on brasses after 1340. The knight pillowed his head upon a helmet, and from it, or rather from a wreath (of two colours, twisted like a turban) rose the crest. Mantling, or a coronet were frequently added. The helm, wreath, crest and mantling, together with the shield of arms, were sometimes placed apart from and above the figure, making what is called an achievement.

Merchants' marks are very frequently found engraved upon shields, especially from *c.* 1450 to *c.* 1550, in the place of armorial bearing.

12

Saints

Saints were often placed in crossheads, on brackets, in canopies, as separate figures, or on the copes or morses of priests. John de Sleford 1401, Balsham Cambs, wears a cope with 10 saints, each helpfully named. Very often labelling was omitted and then we have to identify the haloed figures by the symbols that they carry. This is usually quite easy to do, but some symbols are ambiguous. Some saints were often paired e.g. Peter and Paul, which makes identification easier.

Symbols are listed alphabetically below.

Axe	St Mathias
Axe and book	St Matthew (often grouped with St James the Great)
Anchor	St Nicholas
Balls (3)	St Nicholas
Basket (of bread)	St Philip (from feeding of the five thousand)
Chalice (with serpent)	St John Evang (often grouped with St Andrew)
Child and book	St Agnes (teaching Mary) or St Elizabeth (teaching St John Bapt. with lamb)
Child on shoulder	St Christopher carrying Christ
Club	St Jude, St James the Less (a fuller's bat)
Cross staff	St Philip
Cross saltire (like an 'X')	St Andrew (often grouped with St John Evang.)
Dragon	St George (often grouped with St Katherine), St Margt.
Fish(es)	St Simon
Gridiron	St Laurence, St Faith
Key(s)	St Peter (often grouped with St Paul)
Knife	St Bartholomew, a butcher's flaying knife.
Lamb	St John Bapt., St Agnes

Saw	St Simon
Scallop shell	St James the Great of Compostella (often grouped with St Matthew)
Spear	St Thomas
Square (mason's)	St Jude, St Thomas
Stone	St Stephen
Sword	St Paul (often grouped with St Peter)
Tower	St Barbara
Vase	St Mary Magdalene
Vestments and pall	An Archbishop saint, St. Thos. of Canterbury?
Wheel (and sword)	St Katherine (often grouped with St George)

HOLY TRINITIES

God the Father; a bearded old man seated on a throne behind God the Son; Christ on the Cross, and with God the Holy Ghost; a dove (sometimes omitted) perched on the arm of the Cross, occur on many brasses like inset icons. This stylized composition is found in all the arts. When printing began in the fifteenth century, wooden blocks showing the Trinity were often used as illustrations in religious books. The resemblance to rubbings of Trinities is striking.

THE EIDOLON OF THE SOUL

Abraham holds the naked new-born soul of the deceased in a napkin or in the folds of his clothing—'in Abraham's bosom'. This composition is found mainly on Franco-Flemish or Flemish brasses (Higham Ferrers and Kings Lynn) and is usually in a top centre position. In this context Abraham may equally be described as 'God the Father'. On the ogee arch immediately below this scene at Higham Ferrers are the words, '*Suscipiat me Christus qui vocavit me et in sinu Abrahè Angeli deducant me.*—Accept me Christ who called me and Angels lead me to Abraham's bosom.' Here the seated figure holds an orb which symbolizes God the Father.

13
Brass Rubbing

An oil painting of the interior of the old church at Delft made in 1656 by Hendrik van Vliet, shows a charming group of three children gathered round a little boy who appears to be taking a rubbing of a stone or brass (illustration above). The little girl standing in front of him is perhaps holding a completed rubbing. Such a pastime was no doubt common, and appealed to the artist who painted the same activity in progress in the new church at Delft.[1] Here a red chalk rubbing can just be seen. No rubbings from so early a date have survived but these pictures prove that such an activity existed.

Some of the earliest surviving full-scale copies of brasses were made at the end of the eighteenth century by the antiquary Craven Ord (1756–1832). His method was to spread printer's ink over the brass, wipe the surface clean, so that ink remained only in the lines of engraving, and after placing damp French paper on top, followed by a layer of cloth, to tread them heavily under foot. He finished the outlines at home, cut out the figures and stuck them into a huge portfolio. The results were often pale and incomplete and inscriptions were, of course, in looking-glass writing. Craven Ord commented on an impression that he took in Goring Church Oxfordshire

[1] Jacket/cover. Collection of Lord Northbrook.

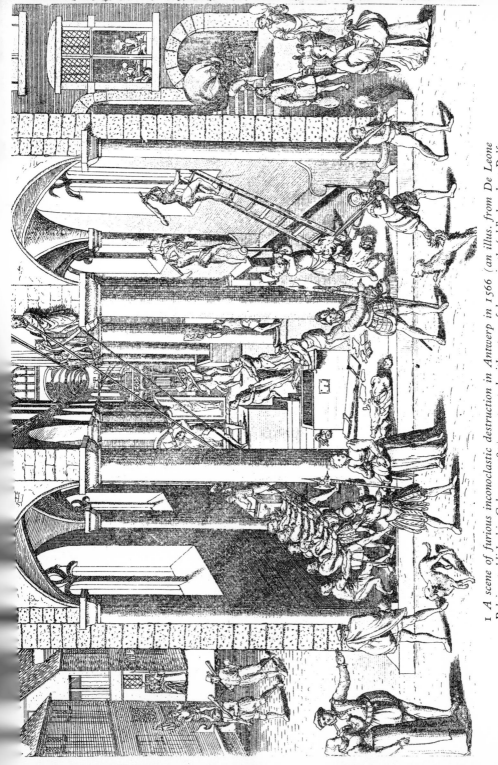

1 A scene of furious inconoclastic destruction in Antwerp in 1566 (an illus. from De Leone Belgico, published in Cologne, 1583), contrasted with a peaceful scene in the 'old' church at Delft (facing), almost a century later (detail of a painting by Hendrick van Vliet 39½ in. × 33 in., by permission of the Baltimore Museum of Art). Children on the left appear to be taking rubbings of a brass or slab.

that it was 'most perfect and was owing to my well soaking the paper in the River Thames about half an hour before I used it'.

Ord's collection, now kept in the British Museum, is of special value as he has recorded some brasses and parts of brasses that have since disappeared. His method of taking impressions would hardly be permitted today.

A clean dry method of copying brasses became popular towards the end of Craven Ord's lifetime, using Ullathorne heelball. The method was like putting a coin under a piece of paper and rubbing on top with a pencil. Using Ullathorne wax the image of the brass appeared black with white lines of engraving, and although this gave a negative effect, inscriptions were no longer in looking-glass writing. Ullathorne was originally designed for colouring and protecting the welts of shoes, not for brass rubbing. It is no longer made, but the small puck-like discs will still be remembered by some people together with its pleasant smell. Hartshorne (*Sepulchral Monuments* p. 56) writing before 1840 refers to 'this little piece of heelball, uniting even fragrance with its economy . . .'

Some heelball can still be bought today but it is inclined to be too grey and greasy for brassrubbing and this led the Monumental Brass Society to collaborate with one of the makers of heelball to formulate a wax specifically for brass rubbing. For a time the Society distributed it to its members, but now this wax (and all other brass rubbing equipment) is marketed by Phillips and Page Ltd, 50, Kensington Church Street, London, W. 8. The wax is in stick and cake form. Sticks are essential, but some people like a larger cake which can be held in both hands for rubbing the main stretches of large brasses.

Paper

The best paper for the purpose is all-rag detail paper 70 grammes per sq. metre in weight. This is thin enough to transmit the engraving and tough enough to withstand the strains of rubbing. Thinner, non-rag papers, down to about 45 gms per sq. metre may be preferred since they are likely to be cheaper and more appropriate for beginners, but they usually tear more easily and do not have the texture and lasting qualities of all-rag paper. Paper such as those used for shelves or walls, although easily available, are not recommended since they tend to go yellow with age. Translucent papers with high 'size' content become brittle with age and crack at the folds.

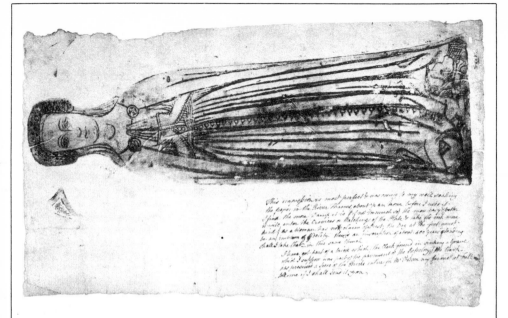

1 *'This impression is most perfect'* wrote Craven Ord, *'and was owing to my well soaking the paper in the River Thames. . . .'* One of the wives of Sir John Foxle, 1378, Bray, Berks. By permission of the British Museum.

2 *Brian Egan re-fixing a brass in Chipping Campden church, Glos, with new bitumen and dowels.*

3 *Most brasses are bedded in bitumen and held by brass dowels set in lead plugs.*

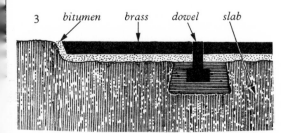

3   bitumen   brass   dowel   slab

Cartridge papers are too thick.

The most useful width is 30in. for single figures, and 40in. for double figures. Still wider paper of 60in. may be necessary for brasses at places such as Kings Lynn and Felbrigg where there are not only two figures but canopy work and inscriptions as well.

Other equipment
Masking tape, brush, duster, and scissors.

Selecting a brass
Lists of brasses are given in various books and are generally selective with the exception of Mill Stephenson's *A List of Brasses in the British Isles* which lists all that were known when it was published in 1926. An Appendix of 1938 gave corrections and additions. This remains the standard list, but a further Appendix is really needed to list brasses since destroyed, discovered, moved, or re-dated. The county lists in this book have been revised to date, and are virtually complete where figure brasses are concerned. Plain inscriptions are mostly omitted.

Having selected a brass that you wish to rub, from the county list, you can look up the place on an indexed map, for example a book map *Three Miles to One Inch Road Atlas of Great Britain* (published by W. and A. K. Johnston and G. W. Bacon Limited).

Permission
It is essential to get permission before you start rubbing. Crockford's Clerical Directory, which should be on the shelves of any good reference library, gives the address of every vicar. A stamped addressed envelope should be enclosed with your application. A fee is usually asked, and sometimes a signed or verbal promise that the rubbing is not being done for commercial purposes. Rubbing is not usually allowed on Sundays, and often not on Saturdays, when the churches are being prepared for Sunday use. Fees vary very much, but it is usual to pay 2s 6d to 7s 6d for ordinary brasses, and between 10s to £1 for fine ones. Some vicars do not charge a specific sum, but expect, and should receive a donation for their fabric fund.

Not every vicar allows brass rubbing. This is sometimes due to the fact that the brass is in need of restoration, and sometimes due to the bad behaviour of brass rubbers in the past, who, in some instances, have even been found at work with sandwiches and transistor radios beside them.

Preparation—floor brasses

Wipe the brass clean with a soft brush or duster, removing all grit and dirt, unroll the paper, and allowing about 6 inches at each end for later trimming, cut a length to cover the brass. Secure the corners and the sides with masking tape placed perhaps at 8-inch intervals across the edge of the paper. Sellotape is not recommended for the purpose since it removes the surface of the paper when you come to peel it off. Hassocks can be helpful to kneel on, but church books should not be used as paper weights.

Feel with your hand for any protruding rivets, and if these are present, make a deliberate hole to allow them to come through the paper. The hole can be patched afterwards.

Preparation—wall brasses

More difficult than floor brasses since they are often partly out of reach and the paper is hard to keep in place. In the days before adhesive tapes the method was to use unconsecrated wafers which were moistened in the mouth and then stuck, one side to the brass and the other to the paper, at intervals. Masking tape is now usually sufficient, but where a brass has been set in plaster or on a wall that is flaking the only retentive surface may be the brass itself. Great care must be taken not to mark the wall. By folding the paper back near the top of the brass a strip of tape can be used along the fold, half on the brass and half on the paper. Tape the bottom if possible. All except the top is then rubbed while holding the paper stretched below with one hand. To finish the top of the brass secure the bottom with masking tape in the same way, the paper creased upwards, remove the tape from the top, and rub the top part holding the paper against the wall with your hand. A helping pair of hands is useful for this. Sometimes a ladder can be placed so that it not only helps you to reach the brass but holds the top of the paper as well. Some wall brasses are held within marble frames so that the paper must be cut to the exact size and stuck to the brass. Pointed pieces of heelball are useful for rubbing near the frame.

Rubbing

Starting at one end, rub to pick up the edges of the design, and then rub hard and evenly to complete the section. Although it does not matter in which direction you rub, you should try and maintain an even pressure in order to obtain a consistent black finish. To avoid going over the edge use one hand as a buffer near the edge of the brass, so that it prevents the other hand from rubbing the stonework. A clean edge to the brass can be achieved by rubbing along the edge rather than across it. Do not hesitate to move your position frequently so that you can rub hard in the best direction depending on the engraving and the shape of the brass. It is easier to rub up and down rather than from left to right as you face the brass, and to keep doing this you will need to reposition your body from time to time.

When you have made certain that every part of the brass has been evenly rubbed polish your work with a duster, as you would polish a pair of shoes, then peel off the masking tape and roll up the rubbing. Note on it where and when it was rubbed—you may not be able to remember later. See that you leave no used bits of masking tape or splinters of heel ball on the floor, return .any borrowed hassocks and leave everything as you found it.

Common faults during rubbing

Blurred Image. This is due to the paper moving. Working slowly piece by piece from one end of the brass to the other helps to eliminate this danger. Naturally the paper must first be stuck down securely.

Paper tears. Too thin a weight of paper. Insufficient cleaning to remove grit. No light rubbing to reveal sharp edges, or no holes made beforehand to allow protruding rivets to come through. Holes can easily be patched afterwards with paste and paper, sellotape is not suitable since the stickiness eventually soaks through the rubbing.

OTHER WAYS OF RUBBING BRASSES

Brass rubbing can be varied in many ways for artistic effect. White, silver, and gold heelball are now obtainable and can be used on black or dark shades of paper to give a positive effect. Another positive effect can be achieved by rubbing with white wax on white paper. When you get home, the rubbing is painted over with indian ink and then wiped clean with rags. The white wax resists the ink, but lines of engraving are stained. This method of making a positive avoids having a margin of black paper, but involves more work. Some people like to blazon heraldic shields and mantles with poster paints.

Dabbing

Just a few brasses are too shallowly engraved for their details to pass through 70 gramme or even 45 gramme paper. Grass-bleached tissue paper available in sheets 20in. × 30in. (only 5 grammes in weight), is recommended. Considering its thinness it is remarkably tough, but calls for special care. Such thin paper can be rubbed successfully and more quickly with a dabber.

A dabber is a home-made tool constructed as follows: cotton wool, rags and other stuffing, up to the volume of a tennis ball, contained in chamois leather, bound round a handle. The chamois leather is rubbed or charged on a dabbing board, with powdered graphite, which is afterwards dabbed onto the paper.

The dabbing board is also home-made: powdered graphite (from chemists) mixed with olive or linseed oil into a dry paste which is spread on the dabbing board (a piece of thick cardboard).

Dabbing is carried out as follows:

(a) charge the dabber, (b) rub off surplus graphite (on part of board specially left without graphite for this purpose) (c) dab on the paper until recharging is necessary.

The technique of dabbing can very happily be combined with normal heelball rubbings, and used to indicate in half tone the presence of indents and help to hide any heelball marks on the stone. Dabbing the whole slab makes sure that no detail is missed.

BRASS RUBBINGS FOR HANGING

Small rubbings can be framed like pictures, but large ones would be expensive and heavy if glazed. Clear plastic polyester film is non-stretching, non shrinking and can be placed over the rubbing as a light substitute for glass (obtainable from stationers). Aerosol or brush varnishes have been used to protect rubbings, but this is unnecessary unless the rubbing smudges. Good black heelball does not smudge. Wooden rollers ('dowelling', from most timber merchants) can be fixed at the top and bottom of a rubbing (hence the need to allow extra paper at each end of a rubbing) but the weight of the roller might make it advisable to mount the rubbing on linen or hessian. Sticking a large rubbing to linen or other surfaces is not easy since the act of rubbing stretches the paper unevenly. 'Heavy duty' wallpaper paste and help from someone used to paper hanging may be advisable if your rubbing is a valuable one. An aerosol glue is simple to control and saves using a brush but is more expensive.

Book-binding cloth, available in various colours, even in 40in. width, can be used for direct rubbing, with only slight loss of detail on account of its thickness. It provides a tough wallhanging without the need to mount on a tougher backing.

14
Bibliography

BOOKS ON ENGLISH BRASSES

Beaumont, Edward T. *Ancient Memorial Brasses*, 1913. A general introduction.

Bouquet, A. C. *Church Brasses*, 1956. An illustrated account but with many inaccuracies. *European Brasses*, 1967. Large illustrations of brasses, some in England and some on the Continent.

Boutell, Chas. *Monumental Brasses and Slabs: an historical and descriptive notice of the Incised Monumental Memorials of the Middle Ages*, 1847. *The Monumental Brasses of England, a Series of Engravings upon Wood, with brief descriptive notices*, 1849. An elaborate appendix to the preceding work.

Busby, Richard J. *Beginner's Guide to Brass Rubbing*, 1969. Various methods are described.

Cambridge Camden Society. *Illustrations of the Monumental Brasses of Great Britain* 1840–6. With essays by various authors.

Catling, H. W. (revised by). *Notes on Brass-Rubbing*. A booklet first published in 1941 by the Oxford University Archaeological Society, and last revised in 1965. Contains a summary list of figure brasses in the British Isles.

Crosley, F. H. *English Church Monuments*, 1921. Including a very brief account of brasses.

Franklyn, Julian. '*Brasses*'. An elementary introduction with a guide to reading inscriptions. Second edition, 1969.

Gawthorp, W. E. *The Brasses of Our Homeland Churches*—1923. An elementary introduction.

Greenhill, F. A. *The Incised Slabs of Leicestershire and Rutland*, 1958. Including a list of all incised slabs known in the country.

Haines, Herbert. *A Manual of Monumental Brasses, comprising an introduction to the Study of these Memorials, and a List of those remaining in the British Isles*, 2 vols, 1861. Still a useful text book, but vol. 2 entirely superseded by Mill Stephenson's 'List' (see below).

Macklin, H. W. *The Brasses of England*, 1907. Written by the original author of this book as a fuller study of the subject.

Mann, James. *Monumental Brasses*, King Penguin, 1957.

Monumental Brass Society. *Transactions*. Cambridge University Assoaiation of Brass Collectors vol. I, 1887–91; vol. II, 1892–6; vol. III, 1897–9; vol. IV, 1900–3; vol. V, 1904–9; vol. VI, 1910–32; vol. VII, 1934–40; Vol. VIII, 1943–51; vol. IX, 1952–62; vol. X, 1963– (publication continuing). Portfolios vols. I–VII (publication continuing).

Norris, Malcolm. *Brass Rubbing*, 1965. A European, up-to-date view of the subject with illustrations.

Oxford University Brass Rubbing Society. *Oxford Journal of Monumental Brasses*, vol. I, 1897–9; vol. II, 1900. *Oxford Portfolio of Monumental Brasses*, 1898–1901.

Stephenson, Mill. *A List of Monumental Brasses in the British Isles*, 1926 with an Appendix by M. S. Giuseppi, and Ralph Griffin, 1938, re-printed in one volume. A list of over 700 pages, giving names, dates, the position of each brass in the church, and where it has been illustrated. No commentary or illustrations.

Suffling, Ernest R. *English Church Brasses from the 13th to 17th century*, 1910.

Trivick, Henry H. *The Craft and Design of Monumental Brasses*, 1969.

Victoria and Albert Museum. *Catalogue of Rubbings of Brasses and Incised Slabs*, 2nd. ed., 1929. Text somewhat out of date, but the many illustrations are useful. Reprinted 1969.

Waller, J. G. and L. A. R. *A series of Monumental Brasses from the Thirteenth to the Seventeenth Century 1842–64*. 62 coloured plates, drawn and engraved by the authors. The positive illustrations are very accurate and fine.

Ward, J. S. M. *Brasses*, 1912. A useful elementary introduction.

AUTHORITIES FOR SEPARATE COUNTIES

Nearly all the old county histories contain references to brasses but their names must be excluded for lack of space. For the same reason notes on brasses in individual churches are omitted unless in book form. Readers will also find useful *The Reports of the Royal Commission on Historical Monuments, The Victoria County History,* Methuen's *Little Guides,* and *The Buildings of England* by Nikolaus Pevsner.

BEDFORDSHIRE

Addington, H. *The Brasses of Bedfordshire, Archaeological Journal*, XL, 1883.

Fisher, Thomas. *Bedfordshire Collections*, 1812–36. *Monumental Remains.*

Sanderson, H. K. St J. 'The Brasses of Bedfordshire', *M.B.S. Trans.*, II–III, 1893–7.

BERKSHIRE

Morley, T. H. *Monumental Brasses of Berkshire*, 1924.

BIBLIOGRAPHY

CAMBRIDGESHIRE

Cave, C. J. P., Charlton, O. J. and Macalister, R. A. S. 'The Brasses of Cambridgeshire', *M.B.S. Trans.*, II–V, 1893–1905 (not completed).

Benton, G. Montagu. *Monumental Brasses now existing in Cambridgeshire* (excluding Cambridge), 1902.

CHESHIRE

See Lancashire.

CORNWALL

Dunkin, E. H. W. *The Monumental Brasses of Cornwall*, 1882.

CUMBERLAND

Bower, R. Brasses in the Diocese of Carlisle, *Cumberland and Westmorland Antiquarian and Archaeological Society*, 1894.

DERBYSHIRE

Field, H. E. 'The Monumental Brasses of Derbyshire', *M.B.S. Trans.*, III and V, 1898–1904.

DEVON

Crabbe, W. R. 'The Monumental Brasses of Devon', *Transactions of the Exeter Diocesan Architectural Society*, 1854.

Rogers, W. H. W. *The Ancient Sepulchral Effigies and Monumental and Memorial Sculpture of Devon*, 1877.

DORSET

Prideaux, W. de C. 'The Ancient Memorial Brasses of Dorset', *Proceedings of the Dorset Natural History and Antiquarian Field Club*, 1897–1907, vols, 19–37.

ESSEX

Chancellor, F. *Ancient Sepulchral Monuments of Essex*, 1890.

Christy, Miller, Porteous, W. W. and Smith, Bartram. *The Monumental Brasses of Essex*, edited by R. H. D'Elboux, 1952, *Memorials of Old Essex*, 1908.

Monumental Brasses

GLOUCESTERSHIRE

Davis, Cecil T. *Monumental Brasses of Gloucestershire*, 1899. Reprinted 1969.

HAMPSHIRE

Cave, C. J. P. 'Monumental Brasses of Hampshire'. *M.B.S. Trans.*, V–VI, 1907–11.

ISLE OF WIGHT

Lewis, R. W. M. 'Complete List of the Monumental Brasses of the Isle of Wight', *M.B.S. Trans.*, II, 1892.

HEREFORDSHIRE

Haines, Herbert. 'The Monumental Brasses of the Cathedral and County of Hereford', *British Archaeological Association Journal*, XXVII, 1871.
Davis, Cecil T. 'The Monumental Brasses of Herefordshire and Worcestershire', *Transactions of the Birmingham and Midland Institute*, 1884–5.

HERTFORDSHIRE

Andrews, W. F. *Memorial Brasses in Hertfordshire*, 2nd ed. 1903.
Page, William. *The Brasses and Indents in St Alban's Abbey*, 1899.

HUNTINGDONSHIRE

French, Valpy. 'The Brasses of Huntingdonshire', *The Antiquary*, IV, 1881.
Macklin, H. W. 'The Brasses of Huntingdonshire', *M.B.S. Trans.*, III, 1898.

KENT

Belcher, W. D. *Kentish Brasses*, I, 1888; II, 1905.
Griffin, R. and Stephenson, Mill. *Monumental Brasses in Kent*, 1923.

LANCASHIRE

Thornely, J. L. *The Monumental Brasses of Lancashire and Cheshire*, 1893.

LINCOLNSHIRE

Jeans, G.E. *A List of Existing Sepulchral Brasses in Lincolnshire*, 1895. 'The Sepulchral Brasses of Lincolnshire', in *Memorials of Old Lincolnshire*, 1911.

BIBLIOGRAPHY

MIDDLESEX

Stephenson, Mill. 'Notes on the Monumental Brasses of Middlesex', *Transactions of the St Paul's Ecclesiological Society*, IV, 1900.

Beloe, E. M. jun. *The Monumental Brasses of Westminster Abbey*, 1898.

Cameron, H. K. 'The Brasses of Middlesex', *Transactions of the London and Middlesex Archaeological Society*. N.S. vol. 10, 1951–vol. 20, 1961 (not yet completed).

NORFOLK

Cotman, John Sell. *Engravings of the most Remarkable of the Sepulchral Brasses in Norfolk*, 1819. *Engravings of Sepulchral Brasses in Norfolk and Suffolk*, 2 vols, 2nd ed., 1839. Includes essays by several early authorities.

Beloe, E. M., jun. *The Monumental Brasses of Norfolk*, 1890–91 (25 lithographs without text).

Farrer, E. *A List of the Monumental Brasses Remaining in the County of Norfolk*, 1890.

NORTHAMPTONSHIRE

Hartshorne, C. H. *An Endeavour to Classify the Sepulchral Remains in Northamptonshire*, 1840.

Hudson, Franklin. *The Brasses of Northamptonshire*, 1853. For errata see *M.B.S. Trans.*, VII, 108–12.

NOTTINGHAMSHIRE

Briscoe, J. P. and Field, H. E. *The Monumental Brasses of Nottinghamshire*, Pt. I, 1904 (all issued).

OXFORDSHIRE

See above. *Oxford Journal of Monumental Brasses*.

Bott, Alan. *Monuments in Merton College Chapel*, 1964.

Günther, R. T. *A Description of Brasses and their Funeral Monuments in the Chapel of Magdalen College*, 1914.

SHROPSHIRE

Stephenson, Mill. 'Monumental Brasses in Shropshire'. *Archaeological Journal*, March 1895, 47–103.

MONUMENTAL BRASSES

SOMERSET

Connor, A. B. *Monumental Brasses in Somerset, Proceedings of the Somerset Archaeological and Natural History Society.* 1932–55. Printed in 22 parts in vols 77 to 98 (with index in vol. 103).

SUFFOLK

Cotman, John Sell. *Engravings of the most Remarkable of the Sepulchral Brasses in Suffolk,* 1819. See also Norfolk. Drawings not entirely accurate.

Farrer, E. *A List of the Monumental Brasses Remaining in the County of Suffolk,* 1903.

SURREY

Stephenson, Mill. 'Monumental Brasses in Surrey', *Transactions of the St Paul's Ecclesiological Society,* III, 1895.

Fairbank, F. R. *Monumental Brasses in the County of Surrey in Memorials of Old Surrey,* 1911.

SUSSEX

Macklin, H. W. *Sussex Brasses in Memorials of Old Sussex,* 1909.

Mosse, H. R. *Monumental Effigies of Sussex,* 2nd ed, 1933.

Davidson-Houston, Mrs C. E. D. 'Sussex Monumental Brasses', *Sussex Archaeological Collections,* LXXVI–VII 1935.

WARWICKSHIRE

Badger, E. W. *The Monumental Brasses of Warwickshire,* 1895.

WILTSHIRE

Kite, E. *The Monumental Brasses of Wiltshire,* 1860. Reprinted 1969.

WORCESTERSHIRE

Thacker, F. J., Barnard, E. A. B. and Parker, J. F. *Transactions of the Worcester Archaeological Association,* vol. III, 107–27; vol. IV, 129–56; vol. XI, 139–43; vol. XV, 1–9; vol. XVI, 1–13.

YORKSHIRE

Stephenson, Mill. 'Monumental Brasses in the East Riding, Yorks', *Archaeological Journal,* XII, 1893; 'Monumental Brasses in the West Riding', XV, 1900; 'Monumental Brasses in the North Riding', XVIII, 1903; 'Monumental Brasses in the City of York', XVIII, 1903; 'Additions', XX, 1909.

BIBLIOGRAPHY

COSTUME HERALDRY AND MERCHANT MARKS

Beaumont, E. T. *Academical Costume, Illustrated by Ancient Monumental Brasses*, 1928.

Boutell's *Heraldry*. First published, 1863. Revised by C. W. Scott-Giles, and J. P. Brooke-Little, 1966.

Clayton, H. J. *The Ornaments of the Ministers as shown on English Monumental Brasses*. Alcuin Club Collections, XXII, 1919. A useful illustrated book.

Druitt, Herbert. *A Manual of Costume as Illustrated on Monumental Brasses*, 1906. Many of the illustrations are reproductions of photographs of brasses.

Edwards, Lewis. 'Professional costume of lawyers illustrated principally by monumental brasses', *M.B.S. Trans.*, VII, 97–108, 145–64.

Girling, F. A. *English Merchants' Marks*, 1964. Includes a chapter on marks on brasses.

Greenhill, F. A. 'A note on the Almuce', *M.B.S. Trans.*, IX, 209–10.

Hope, W. H. St John. *A Grammar of English Heraldry*, revised by A. R. Wagner, 1953.

Kent, J. P. C. 'Monumental Brasses, a new classification of military effigies', in *British Archaeological Association* XII, 1949, 70–97.

Mann, Sir James. 'The Nomenclature of Armour', *M.B.S. Trans.*, IX, 414–28.

Summers, Peter, G. *How to read a Coat of Arms*, The National Council of Social Service, 1967.

BOOKS AND ARTICLES ON FOREIGN BRASSES

Op de Beeck, Dr Roland A. E. 'Flemish Monumental Brasses in Portugal', in *M.B.S. Trans.* X, 151–66.

Belonje and Greenhill, F. A. 'Some brasses in Germany and the Low Countries' *M.B.S. Trans.*, IX, 213–20, 290–6, 379–87, 447–59, 493–508; X, 46–55, 173–85, 232–37.

Cameron, H. K. 'Brasses at Lübeck', *M.B.S. Trans.*, VII, 321–30; IX, 72–6.

Collon-Gevaert, Suzanne. *Histoire des Arts du Metal en Belgique*, 2 vols, Brussels, 1951. A good introduction to the Flemish brass industry, of which the manufacture of monumental brasses was a part.

Creeny, W. F. *Illustrations of Incised Slabs on the Continent of Europe*, 1891; and *A book of Fac-similes of Monumental Brasses on the Continent of Europe*, 1884. These two books show some Franco Flemish Incised slabs and Flemish brasses and help one to appreciate foreign brasses in England.

Eichler, Hans. *Die Gravierten Grabplatten aus Metall in XIV Jahrhundert und ihre Vorstufen*, Cologne, 1933. 'Flandrische gravierte Metallgrabplatten des XIVe Jahrhunderts', *Jahrbuch des preussischen Kunstsammlungen*, LIV, 1933.

Evans, H. F. O. 'Brass at Cues, W. Germany', *M.B.S. Trans.*, X, 25–28.

Greenhill, F. A. 'Brass in Portugal', *M.B.S. Trans.*, IX, 39–42, a Scottish merchant's ledger, recording the import of Flemish brasses *c.* 1500, 184–90; 'Brasses in Norway', X, 2–6, indents in Burgundy, 31–2.

Monumental Brasses

Norris, Malcolm. 'Medieval Trade in Monumental Brasses', *The Geographical Magazine,* March, 1956, 519–25. 'The Schools of Monumental Brasses in Germany', *British Archaeological Association,* XXII, 1959, 34–52. 'Brasses at Zeitz', *M.B.S. Trans.,* IX, 266–70.

Quirk, R. N. *Bishop Robert Hallum and the Council of Constance.* Friends of Salisbury Cathedral 22nd Annual Report. Brass in Constance Cathedral.

Rigold, S. E. 'Early Indents in Laon Cathedral', *M.B.S. Trans.,* X, 275–82; 'Indents of Chalice Brasses in Bruges', 283–4.

Rousseau, Henry. *Frottis de Tombe Plates* 1912. Supplement 1923. A descriptive catalogue of rubbings in the Musée Royaux du Cinquantenaire in Brussels.

ARTISTS

D'Elboux, R. H. 'Nicholas Stone's Monument to Sir John Wyndham at St Decuman's, Watchet', *Somerset Archaeological Society,* vol. 92, 88–92.

Esdaile, Mrs A. J. K. 'The Sculptor and the Brass', *M.B.S. Trans.,* VII, 1935, 49–56.

Esdaile, Mrs and D'Elboux, R. H. 'An Alphabetical List of Post-Reformation brasses of known authorship, chiefly compiled, with additional notes, from Mill Stephenson and the Appendix.' *M.B.S. Trans.,* VIII, 1944, 37–56, 140–4.

Norris, Malcolm. *Vide ut supra.*

TECHNICAL

Cameron, H. K. 'The Metals used in Monumental Brasses', *M.B.S. Trans.,* VIII, 1946, 109–30.

Collon-Gevaert, Suzanne. *Vide ut supra.*

Evans, H. F. O. 'The Fixing of Brasses', *M.B.S. Trans.,* X, 1964, 58–62.

Rigold, S. E. 'Petrology as an aid to Classification of Brasses', *M.B.S. Trans.* X., 1967, 285–6.

County Lists of Brasses

The density of brasses is shown on the map, and has been drawn after dividing the number of brasses in each county into the number of acres per county. Oxfordshire emerges as the densest county with one brass per 1,200 acres, followed in order by Kent, Norfolk, Bucks, Surrey and Herts, Beds, Berks, Essex and Middlesex (including London).

The following lists are intended to include, in a very abbreviated form, the whole series of figure-brasses to be found in the churches of the United Kingdom, together with a few inscriptions of exceptional interest, and most of those which are accompanied by coats-of-arms. Every date implies a separate brass, and where there are many brasses, little more can be given. Where there are only one or two, it is often possible to give the surname, or even the full name of the principal person commemorated. Children and accessories, except canopies, cannot usually be noted. Even so the lists extend to many pages, and include nearly 4,000 brasses. If all known inscriptions were added, the total would probably rise to about 7,500 pre-1700 brasses. It has not been found possible here to include brasses in private possession or in museums, or the matrices of lost brasses, however important. The dates are usually those to be found upon the brasses themselves, unless they were evidently engraved later, when the approximate dates are given of the actual engraving. The note (P) 'palimpsest' implies only that some part of a brass is of that character, the later date, of the obverse, being alone mentioned. The word Priest, without anything further, means one in the

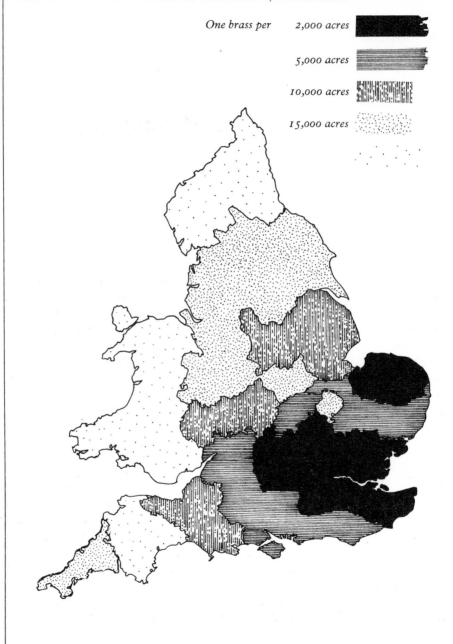

PRESENT DISTRIBUTION OF PRE-A.D. 1700 BRASSES

One brass per   2,000 acres

5,000 acres

10,000 acres

15,000 acres

eucharistic or mass vestments, alb, amice, chasuble, etc., while a bishop or abbot, unless otherwise stated, is understood to be in pontificals.

The principal abbreviations used are as follows:

acad.	academical dress, usually cassock, surplice or tabard, tippet and hood	inscr.	inscription
		kng.	kneeling
alm.	almuce	l.	lady
arm.	a man in armour, of whatever rank, knight, esquire or gentleman	mutil.	mutilated
		(P)	palimpsest, some part re-engraved or re-used
arms.	a shield or coat of arms		
c.	*circa,* about	pecul.	peculiar
can.	canopy, or canopied	pr.	priest
chal.	chalice	qd. pl.	quadrangular plate
civ.	a man in civilian dress, of whatever rank	skel.	skeleton
		sm.	small
demi.	demi-figure, half-effigy	tab.	tabard-of-arms
eccles.	ecclesiastic, usually post-Reformation	trip.	triple
		w.	wife, or with
her.	heraldic, in heraldic dress, of either sex	ws.	wives

A few of the best or most interesting brasses in each county are indicated by an asterisk (*) in the margin. The brasses of Ireland, Scotland and Wales, which are very few in number, follow those of England. None is known in the Channel Islands, or in the Isle of Man, except for a late inscription at Peel.

BEDFORDSHIRE

Ampthill. Wm. Hicchecok, woolman & w., 1450. Lady, 1485. Civ. & w., 1506. Sir Nich. Harvey, arm., 1532.

Arlesey. Inscriptions, 1638, 1759, 1761, 1768, all with coats-of-arms.

Aspley Guise. Priest & St John Bapt., *c.* 1410. Arm., 1501.

Barford Great. Arm. & wife, *c.* 1525.

Barford, Little. Thos. Perys, civ. & wife, 1535.

Barton-in-the-Clay. Priest, demi, 1396. Civ., *c.* 1490.

Bedford, St. Mary. Civ. (covered), 1627. Lady, qd. pl., 1663. Arms, 1671 (copper).

Bedford, St Paul. Sir Wm. Harper, arm. & wife, 1573.

Biddenham. Civ. & w., *c.* 1490. 2 shrouds, *c.* 1530. L., qd. pl., 1639.
Biggleswade. Wm. Halsted, civ. & 2 ws., 1449. Fragments, 1481.
Blunham. Rich. Maulaye, civ. & wife, 1506.
*Bromham. Arm. & 2 wives, canopy, large, 1435 ((P) approp. to 1535).
Caddington. Civ. & wife, 1505. Civ. & 2 wives, 1518.
Campton. Rich. Carlyll, civ. & wife, 1489.
Cardington. Sir Wm. Gascoigne. Arm. in tabard & 2 ws., heraldic, *c.* 1540. Arm. & w., 1638.
Clifton. John Fysher, arm. & wife, 1528.
Cople. Serjeant-at-law & w., *c.* 1410. Arm., *c.* 1415. Arm. & w., 1435, 1507, 1556. Judge & w.;
    1544, 1563.
Dean. Lombardic inscr. *c.* 1300. Thos. Parker, priest in almuce, 1501.
Dunstable. Civ. & w., 1516. 2 civs. & w., 1640. Many fragments.
Eaton Bray. Jane, Lady Bray, kng., qd. pl., 1558.
Eaton Socon. Civ. & w., *c.* 1400. Lady, *c.* 1450.
Elstow. Margery Argentine, 1427. Elizth. Herwy, abbess, *c.* 1520.
Eyworth. Rich. Gadburye, civ. & w., 1624.
Felmersham. Civ. & wife, *c.* 1610.
Flitton. Lady, 1434, 1544. (P) Harry Gray, arm., 1545. Civ. 1628.
Goldington. Rich. Fyssher, civ., 1507. Robt. Hatley, arm., 1585.
Gravenhurst, Lower. An inscr., 1361. Civ. & 3 ws., 1606.
Hatley Cockayne. Arm., *c.* 1430. L., *c.* 1480. Arm. & ws., 1515, 1527.
Haynes. Anth. Newdegate, civ., qd. pl., 1568.
Higham Gobion. Jane Cason, 1602. Kath. Brown, 1603.
Holwell. Chalice & 2 wild men, to Robt. Wodehowse, priest, 1515.
Houghton Conquest. Arm., w. & arm., 1493. Arm. & w., 1500.
Houghton Regis. Priest, demi, 1410. Priest, 1506.
Husborne Crawley. John Carter, civ. & w., 1600.
Langford. Thos. Hundon, priest, 1520.
Leighton Buzzard. 3 civs., qd. pl., 1597. Civ. & w., qd. pl., 1636.
Lidlington. Civ. & w., *c.* 1495. (Brass new church, indent old church).
Luton, St Mary. Civ. 1415. L. & trip. can., *c.* 1490. Arm. & 2 ws., 1513. Pr. in cap & almuce,
    c. 1510. L., 1515. Many fragments.
Marston Mortaine. Walter Papley, pr., demi, 1420. Thos. Reynes, arm. & w., 1451. Inscr.
    & arms, Reynes, 1506.
Maulden. Rich. Faldo, arm. & w., 1576. Anne Faldo, 1594.
Meppershall. Mepertyshale, arm., 1440. Boteler, arm. & w., 1441.
Poddington. John Howard, civ., 1518.
Pottesgrove civ. & w., 1535. 1563 (P).
Pulloxhill. Geo. Fitz, arm & w. (covered), 1608.
Renhold. Edm. Wayte, civ. & w., small, 1518.
Salford. John Peddar, civ. & w., 1505.
Sharnbrook. Cobbe, 2 civs. & w., 1522. Inscr. & arms, 1618.
Shillington. Priest in cope, large, 1400. Pr. in cope, 1485.
Souldrop. John Hanger, civ., qd. pl., 1608.

Stagsden. John Cocke, arm., qd. pl., 1617.

Stevington. Thos. Salle, arm., 1422.

Sutton. A Latin cross fleury, 1516.

Thurleigh. John Harvye, arm., *c.* 1420. Inscr. & arms, 1490.

Tingrith. Robt. Hogeson, civ., qd. pl., 1611.

Toddington. Arms & fragments, *c.* 1480.

Totternhoe. John Warwekhyll, priest w. chalice, 1524. Civ., 1621.

Turvey. Civ., *c.* 1480. Pr. in acad. *c.* 1500. Lady, 1606.

Wilshamstead. Wm. Carbrok, priest, demi, *c.* 1450.

Woburn. Canopy & inscr., 1394.

★Wymington. Civ. & w., canopy, good, 1391. Lady, 1407. Sir Thos. Brounflet, arm., large, 1430. Pr. in cope, w. chalice, *c.* 1510.

Yelden. Priest, 1433. Ecclesiastic, 1617. Civ., qd. pl., 1628.

BERKSHIRE

Abingdon, St Helen. Barbur, civ., demi, 1417. Priest in acad., 1501.

Aldermaston. Arms & inscriptions, *c.* 1425, 1574, (P), 1638.

Appleton. John Goodryngton, in shroud, 1518.

Ashbury. Civ., demi, *c.* 1360. Priest in cope, 1409. Ditto, 1448 (under moveable pew).

Binfield. Priest in cope, demi, 1361. Inscr., 1558. (P).

Bisham. Crekett, civ., 1517. Brinckhurst, civ. & 2 ws., 1581.

Blewbury. John Balam, priest, 1496. Arm. & 2 ws., *c.* 1515. Sir John Daunce, arm. in tab. & w., 1523, 1548. (P).

★Bray. Foxle, arm. & 2 ws., heraldic, bracket, 1378. A judge, 1475. Civ. & 2 ws., *c.* 1490. Civ. & w., qd. pl., 1610. Ditto, 1620.

Brightwell. Pr. w. chalice, 1507. Civ. & w., 1509. Ditto, 1512.

Buckland. John Yate, civ. & w., 1578.

Burghfield. Nich. Williams, arm. & w., 1568.

★Childrey. Fynderne, arm. in tab. & w., canopy, 1444. Pr., *c.* 1480. Civ. & w., *c.* 1480. Pr. w. chalice, *c.* 1490. L. in shroud, 1507. Arm. & w., 1514. Civ. & w. in shrouds, 1516. Civ. & w., *c.* 1520. Pr. in acad., 1529.

Cholsey. John Mere, priest w. chalice, 1471.

Compton Parva. Rich. Pygott, civ. & w., 1520.

Cookham. Civ. & w., 1458, 1503, 1577. (P). Arm. & w., 1510, 1527 (mutil.).

Coxwell, Great. Wm. Morys, civ., 1509. Lady, *c.* 1510.

Cumnor. Arm. & w., 1572. Lady, 1577. (P). Civ. & w., 1599.

Denchworth. Hyde, arm. & w., 1516. Ditto. 1562. (P). Ditto, 1567.

Farringdon. Arm. 1443. Civ. & w., 1485. Pr., 1505. Arm in tab. & 2 ws., 1547.

Fawley. Mary Gunter, qd. pl., 1621.

Finchampstead. Elizth. Blighe, 1635.

Hagbourn, E. Hugh Keate, civ. & w., qd. pl., 1627.

Hampstead, E. Thos. Berwyk, civ., demi, 1443.

Hanney, W. Pr., large, *c.* 1370. Arm., 1557, 1599. Civ. & 2 ws., 1592, Arm. & 2 ws., 1602. Civ. & w., 1611.

Harwell. John Jennens, civ. & w., 1599.

Hatford. Francis Pigott, shields & inscr., 1614.

Hendred, E. Hen. Eldysley, civ., 1439. John Eyston, arm. & w., 1589.

Hurst. Civ. & w., 1574. Lady in bed, qd. pl., *c.* 1600.

Kintbury. John Gunter, civ. & w., 1626.

Lambourn. Civ. & w., demi, 1406. 2 civs., demi, *c.* 1410. Arm. in tabard, *c.* 1485. Civ. & w., 1619.

Letcombe Regis. Lady, *c.* 1440.

Locking, E. Edw. Keate, civ. & w., 1624. Lady, 1628.

Longworth. Priest, demi, 1422. Shrouds, 1500. Lady, 1566.

Newbury. Civilian & wife, 1519.

Reading, St. Giles. John Bowyer, civ. & w., 1521.

Reading, St Laurence. Civ. & w., *c.* 1415, 1584. Civ., 1538. (P).

Remenham. Arm., 1591. Pastor, 1622.

Sandhurst. Rich. Geale, civ. & w., 1608.

Shefford, Little. John Fetyplace, arm. & w., 1524.

*Shottesbrooke. Priest & civ., canopy, *c.* 1370. Lady, 1401. Arm., 1511. Civ. & 3 ws., 1567.

Sonning. Laurence Fyton, arm., 1434. Civ. & w., 1549. Lady, 1575, 1589. Child, sm., 1627.

*Sparsholt. Priest in cross, 1353. Civ., *c.* 1495, 1602. Lady, *c.* 1510.

Stanford-Dingley. Margt. Dyneley, 1444. Civ., 1610.

Stanford-in-the-Vale. Roger Campedene, priest, demi, 1398.

Steventon. Civ. & w., small, 1476. Arm. & w., 1584.

Stratfield-Mortimer. Rich. Trevet, arm., 1441. Lady, 1441.

Streatley. Civ., sm., 1583. (P). Lady, 1570. Civ. & w., 1603.

Swallowfield. Lady, sm., 1466. Christopher Lytkott, arm. & w., 1554.

Tidmarsh. Margt. Wode, 1499. Leyneham, arm. in tabard, 1517.

Tilehurst. Gauwyn More, civ. & w., 1469.

Ufton Nervet. Wm. Smith, civ. & w., sm., 1627.

Waltham, Bright. John Newman, civ., sm., 1517.

Waltham, White. Lady, 1445. Lady, small, 1506.

Wantage. Pr., demi, *c.* 1370. Arm., large, 1414. Pr. in acad., sm., 1512. Civ. & 2 ws., 1522. Lady, 1619.

Welford, Pr. in acad., sm., *c.* 1490. Civ., sm., *c.* 1530.

Windsor, Old. Humfrey Michell, civ. & w., 1621.

*Windsor, St George's Chapel. Canopy, etc., 1380. Arm. & w., heraldic, qd. pl., 1475. Pr. in almuce, qd. pl., 1522. Child in cradle, 1630. Ditto, 1633.

Winkfield. A yeoman-of-the-guard, demi, qd. pl., 1630.

Wittenham, Little. Pr., 1433. Civ., sm., 1454. L., 1472. Civ., 1483. Civ. & w., *c.* 1585. Arm., 1588. Child, qd. pl., 1683.

Wokingham. Civ. & w., *c.* 1520. Ditto, *c.* 1610.

Wytham. Man in armour & w., *c.* 1440.

BUCKINGHAMSHIRE

Amersham. Civ. & w., 1430, 1439, 1521. Civ., *c.* 1450. Child, 1623.

Astwood. Roger Keston, civ. 1409. John Chibnale, civ. & 2 ws., 1534. (P).

Beachampton. Civ., 1600. Lady, small, 1611.

Beaconsfield. John Waren, civ. & w., 1609.

Bledlow. Wm. Herun, priest, small, 1525.

Bletchley. Thos. Sparke, priest, a bust in oval, qd. pl., 1616.

Bradenham. A priest, 1521.

Burnham. Civ. & w., *c.* 1500, 1563. (P). Civ. & 3 ws., 1581. (P).

Chalfont St Giles. Pr., sm., *c.* 1470. Lady, *c.* 1510. Civ. & 2 ws., *c.* 1560 (P). Arm. & w., 1558. Arm. & 2 ws., 1570.

Chalfont St Peter. Arm. & w., *c.* 1446. Ditto, 1446, Pr., 1545. (P).

Chearsley. John Frankeleyn, civ. & w., 1462.

Chenies. Civ. & 2 ws., 1469. Arm. & w., canopy, 1484. Pr., sm., 1494. Lady, heart & canopy, 1510. Lady, 1511, 1524.

Chesham Bois. Arm., 1552. (P). Chrysom, *c.* 1520.

Chicheley. Arm. & w., 1558. (P). Skel. in shroud, qd. pl., sm., *c.* 1560.

Claydon, Middle. Lady, 1523. Pr., demi, w. chalice, 1526. Roger Gyffard, arm. & w., 1542. (P).

Clifton Reynes. Reynes, arm., 1428. Man & w. in shrouds, *c.* 1500.

Crawley, N. John Garbrand, parson, qd. pl., 1589.

Crendon, Long. John Canon, civ. & w., 1468.

Datchet. Arms & inscr., 1559. Hanbery, civ. & w., qd. pl., 1593.

*Denham. Arm. & 2 ws., 1494. Abbess, *c.* 1540. Lady, (P), reverse a friar, 1545. Priest, 1560.

Dinton. Arm. & w., 1424, 1539, 1628. Civ. & w., 1486, 1558. (P). Arm., 1551. (P)'

*Drayton Beauchamp. Arm., 1368, 1375. Pr. w. chalice, sm., 1531.

Dunton. Civ. & w., sm., *c.* 1420. Lady, sm., *c.* 1510.

Edlesborough. John de Swynstede, pr., 1395. Arm & 3 ws., 1540. (P). Civ. & w., 1592.

Ellesborough. Thos. Hawtrey, arm. & w., 1544. (P).

Emberton. John Mordon, priest, *c.* 1410.

*Eton College Chapel. Vice-provost, in cap & almuce, sm., 1489. Provost in alm., triple can., 1503. Fellow, w. chalice, sm., 1509. Arm., 1521. Pr. in cope, 1522. Fellow, 1525. L., 1528. Pr. w. chalice, 1535. Provost, 1535. Vice-prov. in hood, 1545. (P). Lady, 1560. (P). Fellow, kng., 1636, and 11 inscrs.

Haddenham. Priest in cope, *c.* 1420. Pr., demi, 1428. Inscr. 1539. (P).

Halton. Henry Bradschawe, chief baron of exchequer, & w., 1553. (P).

Hambledon. Civ., 1457. Civ. & w., 1497, *c.* 1600. L., kng., 1500. Civ. & w 2s., qd. pl., 1634.

Hampden, Gt. Arm. & w., *c.* 1525. Arm. & 2 ws., 1553. (P).

Hanslope. Mary Birchemore, child, 1602.

Hardmead. Francis Catesby, civ., 1556.

Haversham. Lady, 1427. Skeleton, qd. pl., 1605.

Hedgerley. Robt. Fulmer, civ. & w., sm., 1498. Lady, 1540. (P).

Hitcham. Thos. Ramsey, arm. & w., 1510. Nich. Clarke, arm., 1551.

Horwood, Gt. Hen. Upnore, priest in acad., 1487.

Hughenden. Robt. Thurloe, priest, 1493.

Iver. Rich. Blount, arm. & w., 1508.

Ivinghoe. French inscr., Fallywolle, 1368. Civ. & w., 1517. Civ., 1531, 1576, 1594.
Langley Marsh. John Bowser, civ., 1608.
Lillingstone Dayrell. Paul Dayrell, arm. & w., 1491. Priest, sm., 1493.
Lillingstone Lovell. Hands holding heart. John Merstun 1446. Civ. & w., 1460.
Linford, Gt. Civ. & w., 1473. Ditto, 1536. Ditto, 1611.
Linslade. Civ. & 3 ws., *c.* 1500.
Loughton. Hugh Parke, priest, demi, 1514.
Ludgershall. 3 ladies, *c.* 1600.
Marlow, Little. Alice Ledewich, 1430.
Marston, N. Rich. Sanders, civ., qd. pl., 1602.
Marsworth. Nich. West, judge, arm., 1586. (P). Mary West, 1606. Edm. West, serjeant-at-law, arm. & w., qd. pl., 1618.
Milton Keynes. Adam Babyngton, priest, 1427.
Missenden, Gt. A crest, 1436. Lady, *c.* 1510.
Missenden, Little. John Style, civ., 1613. Inscr. 1646. (P).
Moulsoe. Rich. Rowthall, arm. & w., 1528.
Newport Pagnell. Civ., mutil., large, *c.* 1440.
Penn. L. in shroud, 1540. Arm. & w., 1597 (P), 1638, 1641. Lady, 1640.
Quainton. L., demi, *c.* 1360. Pr. in cassock, kng., sm., 1422. Pr. in cope, 1485. Lady, 1509, 1593. Civ., 1510.
Risborough, Monks. Robt. Blundell, priest, 1431. Civ. & w., demi, *c.* 1460. Children, *c.* 1520.
Saunderton. Isabella Saunterton, demi, *c.* 1430.
Shalston. Dame Susan Kyngeston, vowess, 1540.
Slapton. Priest, demi, 1462. Yeoman-of-crown & 2 ws., 1519.
Soulbury. John Turnay, civ. & w., 1502. John Mallet, civ., 1516.
Stokenchurch. Robt. Morle, arm., 1410. Ditto 1415.
Stoke Poges. Sir Wm. Molyns & w., 1425. Hampdyn, civ. & w., 1577.
Stone. Wm. Gurney, in shroud, & w., 1472. Civ., 1520.(P).
Stow. Alice Saunders, sm., 1479. Child, sm., 1592.
Swanbourn. Thos. Adams, yeoman, & w., 1626.
Taplow. Cross & civ., *c.* 1350. Civ., lady & shroud, 1455. Arm. & 2 ws., 1540.(P).
Thornton. Robt. Ingylton, arm. & 3 ws., canopy, 1472. Lady, 1557.
Tingewick. Eras. Williams, rector, demi, qd. pl., 1608.
Tyringham. Arm., 1484. Mary Catesby, 1508.
Turweston. Priest, *c.* 1450. Civ. & 2 ws., sm., *c.* 1490.
Twyford. Priest, demi, 1413. Thos. Giffard, arm., 1550.(P).
Upton. Agnes Bulstrode, in shroud, kng., sm., 1472. Edw. Bulstrode, arm. & 2 ws., 1517. Arm. & w., 1599.
Waddesdon. Arm., 1490. Priest, 1543. Pr. in shroud, 1548. Arm. & w., 1561.
Wendover. Wm. Bradschawe, civ. & w., kng., sm., 1537.
Weston Turville. Civilian, *c.* 1580.
Weston Underwood. Elizth. Throkmarton (under organ), 1571.
Whaddon. Thos. Pyggot, serjeant-at-law, & 2 ws., 1519. Lady, 1612.
Winchendon, Nether. Arm., *c.* 1420. Lady, *c.* 1420. Civ. & w., 1487.

Winchendeon, Over. An Austin Canon, 1502. Arms and inscr., 1558.
Wing. Civ. & w., 1489, *c*. 1490. A porter, qd. pl., 1648.
Winslow. Thos. Fige, civ. & w., sm., 1578.
Wooburn. Civ., 1488. Civ. & w., *c*. 1500. Priest in cope, 1519. Shroud, *c*. 1520. Child, qd. pl., sm., 1642.
Wootton Underwood. Edw. Greneville, civ. & w., 1587.
Worminghall. Philip King, civ. & w., 1592.
Wyrardisbury. Arm., 1488. Civ., sm., 1512. Arms, etc., 1561.

CAMBRIDGESHIRE

Abingdon Pigotts. Civilian, *c*. 1460.
*Balsham. Priest in cope, canopy, 1401. Ditto, 1462. Arm., *c*. 1480.
Barton. John Martin, cfv. & w., *c*. 1600.
Bassingbourn. Edw. Turpin, civ. & w., 1683.
Burwell. Laurence de Wardeboys, abbot, in almuce, 1542. (P).
Cambridge—
    St Benet. Dr Billingford, in acad., kng., 1442.
    St Mary the Great. Arms, etc., Lorkin, 1596. Ditto, Scott, 1617.
    St Mary the Less. Pr. in acad., 1436. Ditto, demi, *c*. 1500.
    Caius Coll. Arm., *c*. 1500.
    Christ's Coll. Arm. & w., *c*. 1520. Pr. in acad., *c*. 1540. Inscr. 1582. (P).
    Jesus Coll. Arms, etc., Ducket, 1603.
    St John's Coll. Pr. in acad., canopy, 1414. Pr., *c*. 1430.
    King's Coll. Provost in acad., 1496. Ditto, 1507. Provost in almuce, 1528. Ditto, 1558. Arms, etc., 1559. (Brass lectern, *c*. 1525.)
    Queens' Coll. Pr. in cope, *c*. 1480. Pr. in acad., *c*. 1535. Civ., 1591.(P).
    Trinity Hall. Pr. in cope, 1517. Pr. in acad., *c*. 1530. Civ., 1598. Arms, etc., 1611, 1645, 1659.
Croxton. Edw. Leeds, Master of Clare, in gown, 1589.
Dry Drayton. Hutton, arm. & w., *c*. 1550.
Elm. Arms & inscr., Fincham, 1667.
Eltisley. Arms & inscr., Marshall, 1640.
*Ely Cathedral. Bp. Goodryke, 1554. Dean Tyndall, 1614. Arms, etc., Wagstave, 1621.
Fordham. Wm. Cheswryght, civ. & w., 1521.
Fulbourn. Pr., *c*. 1390. Pr. in cope, canopy, 1391. Pr., 1477. Lady, *c*. 1470.
Girton. Priest in cope, 1492. Ditto, 1497.
Haddenham. Canopy, 1405. Civ. & w., 1454.
Hatley, E. A lady, *c*. 1520.
Hatley St George. Sir Baldwin Seyntgeorge, arm., 1425.
*Hildersham. Cross & figs., Robt. de Paris, civ. & w., kng., 1408. Arm. w., 1427. Arm., canopy, 1466. Shroud, *c*. 1530.
Hinxton. Sir Thos. de Skelton & 2 ws., 1416.
Horseheath. Wm. de Audeley, arm., 1365. Civilian, 1552.

Impington. John Burgoyn, arm. in tabard & w., 1505.
★Isleham. Sir John Bernard, arm. & w., can., 1451. Thos. Peyton, arm. & 2 ws., can., 1484.
Civ. & w., 1574. (P).
Kirtling. Edw. Myrfin, civ., kng., 1553.
Linton. Henry Paris, arm., 1424. Arms, etc., 1538, 1558, 1577.
March. Civ. & w., 1501. Arm. in tab. & w., kng., sm., 1507.
Milton. Wm. Coke, judge, & w., 1553. (P). Civ. & w., 1660.
Quy. John Ansty, arm., sons in tabards, 1460.
Sawston. Civ., *c.* 1420. Arm., *c.* 1480. Shrouds, *c.* 1500. Priest w. chalice, sm., 1527.
Shelford, Gt. Pr. in cope, canopy, 1418. Arms, etc., Risley, 1511.
Shelford, Little. Arm. & w., *c.* 1405. Pr. in acad., *c.* 1480.
Stapleford. Wm. Lee, priest, qd. pl., sm., 1617.
Stretham. Joan Swan, 1497.
Swaffham Prior. John Tothyll, arm. & w., sm., 1462. Civ. & w., 1515, 1521, *c.* 1530. Civ., 1638.
★Trumpington. Sir Roger de Trumpington, 1289.
★Westley Waterless. Sir John de Creke & w., *c.* 1325.
Weston Colville. Arm. & w., 1427. Eccles. & w., kng., qd. pl., 1636.
Wicken. Margt. Peyton, sm., 1414. Civilian, sm., *c.* 1520.
Wilbraham, Little. Wm. Blakwey, priest in acad., kng., sm., 1521.
Wilburton. Priest in cope, can., 1477. Civ. & w., 1506. Ditto, 1516.
Wimpole. Priest in cope, 1501. Civ., *c.* 1500. Lady, *c.* 1535.
Wisbech. Thos. de Braunstone, arm., 1401.
Wood Ditton. Henry Englissh, arm. & w., 1393.

CHESHIRE

Chester Cathedral. Thos. Madock & w., 1792.
Chester, Holy Trinity. Inscr. 1545. (P).
Chester, St Peter. Civilian, *c.* 1460.
★Macclesfield. Roger Legh, civ., 1506, and Mass of St Gregory.
Middlewich. Elizth. Venables, qd. pl., 1591.
Over. Hugh Starky, arm., *c.* 1510.
★Wilmslow. Sir Robt. del Bothe, arm. & w., 1460.
Wybunbury. Ralf Dellvys, arm. & w., 1513.

CORNWALL

Anthony, E. Margery Arundell, canopy, 1420.
Blisland. John Balsam, priest, 1410.
St Breock. Civilian & wife, *c.* 1510.
St Budock. John Killigrew, civ. & w., 1567.
★Callington. Nich. Assheton, justice, & w., 1465.
Cardynham. Thos. Awmarle, priest, sm., *c.* 1400.

Colan. Francis Bluet & w., 1572. Cosowarth & w., 1575.

St Columb Major. John Arundel, arm. & 2 ws., 1545. Ditto & w., *c.* 1633.

Constantine. Rich. Geyrveys, civ. & w., qd. pl., 1574. (P). John Pendarves, civ. & w., qd. pl., 1616.

Crowan. St Aubyn, *c.* 1420. Civ. & w., *c.* 1490. Ditto, mutil., *c.* 1550. (P).

St Erme. Robt. Trencreeke, civ. & w., 1596.

Fowey, 2 civs. & w., *c.* 1450. Civ., 1582. Lady, 1602.

St Gluvias. Thos. Kyllygrewe & w., 1484.

Gorran. Lady, kng., *c.* 1510.

Grade. Jas. Eryssy, arm. & w., 1522.

Helston. Thos. Buggins, civ. & w., 1602.

Illogan. Jas. Bassett, arm. & w., 1603.

St Ives. Agnes Trevnwyth, kng., 1462.

St Just. Priest in plain cope, *c.* 1520.

Landrake. Edw. Cowrtney, arm., sm., 1509.

Landulph. Inscr. to Theodore Paleologus, 1636, & 2 others.

Lanteglos-by-Fowey. Mohun, arm. & w., *c.* 1440. Ditto & w., 1525.

Launceston. Lady, sm., *c.* 1620.

Lostwithiel. Tristram Curteys, arm., 1423.

Madron. John Clies, civ. & w., 1623.

★Mawgan-in-Pyder. Pr. in cope, c. 1420. Lady, 1578. (P). Civ., *c.* 1580. Lady, *c.* 1580 (P), & inscrs.

St Mellion. Peter Coryton, arm. & w., 1551. (P).

Minster. Robt. Hender, arm. & w., kng., 4 sm. plates, 1602.

St Michael Penkevil. Arm., 1497. Pr. in acad., 1515. Civ., 1619. Arm., qd. pl., *c.* 1640. Lady, 1622.

St Minver. Roger Opy, 1517.

Probus. John Wulvedon, civ. & w., 1514.

Quethiock. Roger Kyngdon & w., 1471. Rich. Chiverton & w., 1631.

St Stephens-by-Saltash. Fragments, *c.* 1480. Inscr., 1613.

Stratton. Sir John Arundell, arm. & 2 ws., 1561.

Tintagel. Joan Kelly, demi, *c.* 1430.

Truro Cathedral. Civ., 1585. Ditto, 1630. Inscr., 1567.

Wendron. Pr. in cope, mutil., 1535. Civ. & w., mutil., *c.* 1580. (P).

CUMBERLAND

Arthuret. Hands holding heart, *c.* 1500.

Bootle. Sir Hugh Askew, arm., sm., 1562.

★Carlisle Cathedral. Bishop Bell, trip. can., 1496. Bp. Robinson, qd. pl., 1616.

Crosthwaite. Sir John Ratclif, arm. & w., 1527.

Edenhall. Wm. Stapilton, arm. in tabard & w., 1458.

Greystoke. Pr. in almuce, demi, 1526. Lady, *c.* 1540, 1547 (P). Civ., 1551 (P).

MONUMENTAL BRASSES

DERBYSHIRE

Alfreton. Inscr. to John Ormond, Esq., & w., effs. lost, 1507.
Ashbourne. Dedication inscr., 1241. Francis Cockayne, serjt.-at-law in tab. & w., trip. can., 1538.
Ashover. James Rolleston, arm. & w., 1507. Priest, *c.* 1510. Inscr. 1518 (P).
Bakewell. Arms & inscr., 1628, 1653, 1658, 1732.
Chesterfield. Lady, 1451. Arm. & w., 1529, and inscrs.
Crich. Child in swaddling-clothes, qd. pl., 1637, and inscrs.
Dronfield. Thos. & Rich. Gomfrey, priests, 1399. Civ. & w., 1578, and inscrs.
Edensor. John Beton, arm., small, 1570.
Etwall. Lady, 1512. Sir John Porte & 2 ws., heraldic, 1557.
Hathersage. Eyre, arm. & w., 1463. Ditto, heraldic, *c.* 1500, *c.* 1560.
Hope. Henry Balgay, civ., qd. pl., 1685.
Hucknall. Inscr. to Rich, Pawson, vicar, 1537.
Kedleston. Rich. Curzon, arm & w., 1496.
Longstone, Great. Rowland Eyre, civ. & w., kng. w. crucifix, qd. pl., 1624.
★Morley. Stathum, arm. & w., kng., 1453. Ditto & 2 ws., 1470. Ditto & 3 ws., 1481. Sacheverell, arm. & w., *c.* 1525. Ditto, 1558.
Mugginton. Nich. Kniveton, arm. & w., *c.* 1475.
Norbury. Sir Anthony Fitzherbert, Justice of Comm. Pleas, & w., heraldic, 1538 (P).
Sawley. Bothe, arm. & w., 1467. Ditto, 1478. Shylton & w., 1510.
Staveley. Frechwell, arm. in tab., *c.* 1480. Arm. & w., kng., 1503.
Taddington. Rich. Blackwall, civ. & w., 1505.
★Tideswell. Holy Trin., etc., for Sir Sampson Meverell, 1462. Civ. & w., *c.* 1500. Bp. Pursglove, in pontif., 1579.
Walton-on-Trent. Robt. Morley, priest, w. chalice, 1492.
Wilne. Hugh Wylloughbye, arm. & son, in tabards, & w., kng., 1513.
Wirksworth. Thos. Blakewall, civ. & w., 1525. Civ. & w., 1510.
Youlgrave. A lady, 1604.

DEVONSHIRE

Allington, E. John Fortescue, arm. & w., 1595. Lady, kng., *c.* 1600.
Atherington. Sir John Basset, arm. & 2 ws., 1539.
Bickleigh. Inscr. to Nich. Slannyng, 1568.
Bigbury. Lady, *c.* 1440. Elizth. Burton, *c.* 1460.
Blackhauton. Nich. Forde, civ. & w., 1582.
Braunton. Elizth. Chechester, kng., 1548 (P).
Chittlehampton. John Coblegh & 2 ws., 1480.
Clovelly. Cary, arm., 1540, *c.* 1540. Inscr., w. skel. & spade, 1655.
Clyst St George. Julian Osborne, lady, qd. pl., 1614.
Dartmouth, St Petrock. Roope, civ., 1609. Lady, 1610. Ditto, 1617.
★Dartmouth, St Saviour. John Hauley, arm. & 2 ws., canopy, 1408. Lady, *c.* 1470. Civ., 1637.

Ermington. Wm. Strachleigh, civ. & w., kng., 1583.
Exeter Cathedral. Sir Pet. Courtenay, canopy, 1409. Canon Langeton, pr. in cope, kng, 1413.
Filleigh. Rich. Fortescue, arm, qd. pl., 1570.
St Giles-in-the-Wood. Lady, 1430. Ditto, 1592. Ditto, 1610.
Haccombe. Carew, arm., 1469, 1586. Lady, 1589, 1611. Civ. & w., qd. pl., 1656.
Harford. Thos. Williams, arm., 1566. Civ. & w., qd. pl., 1639.
Kentisbeare. Inscr. to Lady Mary Carew, 1558.
Loxhore. Inscr. Rich. Carpenter, rector, 1627.
Luppitt. Lady mutil. *c.* 1440 (P).
Monkleigh. Arm., kng., 1566. Angels and scroll, 1509.
Otterton. Rich. Duke, civ., 1641. Sarah Duke, 1641.
Ottery St Mary. John, Wm. & Rich. Sherman, *c.* 1620.
Petrockstow. Henry Rolle, arm. & w., qd. pl., 1591.
Sampford Peverell. Margt. Poulett, 1602.
Sandford. Mary Dowrich, lying on tomb, 1604.
Shillingford. Sir Wm. Huddesfeld & w., heraldic, qd. pl., 1499.
Staverton. John Rowe, civ., demi, 1592.
★Stoke Fleming. John Corp, civ. & granddau., canopy, 1391.
Stoke-in-Teignhead. Priest, *c.* 1370. Inscr. on heart, 1641.
Tawstock. Arms & inscr., Pagett, 1648.
Tedburn St Mary. Edw. Gee, parson, & w., 1613.
Tiverton. John Greenway, civ. & w., 1529.
Tor Mohun. Wilmota Cary, 1581 (P).
Washfield. Henry Worth, civ. & w., 1606.
Yealmpton. Sir John Crokker, arm., 1508. Inscr., 1580 (P).

DORSETSHIRE

Bere Regis. John Skerne, civ. & w., kng., 1596.
Bryanston. Inscrs. below matrices, 1528 & 1566.
Compton Valence. Thos. Maldon, priest, demi, *c.* 1440.
Corfe Mullen. Rich. Birt, civ., 1437.
Dorchester, St Peter. Scroll & inscr. to Joan More, 1436.
Evershot. Wm. Grey, priest w. chalice, 1524.
Fleet. Mohun, arm. & w., 1603. Ditto, 1612.
Knowle, Church. John Clavell, arm. & 2 ws., 1572.
Litton Cheney. Inscr., 1486 (P), & 2 others.
Lytchett Matravers. Thos. Pethyn, priest in shroud, *c.* 1470 (P).
Langton. John Whitewood, civ. & 2 ws., 1467.
Melbury Sampford. Sir Giles Strangewayes, arm. in tab., 1562. Several arms & inscrs.
Milton Abbey. Sir John Tregonwell, arm. in tabard, kng., 1565. Inscr. & several good matrices.
More Crichel. Isabel Uvedale, 1572.
Moreton. Jas. Frampton, arm, 1523.
Piddlehinton. Inscr. 1562 (P). Thos Browne, parson, sm., qd. pl., 1617.

MONUMENTAL BRASSES

Pimperne. Dorothy Williams, qd. pl., 1694.
Puddletown. Civ., demi, 1517. Arm. in tab., qd. pl., 1524. Arm, 1595.
Puncknowle. Wm. Napper, arm., *c.* 1600.
Purse Caundle. Arm., 1500. Lady, 1527. Priest, sm., 1536.
Rampisham. Thos. Dygenys, civ. & w., 1523.
Shapwick. Mary Oke, *c.* 1440. Vicar, *c.* 1520.
Sturminster Marshall. Henry Helme, vicar, 1581.
Swanage. Wives of Wm. Clavell, *c.* 1490.
Swyre. Arms. & inscr., Russell, 1505. Ditto, 1509.
Thorncombe. Sir Thos. Brook, civ. & w., 1437.
Wimborne Minster. Half-effigy of St Ethelred, engr. *c.* 1440. Second plate (P).
Woolland. Mary Argenton, 1616.
Wraxall. Arms & inscr., Elizth. Lawrence, 1672.
Yetminster. John Horsey, arm. & w., 1531.

DURHAM

Auckland, St Andrew. Priest, *c.* 1380. Cross on qd. pl., sm., 1581.
Auckland, St Helen. Civilian & wife, mutil., *c.* 1470.
Billingham. Robt. Brerely, priest in almuce, 1480.
Brancepath. Arm., *c.* 1400. Rich. Drax, priest in acad., demi, 1456.
Chester-le-Street. Lady, 1430.
Greatham. Hospital chapel. Marginal inscr., *c.* 1350 (recut).
Hartlepool. Jane Bell, 1593.
Houghton-le-Skerne. Dorothy Parkinson, qd. pl., 1592.
Houghton-le-Spring. Margery Belassis, qd. pl., 1587.
Sedgefield. A lady, *c.* 1320. Two skeletons in shrouds, *c.* 1500.
Sockburn. Arms & inscr., Conyers, 1433.

ESSEX

Althorne. B.V.M., etc., to Margt. Hyklott, 1502. Crucifixion, etc., to Wm. Hyklott, 1508.
Arkesden. Rich. Fox, arm., 1439.
Ashen. Arm. & wife, small, *c.* 1440.
Aveley. Arm., qd. pl., sm., 1370. Child, sm., 1583. Arms & chil., *c.* 1520. Inscr., 1584 (P). Two children, 1588.
Baddow, Gt. Jane Paschall, 1614.
Bardfield, Gt. Eleanor Bendlowes, 1584.
Barking. Pr. in acad., w. chalice, *c.* 1480. Pr., demi, 1485. Civ. & w., 1493 (P), 1596. Children, *c.* 1530. Arms & inscr., Merell, 1598.
Belchamp St Paul. Wm. Golding, arm., 1587. Arms, etc., Golding, 1591.
Bentley, Little. Sir Wm. Pyrton, arm. & w., 1490.
Berden. Wm. Turnor, civ. & 2 ws., 1473. Thompson, civ. & w., 1607.
Blackmore. Civ., mutilated, *c.* 1420.

Bocking. John Doreward, arm. & w., 1420. Oswald Fitch, civ., 1613.

Boreham. Alse Canceller, 1573.

*Bowers, Gifford. Sir John Gifford, arm., mutil., 1348.

Bradfield. Joan Rysbye, 1598.

Bradwell-juxta-mare. Margt. Wyott, 1526.

Braxted, Little. Wm. Roberts, arm. & 2 wives, 1508.

Brightlingsea. Civ. & w., 1496. L., 1505, 1514. Civ. & 2 ws., 1521 (P) by appr. Civ. & w., 1525. 2 ladies on appr. bracket, 1536. Civ., 1578.

Bromley, Gt. Wm. Byschopton, priest, canopy, 1432.

Canfield, Gt. John Wyseman, arm. & w., kng., 1558. Lady, *c.* 1530. Thos. Fytch, civ., 1588.

Canfield, Little. 2 ladies, 1578. Ann Pudsey, 1593.

Chesterford, Gt. Lady, *c.* 1530. John Howard, child, sm., 1600.

Chesterford, Little. Isabel Langham, 1462.

*Chigwell. Archbishop Harsnett, in cope, 1631.

*Chrishall. Sir John de la Pole, arm. & w., trip. can., *c.* 1380. Lady, sm., *c.* 1450. Civ. & w., kng., *c.* 1480.

Clavering. Civ. & w., kng., sm., *c.* 1480. Civ. & w., 1591, 1593.

Coggeshall. 2 ladies, *c.* 1490. Civ. & w., *c.* 1520, *c.* 1533. Civ., 1580.

Colchester, St James. John Maynard, civ., *c.* 1584. His wife, 1584 (P).

Colchester, St Peter. Civ. & w., kng., qd. pl., 1530. 2 civs. & w., 1553; civ., 1563; civ. & 2 ws., 1610, all ditto. Civ. & w., kng., 1572.

Corringham. Rich. de Beltoun, pr., demi, *c.* 1340. Civ., sm., *c.* 1460.

Cressing. Dorcas Musgrave, 1610.

*Dagenham. Sir Thos. Urswyk, judge, civ. & w., 1479.

Dengie. Lady, *c.* 1520.

Donyland, E. Nich. Marshall, civ., 1621. Mary Gray, 1627.

Dunmow, Gt. Lady, 1579.

Easter, Good. Margaret Norrington, 1610.

*Easton, Little. Robt. Fyn, pr., *c.* 1420. Henry Bourchier, K.G., Earl of Essex, arm. & w., 1483.

Eastwood. Thos. Burrough, civ., 1600.

Elmdon. Civ. & 2 ws., *c.* 1530.

Elmstead. Two hands holding heart, with scroll, *c.* 1500.

Elsenham. Dr Tuer, vicar, 1615. Anne Fielde, 1615. Alice Tuer, 1619.

Epping. Thos. Palmer, barrister, 1621.

Fambridge, N. Wm. Osborne, civ. & w., 1590.

Faulkbourn. Henry Fortescue, arm., 1576. Mary Darrell, 1598.

Felstead. Cristine Bray, demi, 1420. Arm., *c.* 1415.

Finchingfield. John Berners, arm. & w., heraldic, 1523.

Fingringhoe. John Alleyn, civ., inscr. *c.* 1600, (P).

Fryerning. Lady, 1563, (P) and fragments.

Goldhanger. Audrey Heyham, 1531. Arms, etc., Heyham, 1540.

Gosfield. Thos. Rolf, lawyer, in acad., 1440.

Halstead. Bartholomew, Lord Bourgchier, & 2 ws., 1409. Lady, 1604.

Hanningfield, W. Isabel Clonvill, demi, 1361.

Harlow. Arm. & w., sm., *c.* 1430. Civ., 1559, 1602, 1615. Civ. & w., *c.* 1490, 1518, Inscr. 1575, (P). 1582, *c.* 1585, 1642.

Hatfield Peverel. John Allen, civ. & w., 1572.

Hempstead. Civ., *c.* 1475, *c.* 1480. Civ. & w., *c.* 1475, 1498, 1518, *c.* 1530.

Henny, Gt. Wm. Fisher, civ. & w., *c.* 1530.

Heybridge. John Whitacres, civ., 1627.

*Horkesley, Little. Sir Robt. & Sir Thos. Swynborne, arm., canopies 1412. Shroud, 1502. 2 arm. & w., heraldic, 1549, (P).

Hornchurch. Civ. & w., 1591, 1604. 2 ladies, 1602. Many fragments.

Horndon, E. Anne Tyrell, *c.* 1476. Arm., sm., kng., mutil., *c.* 1520.

Hutton. Arm. & w., *c.* 1525.

Ilford, Little. Thos. Heron, schoolboy, 1517. Anne Hyde, 1630.

Ingrave. Margt. Fitz Lewis, 1466. Rich. Fitz Lewis & 4 ws., heraldic, 1528.

Laindon. Priest w. chalice, *c.* 1470. Ditto, *c.* 1510.

Lambourne. Robt. Barfott, civ. & w., 1546, (P).

Latton. Sir Peter Arderne, judge, arm. & w., 1467, *c.* 1485. Lady, 1604. Civ. & w., *c.* 1600.

Laver, High. Edw. Sulyard, arm. & w., *c.* 1495.

Leigh. Rich. & John Haddok, civs. & ws., 1453. Rich. Chester, civ. & w., 1632. Ditto, 1640.

Leighs, Gt. Ralph Strelley, priest, demi, mutil., 1414. Head, *c.* 1370.

Leyton, Low. Ursula Gasper, 1493. Tobias Wood, civ. & w., *c.* 1620.

Lindsell. Thos. Fytche, civ. & w., 1514.

Littlebury. Civ., *c.* 1480, *c.* 1520. Pr. w. chalice, *c.* 1510. Civ. & w., *c.* 1510. Lady, 1578, 1624.

Loughton. Civ. & w., 1541. Arm. & w., 1558, 1637. Civ., 1594.

Margaretting. Arm. & w., curious, *c.* 1550.

Matching. John Ballett, civ. & w., 1638.

Messing. Lady, *c.* 1540.

Nettleswell. Thos. Laurence, civ. & w., 1522. Civ. & w., 1607.

Newport. Thos. Brond, civ. & w., 1515. Nightingale, ditto, 1608.

Norton, Cold. A lady, *c.* 1520.

Ockendon, N. Wm. Poyntz, arm. & w., 1502. Thomasyn Ardall, 1532.

*Ockendon, S. Sir Ingram Bruyn, canopy, large, 1400. Lady, 1602.

Ongar, High. A civilian, *c.* 1510.

Orsett. A civilian, sm., kng., *c.* 1535. Fragments, etc.

Parndon, Gt. Rowland Rampston, civ., 1598.

*Pebmarsh. Sir Wm. Fitzralph, cross-legged, canopy, large, 1323.

Rainham. A lady, *c.* 1475. Civilian & wife, *c.* 1500.

Rawreth. Edm. Tyrell, arm. & w., kng., 1576.

Rayleigh. A civilian and wife, mutil., *c.* 1450.

Rayne. Arms & inscr., Capell, 1572.

Rettendon. Civ. & 2 ws., *c.* 1535. Civ., 1605. Ditto, 1607.

Rochford. Maria Dilcock, sm., 1514.

Roydon. Thos. Colte, arm. & w., 1471. John Colt, arm. & 2 ws., heraldic, 1521. Civ., *c.* 1570. Lady, 1589.

Runwell. Eustace Sulyard, arm. & w., kng., 1587.

Saffron Walden. Priest, *c.* 1430, *c.* 1480. 2 ladies, *c.* 1480. Lady, *c.* 1500, *c.* 1530. Civ. & w., *c.* 1510, *c.* 1530. Civ. *c.* 1530.

Sandon. Patrick Fearne, parson, & w., 1588. Fragments.

Southminster. Civ. & 2 ws., *c.* 1560. Civ., 1634. Arms, etc., 1556.

Springfield. Thos. Coggeshall, arm., 1421.

Stanford Rivers. Chrysom, 1492. Borrow, arm. & w., 1503. Arm. & w., *c.* 1540.

Stapleford Tawney. Arms & marginal inscr., Scott, 1505.

Stebbing. Lady, large, *c.* 1390.

Stifford. Pr., demi, 1378. Shroud, *c.* 1480. Civ. & w., 1504, 1622. Lady, 1627, 1630.

Stisted. Elizth. Wyseman, kng., 1584.

Stock. Rich. Twedye, arm., 1574.

Stondon Massey. Carre, civ. & w., 1570. Civ. & w., 1573, (P).

Stow Maries. Mary Browne, 1602.

Strethall. Priest in acad., *c.* 1480. Inscr., 1539, (P).

Sutton. Thos. Stapel, serjeant-at-arms, arm., mutil., 1371.

Terling. Rochester, civ. & w. Civ. & 2 ws., 1584, (P).

Thaxted. Priest in acad., *c.* 1450.

Theydon Gernon. Priest in cope, 1458. Ellen Braunche, 1567.

Thorington. A lady, 1564.

Thurrock, Grays. Two ladies, *c.* 1510.

Thurrock, West. Humphrey Heies and son, 1585.

Tillingham. Edw. Wiot, civ., kng., 1584.

Tilty. Arm. & w., 1520, 1562. Margt. Tuke, 1590.

Tollesbury. Civilian & wife, 1517.

Tolleshunt Darcy. Inscr., (P). Arm., & w., *c.* 1420. Lady, *c.* 1535, (P). Arm., 1540, (P). Inscr., 1559.

Toppesfield. John Cracherood, civ. & w., 1534, (under organ).

Twinstead. Isake Wyncoll, civ. & w., 1610.

Upminster. L., heraldic, 1455. Civ., *c.* 1530, (P), 1545, (P). Lady, *c.* 1555, 1636. Arm., 1591. Fragments.

Waltham Abbey. Stacy, civ. & w., qd. pl., 1565. Colte, civ. & w., 1576.

Waltham, Great. Civ. & 2 ws., 1580. Rich. Everard, civ., 1617.

Waltham, Little. John Maltoun, arm., 1447.

Warley, Little. Anne Hanmer, demi, 1592.

Weald, N. Walter Larder, civ. & w., 1606.

Weald, S. Fragments of ten brasses, *c.* 1450–1634. Marg. inscr. 1567, (P).

Wendens-Ambo. Wm. Loveney, arm., *c.* 1410.

Wenden-Lofts. Wm. Lucas, civ. & w., *c.* 1460.

Widdington. A civilian, *c.* 1450.

Willinghale Doe. Thos. Torrell, arm., *c.* 1442. Lady, 1582, 1613.

★*Wimbish.* Sir John de Wautone & w., sm., in head of cross, 1347.

Woodham Mortimer. Dorothie Alleine, child, 1584.

Writtle. Arm. & w., *c.* 1500. 2 ditto, 1513. Civ. & 4 ws., *c.* 1510. Lady, 1524, 1592. Civ. & w., 1576, 1606, 1609.

Wyvenhoe. Viscount Beaumont, arm., canopy, 1507. Pr. w. chalice, 1535. Elizth., Countess of Oxford, heraldic, canopy, 1537, (P).
Yeldham, Gt. Rich. Symonds, civ. & w., *c.* 1612.

GLOUCESTERSHIRE

Abbenhall. Rich. Pyrke, civ. & w., 1609.
Berkeley. Wm. Freme, civ., holding a heart, 1526.
Bisley. Kath. Sewell, 1515.
Bristol—
    St James. Henry Gibbes, civ. & w., 1636.
    St John. Thos. Rowley, civ. & w., 1478.
    St Mary Redcliff. Chief Justice Sir John Juyn, 1439. Pr. in cope *c.* 1460 (P). Arm. in
        tab. & 2 ws., qd. pl., 1475. Civ. & w., canopy, 1480. Serjt.-at-law & w., 1522.
    Trinity Almshouses. John Barstaple, civ., 1411. Lady, *c.* 1411. (17th cent. restoration?).
    Grammar School. Nich. Thorne, civ. & 2 ws., *c.* 1570 (under glass).
Cheltenham, St Mary. Sir Wm. Greville, judge, & w., 1513.
Chipping Campden. Wool-merchant & w., can., 1401. Civ. & w., 1450, 1467. Civ. & 3 ws.,
    1484.
Cirencester. Arm. & w., can., 1438. Pr. w. chalice, 1478. Pr. in cassock, *c.* 1480. 12 brasses
    of civs. (wool-merchants) & ws., *c.* 1400, 1440, 1442, 1462, *c.* 1470, *c.* 1480, 1497, *c.* 1500,
    c. 1500, *c.* 1530, 1587, 1626, and fragments.
Coaley. Priest, 1630.
Deerhurst. Sir John Cassy, judge, & w., can., 1400. L., *c.* 1520, 1525.
Dowdeswell. Priest in cope, *c.* 1520.
Doynton. Civ. & w., 1529.
Dyrham. Sir Morys Russel & w., canopy, large, 1401.
Eastington. Elizth. Knevet, heraldic, 1518.
Fairford. Tame, arm. & w., 1500. Ditto & 2 ws., heraldic, 1534.
Gloucester, St Mary de Crypt. Alys & Agnes Henshawe, 1519. John Cook, civ. & w., can.,
    1544.
Kempsford. Walt. Hichman, civ. & w., 1521.
Lechlade. Woolman & w., 1450. Civ., *c.* 1510.
Leckhampton. Wm. Norwood, civ. & w., qd. pl., 1598.
Micheldean. Margery & Alice Baynham, *c.* 1500.
Minchinhampton. Civ. & w., *c.* 1500, 1519. Ditto in shrouds, *c.* 1510.
Newent. Roger Porter, arm., sm., 1523.
Newland. Arm. & w., 1443.
Northleach. 7 brasses of civs. (wool-merchants) & ws., *c.* 1400, 1447, 1458, *c.* 1485, *c.* 1490,
    1501, 1526. Pr. in surplice, kng., *c.* 1530.
Olveston. Morys & Sir Walt. Denys, arm. in tabards, 1505.
Rodmarton. John Edward, lawyer, 1461.
Sevenhampton. John Camber, civ., 1497.
Thornbury. Avice Tyndall, 1571.

Todenham. Wm. Molton, civ. & w., 1614.
Tormarton. John Ceysyll, civ., 1493.
Whittington. Rich. Coton, civ. & w., 1560.
Winterbourne. A lady, *c.* 1370.
Wormington. Anne Savage, in a bed, 1605.
*Wotton-under-Edge. Thos. Lord Berkeley & w., large, 1392.
Yate. Alex. Staples, civ. & 2 ws., 1590.

HAMPSHIRE

Aldershot. Arms & inscr., Sir John Whyte, *c.* 1573. Inscr., 1583, (P).
Alton. Lady, *c.* 1510. Several frags. & inscrs.
Andover. Arms & inscr., Nich. Venables, 1602.
Basingstoke. Robt. Stocker, civ. & w., 1606. Child, 1621.
Bramley. Wm. Joye, civ., 1452. Gwen Shelforde, 1504. Civ. & w., sm., 1529.
Bramshott. John Weston, civ. & w., *c.* 1430.
Candover, Brown. Civilian & wife, *c.* 1490.
Candover, Preston. Kath. Dabrigecort, 1607.
Chilbolton. Arms & inscr., Thos. Tutt, *c.* 1610.
Christchurch. Many empty matrices to priors and monks, etc.
*Crondall. Nich. de Kaerwent, priest, large, 1381. John Gyfford, arm., kng., sm., 1563.
    Skeleton, qd. pl., 1641.
Dogmersfield. Anne Sutton, qd. pl., 1590.
Dummer. Wm. at Moore, civ., kng., *c.* 1580. Inscr., 1591, (P).
Eling. Arms & inscr., Wm. Pawlet, 1596.
Eversley. Large cross to Rich. Pendilton, 1502.
Fareham. Arms & inscr., Constance Riggs, 1653.
Farlington. Arms & inscr., Antony Pounde, 1547.
Fordingbridge. Wm. Bulkeley, arm. & w., kng., qd. pl., 1568.
Froyle, John Lighe, civ., 1575.
Hale. Arms & inscr., Sir John Penruddocke, 1600.
Hartley Wespall. Arms & inscr., John Waspaill, 1452.
Havant. Thos. Aileward, priest in cope, 1413.
Headbourne Worthy. John Kent, civ., sm., 1434.
Headley. Civilian & wife, sm., *c.* 1510.
Heckfield. Elizth. Hall, 1514. Several inscrs.
Hinton Ampner. Arms & inscr., Stewkeley, 1642. Several inscrs.
Itchen Stoke. Lady, *c.* 1500. Joan Batmanson, 1518.
Kimpton. Robt. Thornburgh, arm. & 2 ws., kng., 1522.
Kingsclere. Lady, sm., 1503. Wm. Estwood, priest, sm., 1519.
Lymington. Arms & inscr., Joan Guidott, 1668.
Mapledurwell. John Canner, civ. & w., sm., *c.* 1520.
Monxton. Alice Swayne, kng., sm., 1599.
Mottisfont. Arms & inscr., Sir Wm. Sandys, 1628.

Nursling. Arms & inscr., Andrew Mundy, 1632.

Oakley, Church. Robt. Warham, civ. & w., 1487.

Odiham. Civ. & w., *c.* 1480. Pr., 1498. Lady, 1504, 1522. Civ., *c.* 1535. Arm., *c.* 1540, (P). Child, 1636.

Prior's Dean.. John Compton, civ. & w., 1605.

*Ringwood. John Prophete, priest in cope, w. saints, can., 1416.

Sherborne St John. Brocas. civ. & w., demi, *c.* 1360. Arm. in tab., kng., 1488. Arm., kng., sm., 1492. Arm. & 2 ws., sm., 1492. Arm., kng., sm., *c.* 1540.

Sherfield-on-Loddon. Lady, qd. pl., 1595. Civ., kng., sm., *c.* 1600.

*Sombourne, King's. Two civilians, *c.* 1380.

Southampton, God's House. Priest in cope, *c.* 1500, (mutil.).

Southwick. Arm. & w., sm., 1548, (P).

Stoke Charity. Wayte, arm., 1482. Hampton, arm. & w., 1483. Inscr., 1552, (P).

Sutton, Bishops. Arm. & wife, *c.* 1520.

*Thruxton. Sir John Lysle, canopy, *c.* 1425.

Tytherley, W. Anne Whitehede, 1480.

Wallop, Nether. Dame Mary Gore, prioress, 1436.

Warnborough, S. Robt. Whyte, arm., kng., sm., 1512.

Weeke. Fig. of St Christopher, for Wm. Complyn & w., 1498.

Whitchurch. Rich. Brooke, civ. & w., 1603.

Winchester College, Chapel & Cloisters. Facsimiles of lost originals, 3 wardens & 8 fellows, some demi, 5 in euch., 1 in almuce, 4 in cope, 1 in acad., 1413–1559, & Civ., 1498. Many inscrs. in cloisters. Frag., 1560, (P).

*Winchester, St Cross. John de Campeden, pr. in cope, 1382. Pr. in alm., 1493. Pr., 1518, & inscrs.

Winchester, St Maurice. Children in swaddling-clothes, 1612.

Winchfield. Arms & inscr., Rudyerd, 1652 & 1659.

Yateley. Civ. & w., 1517, 1532. Lady, mutil., 1578. Civ., *c.* 1590.

HEREFORDSHIRE

Brampton Abbotts. Joan Rudhale, sm., 1506.

Burghill. John Awbrey, civ. & w., qd. pl., 1616.

Clehonger. Arm. & w., *c.* 1470.

Colwall. Anth. Harford, arm. & w., qd. pl., *c.* 1590.

*Hereford Cathedral. Bp. Trilleck, canopy, 1360. Priest in cope, in head of cross, 1386. Pr. in cope, 1428, 1434, 1476. Dean Frowsetoure, in cope, canopy, 1529. Arm. & w., can., large, 1435. Arm. & 2 ws., 1514. Fragments, one *c.* 1285 St Ethelbert.

Ledbury. Pr. in acad., kng., *c.* 1410. Arm., 1490. Arm., qd. pl., 1614.

Ludford. Wm. Fox, arm. & w., 1554.

Marden. Margt. Chute, 1614.

HERTFORDSHIRE

Albury. Arm. & w., *c.* 1475. Civ. & w., 1588. Arm. & w., qd. pl., 1592.

Aldbury. Civ., sm., 1478. Verney, arm. in tab. & w., heraldic, 1547.

Aldenham. 5 civ. brasses, 3 ladies, *c.* 1520–*c.* 1535, 1608. Shroud, 1547. Inscr., 1569, (P).

Amwell, Gt. Civ. & 2 ws., *c.* 1490.

Ardeley. Philip Metcalff, priest, 1515. Thos. Shotbolt, civ. & w., 1599.

Aspenden. Civ. & w., 1500. Clyfford, arm. in tab. & w., kng, 1508.

Aston. John Kent, civ. & w., 1592.

Baldock. L., *c.* 1410. Civ. & w., *c.* 1420, *c.* 1480. Shrouds, *c.* 1480.

Barkway. Robt. Poynard & 2 ws., 1561.

Barley. Inscr., 1566, (P). Andrew Willet, minister, 1621.

Bayford. Arm. & w., *c.* 1545, (P). Arm., *c.* 1630.

Bennington. A Canon of Windsor, in cope, mutil., *c.* 1420.

Berkhamstead, Gt. Civ. & w., 1356. Arm., *c.* 1365. Lady, *c.* 1370. Pr., demi, *c.* 1400. Civ., 1485. Lady in shroud, sm., 1520. Inscr., 1558, (P).

Braughing. Barbara Hanchett, 1561.

Broxbourne. Pr. w. chalice, *c.* 1470. Sir John Say. Arm. in tab. & w., heraldic, 1473. Pr. in acad., *c.* 1510. Serjeant-at-arms, 1531.

Buckland. Lady, 1451. Pr. in cope, w. chalice, 1478. Civ., 1499.

Cheshunt. Canopy, etc., for Nich. Dixon, pr., 1448. Civ. & w., 1449. Lady, 1453, 1502, 1609.

Clothall. John Wynter, pr. 1404. Pr. w. chalice, 1519. Pr. in cope, 1541. Lady, 1578 (covered). Ecclesiastic, 1602.

Datchworth. Device & inscr., 1622.

Digswell. Arm. & w., large, 1415. Arm., 1442. Shrouds, 1484. Civ. & w., 1495, *c.* 1530, (P).

Eastwick. Joan Lee, 1564.

Essendon. Wm. Tooke, civ. & w., kng., 1588.

Flamstead. Priest in cope, 1414. Civ. & w., *c.* 1470.

Gaddesden, Gt. Wm. Croke, civ. & w., 1506. Civ. & w., *c.* 1525.

Hadham, Gt. Priest in acad., demi, *c.* 1420. Civ. & w., 1582. Civ. & 2 ws., 1610.

Hadham, Little. Pr. in cope, sm., *c.* 1470. Arm. & w., *c.* 1485.

Harpenden. Anabull, civ. & w., 1456. Cressye, civ. & w., 1571.

Hatfield. Arms & inscr., Fulke Onslowe, 1602.

Hemel Hempstead. Robt. Albyn, arm. & w., 1390.

Hinxworth. Civ. & w., *c.* 1450, 1487.

Hitchin. 6 civ. brasses w. ladies, 1421–*c.* 1550. 4 shroud brasses, *c.* 1480–1490. Priest in cope, 1498.

Hunsdon. Lady in shroud, 1495. Jas. Gray, park-keeper, w. Death, etc., qd. pl., 1591.

Ickleford. Thos. Somer, civ. & w., demi, *c.* 1400.

Ippolyts. Rice Hughes, civ. & w., qd. pl., 1594.

Kelshall. Rich. Adane, civ. & w., 1435.

Kimpton. A lady, *c.* 1450.

Knebworth. Priest in cope, w. saints, 1414. Arm. & 2 ws., 1582.

Langley, Abbot's. 2 ladies, sm., 1498. Civ. & 2 ws., 1607.

Langley, King's. Lady, 1528, (P). 1578, (P). Civ. & 2 ws., 1588.

Letchworth. Civ. & w., demi, *c.* 1400. Priest w. heart & scrolls, 1475.

Mymms, N. Wm. de Kestevine, 1361. L., 1458. Arm., 1488. Civ. & w., *c.* 1490. Arm. & w., *c.* 1560.

Nettleden. Sir Geo. Cotton, arm., 1545. Appr. (P).
Newnham. Civ. & 2 ws., *c.* 1515, (P). Lady, 1607.
Northchurch. Oval. Peter the wild boy, 1785.
Offley. Samwel, civ. & 2 ws., 1529. Civ. & 3 ws., *c.* 1530.
Pelham, Brent. Two ladies, 1627.
Pelham, Furneux. Civ. & w., canopy, *c.* 1420. Arm. & w., 1518.
Radwell. Civ. & w., 1487. Civ. & 2 ws., 1516. Lady, 1602.
Redbourn. Pecok, civ., 1512. Rede, arm. & w., kng., 1560.
Rickmansworth. Thos. Day, civ. & 2 ws., 1613.
Royston. Pr. in acad., canopy, 1421. Cross, w. heart & wounds, *c.* 1500. Civ. & w., *c.* 1500.
★St Alban's, Abbey. Abbot Delamere, *c.* 1360. Frag. of abbot, *c.* 1400, (P). 4 monks, *c.* 1450,
    c. 1470, *c.* 1470, 1521. Arm. & w., 1468, 1519. Arm., 1480. Civ. & w., 1411. Civ., *c.* 1465,
    c. 1470, and fragments.
★St Alban's, St Michael. John Pecok, civ. & w., *c.* 1380. Arm., *c.* 1380. Civ. in cross, *c.* 1400.
St Alban's, St. Peter. Roger Pemberton, civ., 1627.
St Alban's, St Stephen. Wm. Robins, arm. & w., 1482.
Sandon. John Fitzgeffrey, arm. & w., 1480.
Sawbridgeworth. Arm. & w., 1437, *c.* 1600. Arm. *c.* 1480. Civ. & 2 ws., 1470. Shrouds, 1484.
    Lady, 1527, *c.* 1600.
Standon. Civ., *c.* 1460. Civ. & arm., 1477. Arm., 1557, (P).
Stanstead Abbots. Arm., *c.* 1490. Civ. & w., *c.* 1540, (P). Ditto, 1581.
Stevenage. Steph. Hellard, priest in cope, *c.* 1500.
Tewin. Thos. Pygott, civ., 1610.
Walkerne. Civ. & w., *c.* 1480. Ditto, 1583, (P). Ditto, 1636.
Ware. Lady, *c.* 1400. Ditto, 1454. Civ. & 2 ws., *c.* 1470.
Watford. Sir Hugh de Holes, judge, large, 1415. Lady, 1416. 3 civs., qd. pl., 1613.
Watton. Arm., canopy, 1361. Pr. in cope, can., *c.* 1370. Civ., *c.* 1450, *c.* 1470. Lady, 1455.
    Arm., 1514. Lady, 1545.
Wheathamstead. Civ. & w., *c.* 1450, *c.* 1510. Arm., much mutil., *c.* 1500. John Heyworth, &
    w., 1520.
Willian. Rich. Goldon, priest w. heart, 1446.
Wormley. Civ. & w., 1479. Ditto, *c.* 1490. Ditto, 1598.
Wyddiall. John Gille, civ. & w., 1546, (P). Margt. Plumbe, demi, 1575.

HUNTINGDONSHIRE

Broughton. Laurence Martun, civ., mutil., *c.* 1490.
Diddington. Wm. Taylard, arm. & w., kng., w. saints, 1505. Lady, 1513.
Gidding, Little. Arms & inscr., 1656, 1657, 1717, 1719.
Godmanchester. Civilian, *c.* 1520, (P).
Offard Darcy. Arm. & 2 ws., *c.* 1440, (P). Priest in acad., kng., *c.* 1530.
★Sawtry All Saints'. Wm. Le Moigne, arm. & w., 1404.
Somersham. Priest, *c.* 1530.
Stanground. Arms & inscr., Elias Petit, 1634.

Stilton. Rich. Curthoyse, civ. & w., 1606. 2 civs., 1618.
Stukeley, Little. Civilian, *c.* 1590.
Tilbrook. Civ. & wife, *c.* 1400 (covered).

ISLE OF WIGHT

Arreton. Harry Hawles, arm., mutil., *c.* 1430.
Calbourne. Arm., *c.* 1380. Arms & inscr., Price, 1638. Time, Death, etc., to Daniel Evance, rector, 1652.
Carisbrooke. Arms, Keeling, 1619.
Freshwater. Adam de Compton, arm., 1367.
Kingston. Rich. Mewys, civ., 1535.
Shorwell. Rich. Bethell, pr. in cassock & scarf, 1518. Wives of Barnabas Leigh, qd. pl., 1619. Arms, etc., Leigh, 1621.

KENT

Acrise. Mary Heyman, 1601. Arms, etc., Hamon, 1613.
Addington. Arm., demi, 1378. Arm & w., canopy, 1409. Arm., *c.* 1415, *c.* 1445. Arm. & w., 1470. Priest, demi, w. chalice, 1446.
Aldington. Arm. & w., 1475, (P).
Ash, near Sandwich. Lady, mutil., can., 1455. L., 1455. Civ. & w., sm., 1525. Arm. & w., 1602. Civ. & w., 1642.
Ash, near Wrotham. Rich. Galon, priest, demi, 1465.
Ashford. Lady, mutil., canopy, 1375. Several fragments.
Aylesford. Cosyngton, arm. & w., 1426. Inscr., Savell, 1545, (P).
Barham. Civilian, *c.* 1375. Arm. & w., *c.* 1460.
Bearstead. Civ. & w., 1634.
Beckenham. Arm. in tabard & 2 ws., heraldic, kng., 1552. Lady, 1563.
Bethersden. Wm. Lovelace, civ., 1469, (P). Thos. Lovelace, civ., sm., 1591.
Bexley. A hunting-horn, etc., *c.* 1410. Civ., sm., 1513.
Biddenden. 2 civs. & w., sm., *c.* 1520. Arm. & w., kng., 1566. Civ., 1572, (P). Civ., 1593. Civ. & w., 1628, 1641. Civ. & 2 ws., 1584, 1598, 1609.
Birchington. Civ., 1449, 1454. Lady, 1518, 1528, 1533. John Heynys, priest w. chalice, 1523.
Birling. Walter Mylys, civ., 1522.
Bobbing. Arm. & w., *c.* 1420. Arm., mutil., can., 1420. L. 1496.
Borden. Civilian, *c.* 1450. Priest in almuce, 1521.
Boughton Malherbe. Civ. & w., kng., sm., 1499. Arm. & w., 1529.
Boughton-under-Blean. Civ. & w., 1508, 1591. Arm., 1587.
Boxley. Wm. Snell, priest in acad., 1451. Arm., 1576.
Brabourn. Arm., canopy, 1433. Lady, 1450, 1528. Arm., 1524.
Bredgar. Thos. Coly, priest in acad., w. chalice, 1518.
Brenchley. Civilian & 3 ws., 1517. Civ. & w., *c.* 1540.
Brookland. Thos. Leddes, priest, sm., 1503.

Canterbury—
    Cath. Chapter Office. John Lovelle, priest in cope, without almuce, 1438.
    St Alphege. Arms, etc., Prude, 1468. Priest in acad., 1523.
    St Margaret. John Wynter, civ., 1470.
    St Martin. Civ. & w., 1587. Arm., 1591, and inscrs.
    St Gregory Northgate. Raff Brown, civ., 1522.
    St Paul. Geo. Wyndbourne, civ. & w., 1531.
Capel-le-Ferne. John Gybbis, civ. & w., sm., 1526.
Challock. Thos. Thorston, civ. & w., sm., 1504.
Chart, Great. Notary, *c.* 1470. Civ. & w., 1485, 1500, 1565, (P). Civ. & 5 ws., 1499. Arm. &
    2 ws., 1513. Civ., kng., 1680. Slabs in churchyard.
*Chartham. Sir Robt. de Setvans, 1306. Engr., *c.* 1323. Priest in cope, 1416, 1454. Priest in
    almuce, 1508. Lady, sm., 1530.
Chelsfield. Crucifix, etc., mutil., to Robt. de Brun, priest, 1417. Priest, sm., *c.* 1420. Lady,
    c. 1480, 1510.
Cheriton. Priest in acad., 1474. Priest, 1502. Lady, 1592.
Chevening. Arms & inscr., Lennard, 1556. Civ. & wife, 1596.
Chiddingstone. Arms, etc., Birchensty, 1637, and other inscrs.
Chislehurst. Alan Porter, priest, demi, 1482.
Cliffe. Thos. Faunce, civ. & w., 1609. Civ. & 2 wives, 1652.
*Cobham. Lady, *c.* 1315, 1375, 1380, 1395. Arm., 1354, *c.* 1365, 1367, 1405, 1407, all large w.
    fine canopies. Priest in almuce, demi, 1418. Pr. in cope, 1402, *c.* 1450, 1498. Ditto on
    bracket, *c.* 1420. Cross, mutil., 1447. Arm., demi, 1402. Lady, 1433. Lady, canopy, 1506.
    Arm. & w., 1529. Inscr. 1473, (P).
Cowling. Feyth Brooke, sm., 1508, and inscrs.
Cranbrook. Civ. & chrysom, 1520. Civ. & w., kng., 1627.
Cray, St Mary. Civ. & 3 ws., 1508. L., 1544. Civ. & w., 1604. L., qd. pl., & Civ., qd. pl.,*c.* 1773.
Cudham. Alice Waleys, 1503.
Cuxton. Inscrs. 1545, (P).
Dartford. Civ. & w., can., 1402. Lady, 1454, 1464, 1590, and 1612. Civ. & w., 1496. Civ., 1508.
    Civ. & 2 ws., 1590. Inscr. 1574, (P).
Davington. Civ. & w., kng., qd. pl., 1613. Lady, kng., qd. pl., 1616.
Deal, Upper. Civ. & w., 1508. Arm., kng., 1562. Chrysom, 1606.
Denton. Arms & inscr., John Boys, 1543.
Ditton. Rowland Shakerley, arm., mutil., 1576.
Dover, St Mary. Wm. Jones, civ. & w., 1638.
Downe. Civilian & w., *c.* 1400. Civ., *c.* 1420. Jacob Verzelini & w., 1607.
Eastry. Thos. Nevynson, arm. & w., 1590.
Edenbridge. John Selyard, civ., 1558.
Elmsted. Lady, 1507, and several inscriptions.
Erith. Civ., sm., 1425. Civ. & w., 1435, 1511. Lady, 1471. Edw. Hawte, arm. & w., 1537.
    Inscr., 1574, (P).
Farningham. Priest, demi, 1451. Lady, sm., 1514. Civ., kng., 1517. Thos. Sibill, civ. & w.,
    1519.

Faversham. Civ., mutil., can., 1414. Pr. in cope, can., 1480. Pr. w. chalice, 1531. Civ., *c.* 1500, *c.* 1580, 1610. Civ. & w., can., 1533. Civ. & 2 ws., 1533, and many fragments, arms (some (P)) and inscrs.

Fordwich. Aphra Hawkins, 1605.

Gillingham. Arms & inscr., Wm. Beaufitz, 1433.

Godmersham. Inscr., 1516, (P).

Goodnestone. Civilian and wife, 1507, 1558 and 1568.

Goudhurst. Arm., canopy, 1424. Sir John Culpeper & w., 1481. Arm., *c.* 1520.

★Graveney. Lady & son, demi, *c.* 1360. Rich. de Feversham, arm., 1381. John Martyn, judge, & w., can., 1436.

Halling. Silvester Lambarde, in a bed, qd. pl., 1587.

Halstead. Wm. Burys, arm., 1444. Wm. Petley, civ. & w., 1528.

Halstow, High. Wm. Palke, minister, & w., sm., 1618.

★Hardres, Upper. John Strete, pr. in acad. & bracket, 1405. Arms & inscrs., Hardres, 1533 and 1575. Inscr. & shs., 1579 (P sh. lost).

Harrietsham. Susanna Parthericke, kng., qd. pl., 1603.

Harty. Habram Fare, civ., mutil., 1515. Arms & inscr., Haward, 1610.

Hawkhurst. John Roberts, civ. & w., 1499. Inscr., 1612, (P).

Hayes. Priest, demi, *c.* 1460. Priest, sm., 1479. Ditto, 1566.

Headcorn. John Byrd, child, kng., qd. pl., 1636.

Herne. Arm. & w., *c.* 1430. Pr. in acad., *c.* 1450. Lady, 1470, 1539. Civ. & 2 ws., 1604.

Hever. Margt. Cheyne, 1419. Sir Thos. Bullen, K.G., 1538. Kng., civ., 1584. Inscr., *c.* 1520, (P).

Higham. Arms & inscr., Boteler, 1615.

Hoath. Lady, *c.* 1430. Civilian & w., sm., 1532.

Hoo, All Hallows. Wm. Copinger, arm., kng., 1594.

Hoo, St Werburgh. Pr., demi, 1406. Pr., large, 1412. Civ., *c.* 1430. 2 civs., 1446. Arm. & w., 1465. Lady, 1615. Civ. & w., 1640.

★Horsmonden. Priest, large, can., *c.* 1340. Lady, 1604.

Horton Kirby. Lady, *c.* 1460. Civilian & wife, 1595.

Hunton. Civilian, 1513. Arms, etc., Francis Fane, 1651.

Ightham. Clement, arm. in tabard & w., 1528. Lady, 1626, and inscrs.

Iwade. Simon Snellyng, civ. & w., 1467.

Kemsing. Thos. de Hop, priest, demi, 1347.

Kingsnorth. Humf. Clarke arm. & wife, 1579.

Langdon, E. Martha Master, 1591.

Lee. Lady, sm., 1513, 1545. L., 1582, (P). Nich. Ansley, arm., kng., 1593. Inscr., 1545, (P).

Leeds. Wm. Merden, civ. & w., sm., 1509. Kath. Lambe, sm., 1514.

Leigh. Lady in a tomb, qd. pl., sm., *c.* 1580, and several inscriptions.

Lenham. Arms, etc., Codd, 1631.

Luddesdown. Man in armour, mutilated, *c.* 1450.

Lullingstone. Arms, etc., Rokesle, 1361. Sir Wm. Pecche, arm., 1487. Alice Baldwyn, sm., 1533. Elizth. Hart, 1544.

Lydd. Priest in acad., 1420. Civ. & w., canopy, 1430. Civ., 1508, *c.* 1520, 1578, *c.* 1590. Civ. & w., 1557, 1566, and Lady, *c.* 1590.

Lynsted. Lady, 1567. Civ. & w., 1621. Arms, etc., 1637, 1642.

Maidstone, All Saints. Thos. Beale, civ. & w., qd. pl., 1593. Civ. & w., qd. pl., 1640.

Malling, E. Selby, civ. & w., 1479. Pr. in almuce, w. chal., sm., 1522.

Malling, W. Civilian, sm., 1497. Ditto, 1532. Lady, mutilated, 1543, (P).

*Margate, St John. Civ., 1431. Heart & scrolls, 1433, (P). Civ. & w., 1441. Civ., 1442. Arm., 1445. Skeleton, 1446. Priest, sm., 1515. Inscr., 1582, (P). Arm., *c.* 1590. Inscr. & ship, 1615.

Mereworth. Sir John de Mereworth, arm. & canopy, mutil., 1366. Civ. & w., 1479. Civ., kng., 1542.

Mersham. Priest, *c.* 1420. Civ. & w., *c.* 1520.

Milton-next-Sittingbourne. Arm., *c.* 1470. John Northwood, arm. in tabard & w., 1496. Margt. Alefe, 1529.

*Minster-in-Sheppey. Sir John de Northwoode? *c.* 1330, (P). Lady, *c.* 1335.

Monkton. A priest, *c.* 1460. Inscr., 1580, (P).

Murston. John Eveas, arm. & w., 1488.

Newington. Two civs., 1488. Lady, 1580, 1600. Civ. & 2 ws., 1581.

Newington-juxta-Hythe. Lady, mutil., *c.* 1480. Civ. in shroud & w., 1501. Priest w. chal., sm., 1501. Civ. & 3 ws., 1522. Civ. *c.* 1600. Arm. & w., 1630, and seven inscriptions.

Nonington. Inscr., 1581, (P).

Northfleet. Priest, large, 1375. Pr., demi, 1391. Arm. & w., 1433.

Orpington. Arms, etc., Gulby, 1439. Priest in cope, 1511. Inscr., 1522, (P).

Otham. Thos. Hendley, civ. & 3 ws., kng., qd. pl., 1590, (P).

Otterden. Man in armour, 1408, 1502, 1508. Lady, 1488, 1606.

Peckham, E. A civilian & wife, small, *c.* 1525.

Peckham, W. Elizth. Culpepir, *c.* 1460.

Pembury. Elizth. Rowe, child, 1607.

Penshurst. Small cross, *c.* 1520. Civ. & w., 1514. Inscr., 1558, (P).

Pluckley. Arm., 1440. Lady, 1526. Arm & w., 1610. Dering brasses restored in 17th cent.

Preston, near Faversham. Arm. & w., 1442. Arm., 1459. Lady, 1612.

Rainham. Arm. 1514. Civ., 1529. Lady, *c.* 1530. Civ. & w., *c.* 1580.

Ringwould. Lady, mutil., sm., 1505. Civ., sm., 1530.

Ripple. Arms & inscr., Warren, 1591, 1612.

Rochester, St Margaret. Thos. Cod, priest in cope, 1465, (P).

Romney, New. Arms & inscr., 1375. Civ., 1510. Civ. & w., 1610.

Romney, Old. John Ips, civ. & w., sm., 1526.

St Laurence, Thanet. Arm., 1444. Lady, 1493. Arms & inscr., 1610.

St Mary-in-the-Marsh. Maud Jamys, 1499. Wm. Gregory, civ., 1502.

St Nicholas, Thanet. Two civs., Edvarod & Parramore, & w., 1574, (P).

St Peter, Thanet. Rich. Colmer, civ. & w., 1485. Nich. Esstone, civ. & w., sm., 1503.

Saltwood. Priest, demi, 1370. Arm. & w., 1437. Angel & heart, etc., for Anne Muston, 1496.

Sandwich, St Clement. Civ., can., *c.* 1490. Arms & inscr., 1583, 1583.

*Seal. Sir Wm. de Bryene, arm., 1395. Civ., 1577, (P).

Selling, near Faversham. A civilian, *c.* 1525. Fragments, *c.* 1530.

Sheldwich. Arm. & w. & canopy, 1394. Arm. & w., 1426. Joan Mareys, in shroud, demi, 1431.

Shepherdwell. Inscr., 1660, (P).

Shorne. Civ. & w., demi, 1457. Lady, *c.* 1470, 1583 chalice, 1519.

Snodland. Civ., sm., 1441. Ditto, 1486. Civ. & w., 1487. Civ. & 2 ws., *c.* 1530.

Southfleet. Joan Urban, on bracket, 1414. Civ. & w., 1420. Priest in cope, demi, 1456. Shroud, *c.* 1520. Civ. & w., *c.* 1520.

Staple. A civilian, *c.* 1510.

Staplehurst. A lady, *c.* 1580.

Stockbury. Hooper, civ. & w., qd. pl., 1617. Lady, qd. pl., 1648.

Stoke. Wm. Cardiff, priest, 1415. Arms, etc., Wilkins, 1575.

⋆Stone. Priest in head of cross, 1408. Arms & inscr., 1574.

Stourmouth. Thos. Mareys, priest in acad., 1472.

Sturry. Inscr., *c.* 1570, (P).

Sundridge. Roger Isly, arm., 1429. Civ., *c.* 1460. Arm. & w., 1518.

Sutton, E. Sir Edw. Filmer, arm. & w., qd. pl., 1629.

Teynham. Arm., 1444. Civ., 1509. Ditto, sm., 1533. Civ. & w., 1639.

Thannington. Thos. Halle, arm., 1485.

Tilmanstone. Rich. Fogg, civ. & w., kng., qd. pl., 1598.

Trotterscliffe. Wm. Crofton, civ. & w., 1483.

Tunstall. Priest, 1525. Lady, *c.* 1590, and several inscriptions.

Ulcombe. Arm. & canopy, 1419. Arm., 1442. Arm. & w., 1470.

Upchurch. Civilian & wife, demi, *c.* 1350.

Westerham. Civ. & w., 1529, (P). Civ., 1531. Civ. & 2 ws., 1533. Two civs., *c.* 1545. Civ. & 2 ws., 1557, (P), 1566. Wm. Dye, parson, 1567. Inscr., 1563, (P).

⋆Wickham, E. John de Bladigdone, civ. & w., demi, in head of cross, *c.* 1325. Yeoman of the Guard & 3 ws., 1568.

Wickham, W. Wm. de Thorp, pr., sm., 1407. Stokton, ditto, 1515.

⋆Woodchurch. Priest in head of cross, *c.* 1330. Arm. 1558.

Wrotham. Civ. & w., 1498. Civ., *c.* 1500. Arm. & w., 1512. Ditto, heraldic, 1525. Arm. & w., 1611. Lady, 1615.

Wye. Two civs., John Andrew and Thos. Palmere, & w., *c.* 1440.

LANCASHIRE

Childwall. Henry Norris, arm. & w., heraldic, 1524.

Eccleston. Priest in cope, *c.* 1510.

Flixton. R. Radclyffe, civ. & 2 wives, 1602.

Lancaster, St Mary. Thos. Covell, civilian, 1639.

Manchester Cathedral. Priest, 1458. Arm. & w., much mutil., *c.* 1460. Stanley, Bishop of Ely, 1515. Arm., *c.* 1540, (P). Civ. & w., qd. pl., 1607. Ditto, 1629.

Middleton. Priest w. chalice, 1522. Arm. & w., *c.* 1510, 2 arm. & w., 1531. Assheton, civ. & w., 1618. Ditto, arm & w., 1650.

Newchurch. Children & inscr., Ratclyff, 1561.

Ormskirk. Arm. in tabard, Scarisbrick, *c.* 1500.

Preston. Seath Bushell, civ., 1623.

Prestwich. Inscr., 1634, (P).
Rivington. Qd. pl., skeleton, 1627.
Rufford. Sir Robt. Hesketh, arm., 1543, (P).
Sefton. Margt. Bulcley, canopy, 1528. Sir Rich. Molineux, arm. & 2 ws., 1568. Ditto,
  c. 1570.
Ulverstone. Myles Dodding, civ. & w., 1606.
Walton-on-the-Hill. Thos. Beri, civilian, 1586.
Whalley Abbey. Raffe Caterall, arm. & w., 1515.
*Winwick. Peers Gerard, arm. in tab., canopy, 1492. Sir Peter Legh, arm. w. chasuble over,
  & w., 1527.

LEICESTERSHIRE

Aylestone. Wm. Heathcott, parson, 1594.
Barwell. John Torksay, eccles. & w., qd. pl., 1614. Civ. & w., 1659.
*Bottesford. Henry de Codyngtoun, priest in cope, w. saints & canopy, 1404. John Freman,
  pr. in cope, *c.* 1440.
Bowden, Gt. Inscr., Wolstanton, 1403, (P).
*Donington Castle. Robt. Staunton, arm. & w., w. canopy, 1458.
Hinckley. Civilian & wife, *c.* 1420.
Hoby. Man in armour & w., mutil., *c.* 1480.
Leicester, Wigston's Hospital. Priest in shroud, *c.* 1540.
Loughborough. Civ. & w., inscr., 1445, (P). Civ. & w., 1480, and fragments.
Lutterworth. John Fildyng, civ. & w., 1418. Civ. & w., *c.* 1470.
Melton Mowbray. A large inscribed heart and inscr., 1543.
Queeniborough. A lady, 1634.
Saxelby. A lady, 1523.
Scalford. A civilian, kng., *c.* 1520, and inscriptions.
Sheepshed. Thos. Duport, arm. & w., qd. pl., 1592.
Sibson. John Moore, priest in almuce, & Saviour, 1532.
Stapleford. Geoffrey Sherard, arm. & w., 1492.
Stokerston. John Boville, arm. & w., 1467. Arm. w., 1493.
Swithland. Agnes Scot, *c.* 1455.
Thurcaston. John Mershden, priest in cope, 1425.
Wanlip. Sir Thos. Walsch, arm. & w., 1393.
Wymondham. Margery Barkeley, 1521.

LINCOLNSHIRE

Algarkirk. Nich. Robertson, civ. & 2 wives, 1498.
Althorpe. Wm. de Lound, priest, *c.* 1360.
Asgarby-by-Sleaford. Arms & inscr., Butler, 1603.
Ashby Puerorum. Lytleburye, arm. & w., *c.* 1560. Ditto, *c.* 1560.
Barholm. Arms & inscr., Fordham, 1641.

Barrowby. Nich. Deen, civ. & w., 1479. Margt. Deen, heraldic, 1508.

Barton-on-Humber, St Mary. Lady, demi, *c.* 1380. Seman, civ., 1433.

Bigby. Elizth. Skypwith, *c.* 1520. Nayler, rector, & w., qd. pl., 1632.

★*Boston.* Civ., canopied, 1398. Pr. in cope, *c.* 1400. Civ. & 2 ws., bracket & can., mutil., *c.* 1400. Civ. & w., *c.* 1470. Civ., 1659, and many fragments and matrices.

Broughton. Sir Hen. Redford & w., canopied, *c.* 1390.

Burton Coggles. Cholmeley, civ., 1590. Ditto, arm. & w., 1620.

★*Buslingthorpe.* Sir Rich. de Boselyngthorpe, arm., demi, *c.* 1310.

Conisholme. John Langholme, arm. & w., kng., 1515.

Corringham. Civ. & w., kng., qd. pl., 1628. Arms & inscr., 1631.

Cotes-by-Stow. Butler, arm. & w., 1590. Ditto, kng., 1602.

Cotes, Great. Isabella Barnardiston, *c.* 1420. Arm. & w., kng., 1503.

Covenham, St Bartholomew. John Skypwyth, arm., 1415.

★*Croft.* Man in armour, demi, *c.* 1310.

Driby. Jas. Prescot, civ. & w., kng., 1583.

Edenham. An archbishop, small, *c.* 1500.

Evedon. Dan. Hardeby, civ. & w., kng., 1630.

Fiskerton. Priest in cope, *c.* 1490.

Gedney. A lady, *c.* 1390.

Glentham. Elizth. Tourney, demi, 1452.

Grainthorpe. A large cross, *c.* 1380.

★*Gunby, St Peter.* Massyngberd, arm. & w., can., 1552, (P). Wm. Lodyngton, justice, can., 1419.

Hainton. John Henege, civ. & w., 1435. Sir Thos. Henneage, arm. & w., heraldic, 1553.

Hale. Arms & inscr., Cawdron, 1625.

Halton Holgate. Bridgett Rugeley, qd. pl., 1658.

Harpswell. Arm. & w., kng., *c.* 1480.

Harrington. Margt. Copledyk, 1480. Copledike, arm. & w., 1585.

Holbeach. Arm., *c.* 1410. Joan Welby, 1488.

Horncastle. Sir Lionel Dymoke, arm., (P), also in shroud, 1519 (P).

Ingoldmells. Wm. Palmer, w. a 'stylt', 1520.

Irnham. Sir Andrew Luttrell, canopied, 1390. Arm., *c.* 1440.

Kelsey, South. Arm. & w., *c.* 1410.

Kyme, South. 1530. Inscr., (P).

Laughton. Arm., canopied, 1549, (P).

Leadenham. Lady Elizth. Beresforde, qd. pl., 1624.

Lincoln, St Mary-le-Wigford. Cross & inscr., Horn, 1469, (P). Inscr. 1525, (P).

Lincoln, Cathl. Ch. of B.V.M., Bp. Wm. Smyth, *c.* 1495 (replica).

★*Linwood.* John Lyndewode, woolman & w., canopied, 1419. Woolman, canopied, 1421.

Mablethorpe St Mary. Elizth. Fitzwilliam, 1522.

Northope. Francis Yerburgh, civ. & 2 ws., 1595.

Norton Disney. Wm. Disney, arm. & w. and arm. & 2 ws., 1578, (P).

Ormsby, South. Lady, *c.* 1410. Skypwyth, arm. & w., can., 1482.

Pinchbeck. Margt. Lambart, w. 27 shields, qd. pl., 1608.

Rand. Lady, 1590, and several fragments.

Rauceby. Wm. Styrlay, priest, 1536.

Scampton. Arms, etc., Fitzwilliam, 1581. Bolles, 1644, 1648.

Scotter. Marmaduke Tirwhit, civ. & w., kng, qd. pl., 1599.

Scrivelsby. Sir Robt. Demoke, arm., 1545.

Sleaford. Geo. Carre & w., 1521, and inscrs.

Somerby. Arms & inscr., Bradshaw, 1673.

Somersby. Geo. Littlebury, civ., kng., 1612.

Spilsby. Margt. de Wylughby, 1391. Lord Willoughby d'Eresby & w., canopied, *c.* 1400.

Stallingborough. Ayscugh, arm. & w., heraldic, 1509. Lady, 1610.

★Stamford, All Saints. Woolman & w., 1460. Ditto, canopied, *c.* 1460. Lady, 1471. Civ. & w., 1475. Ditto, *c.* 1500. Pr. in cope, 1508.

Stamford, St John. Civ. & w., 1489. Priest, 1497.

Stoke Rochford. Hen. Rochforth, arm. & w., 1470. Arm & w., 1503.

★Tattershall. Civ., 1411. Ralph, Lord Cromwell, canopied, 1455 Priest, 1456. Lady, can., 1479. Ditto, 1497. Pr. in cope, *c.* 1510. Priest, 1519.

Theddlethorpe, All Saints. Robt. Hayton, arm., 1424.

Waltham. Joan Waltham, son & dau., demi, 1420.

Welton-le-Wold. Arms & inscr., Dyon, *c.* 1600.

Wickenby. Arms & inscr., Millner, 1635.

Winterton. Two ladies, 1504.

Winthorpe. Rich. Barowe, civ. & w., 1505. Robt. Palmer, 1515.

Witham, North. Wm. Misterton, civ., mutil., 1424.

Witham, South. Arms & inscr., Harington, 1597.

Wrangle. John Reed, civ. & w., 1503.

MIDDLESEX

LONDON (anticlockwise starting in the east, north of the Thames)

North of the Thames

E.6   *East Ham, St Mary Magdalene.* Hester Neve, 1610, Elizth. Heigham, 1622.

E.17   *Walthamstow, St Mary.* Monox, civ. & w., 1543. Hale civ. & w., 1588, (P).

E.15   *West Ham, All Saints.* Thos. Staples, civ. & 4 ws., 1592.

E.14   *St Kath, Butcher Row, Radcliffe.* Wm. Cutinge, civ. & w., 1599.

E.8   *Hackney, St John Bapt.* Christopher Urswic. Priest in cope, 1521. Arm. & 4 ws., 1562.

N.9   *Edmonton, All Saints.* Civs. Asplyn, Askew & w., *c.* 1500. Nich. Boone, civ. & w., 1523. Edw. Nowell, civ. & w. 1616.

N.17   *Tottenham, All Hallows.* John Burrough, civ. & w., 1616. Margt. Irby, qd. pl., 1640.

N.1   *Islington, St Mary.* Arm. & w., 1540, (P). Ditto, 1546, (P).

N.3   *Finchley, St Mary.* Lady, 1487. Civ. & w., 1609. Lady, 1609. Civ. & 3 ws., qd. pl., 1610.

E.1   *Minories, Holy Trinity.* Constantia Lucy, child, 1596.
E.C.1   *St Bartholomew-the-Less, Smithfield Gate.* Wm. Markeby, civ. & w., 1439.
E.C.1   *Clerkenwell, St James.* John Bell, Bp. of Worcester, 1556.
E.C.2   *Bishopsgate, Great St Helen.* Civ. & w., *c.* 1465. Priest in acad., 1482. Civ. & w., 1495. Pr. in acad., *c.* 1500. Arm., 1510, 1514. Lady, heraldic, *c.* 1535.
E.C.3   *★All Hallows, Barking, Tower Hill.* Woolman & w., 1437. Civ. & w., 1477. The Resurrection, *c.* 1500. Civ., 1498. Civ. & 2 ws., 1518. Civ. & w., qd. pl., Flemish, 1533. Arm. & w., 1546, (P). Ditto, qd. pl., 1560. Arms, 1552, (P), 1556, (P). Civ., 1591.
E.C.3   *St Andrew, Undershaft, Leadenhall St.* Nich. Leveson, civ. & w., 1539. Simon Burton, civ. & 2 ws., qd. pl., 1593.
E.C.3   *St Olave, Hart St.* 2 ladies Haddon, 1516. Civ. & w., 1584. Inscr., 1566, (P).
E.C.4   *Ludgate, St Martin.* Thos. Beri, civ., qd. pl., 1586.
E.C.4   *St Dunstan-in-the-West, Fleet St.* Helen Dacres, civ. & w., 1530.
E.C.4   *Temple Church.* Qd. pl., 1597.
S.W.1   *★Westminster Abbey.* Bp. John de Waltham, can., 1395. Archbp. Robt. de Waldeby, can., 1397. Alianora de Bohun, can., 1399. Sir John Harpeden, 1438. Sir Thos. Vaughan, 1483. Abbot Estney, can., 1498. Sir Humf. Stanley, 1505. Dean Bill, 1561, 4 shs., 1560, (P).
S.W.1   *Westminster, St Margt.* Cole, civ. & w., qd. pl., 1597.
S.W.3   *Chelsea Old Church.* Lady Jane Guyldeford, heraldic, 1555. Sir Arthur Gorges, arm. & w., 1625.
S.W.6   *Fulham, All Saints.* Margt. Saunders, demi, on lozenge plate, Flemish, 1529.
W.3   *Acton, St Mary.* Humfrey Cavell, civ., 1558.
W.5   *Ealing, St. Mary.* Rich. Amondesham, civ. & w., *c.* 1490.

South of the Thames
S.W.13   *Barnes, St Mary Virgin.* Edith & Elizth. Wylde, small, 1508.
S.W.15   *Putney, St Mary.* John Welbeck, arm., 1478, (P). Lady, *c.* 1585.
S.W.15   *Wandsworth, All Saints.* Serjeant-at-arms with mace, 1420.
S.W.17   *Tooting Graveney, St Nicholas.* Wm. Fitzwilliam, civ. & w., qd. pl., 1597.
S.W.16   *Streatham, St Leonard.* Wm. Mowfurth, priest, 1513.
S.E.1   *Lambeth, St Mary.* Cath. Howard, heraldic, 1535. Thos. Clere, arm., 1545.
S.E.5   *Camberwell St Giles.* Arm., 1538, (P). Civ., 1492, 1497, 1507. Arm., & w., kng, 1532. Civ. & w., kng., 1577. Civ. & w., 1577. Inscr. 1582, (P).
S.E.16   *Rotherhithe, SS Mary & Paul.* Peter Hills, mariner, & 2 ws., qd. pl., 1614, almost effaced.
Ashford. Civilian & w., 1522.
Bedfont. Civilian & lady, 1631.
Brentford, New. Hen. Redmayne, civ. & w., 1528.
Cowley. Walter Pope, civ. & w., inscr., 1502, (P).
Cranford. Inscr., 1581, (P).
Drayton, West. Civ., sm., *c.* 1520. Lady, 1529. Jas. Good, M.D. & w., 1581, (P).
Edgware. Anth. Childe, in swaddling-clothes, 1599.

Enfield. Joyce, Lady Tiptoft, heraldic, can., *c.* 1470. Civ. & w., 1592.

Greenford, Great. Priest, demi, *c.* 1450. Lady, *c.* 1480. Pr., 1521. Lady, 1544.

Greenford, Little. Hen. Myllet, civ. & 2 ws., 1500.

Hadley. 2 ladies, 1442. Civ. & w., 1500. Lady, *c.* 1504. Civ. & w., 1518, 1614.

Harefield. Lady, 1444. Serjeant-at-law, 1528. Inscr. 1533, (P). Arm. & w., *c.* 1537, (P), 1537. Civ. & w., 1545.

Harlington. Priest, demi, 1419. Lovell, arm. & w., 1545; (P).

Harrow. Arm. on canopied bracket, *c.* 1370. Arm., *c.* 1390. Priest in cope, 1442. Pr. in acad., demi, *c.* 1460. Pr. in cope, 1468. Civ. & 3 ws., 1488. Inscr. & verses, 1574, (P). Arm. & w., 1579, (P). John Lyon & w., 1592. Civ., 1603.

Hayes. Priest, *c.* 1370. Arm., 1456. Arm. & w., 1576.

Hendon. John Downner, civ., 1515.

Heston. Lady in childbed, qd. pl., 1581.

Hillingdon. Lord Le Strange & w., can., 1509. Arm., 1528. Civ. & w., 1579. Civ., 1599. Arms., 1561, (P).

Hornsey. John Skevington, child in shroud, *c.* 1520. Inscr., 1615, (P).

Ickenham. Civ., *c.* 1580, 1582. Edm. Shorditche, arm. & w., 1584.

Isleworth. Arm., *c.* 1450. Inscr., 1544, (P). A nun, sm., 1561. Civ., *c.* 1590. Inscr., 1575, (P).

Kingsbury. John Shephard & 2 ws., 1520.

Littleton. Inscr. and roses, 1553, (P).

Mimms, South. Lady, 1448.

Northolt. Arm., sm., 1452. Arm. & w., 1560, (P). Vicar, 1610.

Norwood. Matth. Hunsley, 1618. Francis Awsiter, 1624.

Pinner. Anne Bedingfeld, in swaddling-clothes, 1580, (P).

Ruislip. John Hawtrey, civ. & w., 1593. Civ., *c.* 1600. Civ. & w., 1574.

Stanwell. Rich. de Thorp, priest, demi, 1408.

Teddington. John Goodyer, civ. & w., sm., 1506.

Willesden. Civ. & w., 1492. Lady, 1505, *c.* 1550. Priest in cope, 1517. Arm. & 2 ws., 1585. Lady, 1609.

MONMOUTHSHIRE

Abergavenny. Hughes, vicar, 1631. Margt. Robertes, qd. pl., 1637.

Llangattock-nigh-Usk. Zirophaeniza Powell, qd. pl., 1625.

Llanover. Qd. pl., 1610.

Matherne. Philip Williams, civ. & w., 1590.

Usk. A Welsh inscr., 1421.

NORFOLK

Acle. Swanne, civ., sm., 1533. Thos. Stones, 'minister', demi, 1627.

Aldborough. Herward, arm., 1481. Lady, 1485. Civ., *c.* 1490.

Antingham. Rich. Calthorp, arm., 1562. Arms & inscr., 1596.

Attlebridge. Chalice for Geo. Cuynggam, priest, *c.* 1525.

Aylsham. Priest in almuce, *c.* 1490. Civ. & w., *c.* 1490. 2 shrouds, 1499. Civ. & w., *c.* 1500. Shroud, 1507.

Baconsthorpe. Arms, Heydon, 1550. Lady, kng., heraldic, 1561. Arms, etc., Heydon, 1642.

Barnham Broom. Bryghteve, civ., 1467, (P). Dorant, civ. & w., 1514.

Barningham Northwood. Hen. Pagrave, arm. & w., 1516.

Barningham Winter. John Wynter (?) arm., *c.* 1410.

Barsham, West. Arms & inscr., Gournay, 1641.

Bawburgh. Civ. & w., 1500. Priest in shroud, 1505. Chalice for priest, 1531. Priest in shroud, curious, 1660.

Beechamwell. Priest, *c.* 1385. Grymston, priest, demi, 1430.

Beeston Regis. John Deynes, civ. & w., 1527. Fragments, etc.

Beeston St Laurence. Arms & inscr., Preston, 1630.

Belaugh. Chalice for John Feelde, priest, 1508.

Binham. Civ. & w., demi, *c.* 1530.

Bintry. Chalice for Thos. Hoont, priest, 1510.

Blakeney. Arms & inscr., Calthorp, 1503.

Blickling. Bust of civ., *c.* 1360. Sir Nich. Dagworth, arm., 1401. Civ. & w., 1454. Lady, 1458. Child, 1479. Isabel Cheyne, 1485. Lady, 1512, and many inscrs.

Blofield. Arms & inscr., Paston, 1630, 1641.

Brampton. Robt. Brampton & w., shrouds, 1468. Arm. & 2 ws., 1535. Civ. & w., 1622.

Brisley. John Althowe, priest, w. chalice, 1531. Inscr., 1544, (P).

Broome. Arms & frag., 1455.

Buckenham, Old. A crane with scroll, *c.* 1500. Chalice, *c.* 1520.

Burgh St. Margt. John Burton, rector, kng., 1608.

Burlingham, North, St Andrew. Inscr., 1559, (P), 1563, (P).

Burlingham, South. Chalice for Wm. Curtes, 1540.

★Burnham Thorpe. Sir Wm. Calthorp, arm., canopied, 1420.

Burnham Westgate. Wife of John Hunteley, 1523.

Buxton. Chalice for Robt. Northen, priest, 1508.

Bylaugh. Sir John Cursun, arm. & w., 1471.

Cley. Civ., *c.* 1450, *c.* 1500. Merchant & w. in shrouds, 1512. Priest in acad., w. chalice, *c.* 1520. Inscr., 1578, (P).

Clippesby. Thos. Pallyng, civ. & w., 1503. John Clippesby, arm. & w., 1594.

Colby. Scrolls, *c.* 1530, (P).

Colney. Chalice for Hen. Alikok, priest, 1502.

Creake, North. Man in civil or monastic dress, w. church, canopied, *c.* 1500.

Creake, South. Pr. in cope, *c.* 1400. Ditto, with staff, & civ., 1509.

Cressingham, Gt. Arm. & w., 1497. Wm. Eyre, lawyer, civ., 1509. Priest in almuce, 1518. Lady, 1588.

Cromer. Margt. Counforth, 1518.

Dereham, East. Priest, demi, 1479. Lady, 1486. Arms, etc., 1503.

Ditchingham. Philip Bosard, civ. & w., 1490. Civ. and son, 1505.

Dunham, Gt. Arms & inscr., Bastard, 1624.

Dunston. Civilian and 2 wives in shrouds, 1649.

Ellingham, Gt. A lady, *c.* 1500.
*Elsing. Sir Hugh Hastings, canopied, w. saints & weepers, 1347.
Erpingham. Sir John de Erpingham, *c.* 1415.
Fakenham. Priest in cope, 1428. Civ. & 2 ws., *c.* 1470. 4 inscribed hearts, *c.* 1470. Lady, *c.* 1510.
*Felbrigg. Civ. & w. and arm. & w., *c.* 1380. Sir Symon Felbrygge, K.G., 1416. Lady, *c.* 1480. Arm., *c.* 1608. Lady, 1608.
Felmingham. Inscrs., *c.* 1530, (P) and 1591, (P). Arms & inscr., 1628.
Feltwell St Mary. Francis Hetht, arm., 1479. Lady, 1520.
Fincham. A lady in shroud, *c.* 1520.
Forncett St. Peter. Arms & inscr., Baxter, 1535.
Fransham, Gt. Geoff. Fransham, arm., 1414. Lady in shroud, *c.* 1500.
Frenze. Arm., 1475, (P) 1510. Lady, 1519, 1521, 1551. Shroud, *c.* 1520.
Frettenham. Alys Thorndon, *c.* 1420. Lady, *c.* 1460.
Garboldisham. Merchant's mark & inscr., Carlton, 1579.
Gissing. Arms & inscr., Kemp, 1596. Shield, *c.* 1600.
Gressenhall. Arms & inscr., Estmond, 1604, 1609.
Guestwick. Civilian, 1505, *c.* 1520. Chalice for priest & father, 1504.
Halvergate. Bust of lady, 1540, (P). Inscr., 1543, (P).
Hardwick. Arms & inscr., Bakon, *c.* 1500.
Harling, West. Ralf Fuloflove, priest, 1479. Wm. Berdewell, arm. & w., *c.* 1490. Ditto, 1508.
Haveringland. Arms & inscr., Davye, 1561.
Heacham. Man in armour, *c.* 1485.
Hedenham. Chalice for Rich. Grene, pr., 1505. Arms, etc., Beddingfeld, 1594.
Helhoughton. Heart, with hand and scrolls, Stapilton, *c.* 1450.
Hellesdon. Rich. de Heylesdone, civ. & w., demi, *c.* 1370. Rich. Thaseburgh, priest, 1389.
Heydon. Arms, etc., 1517, 1580, 1618, 1630, and many inscriptions.
Hellington. Arms & inscr., Gaudy, 1642.
Hindolvestone. Edm. Hunt, civ. & w., 1568.
Holkham. Arms & inscr., Osborne, 1618.
Holme Hale. French inscr. for Sir Esmon de Illeye & w., 1349.
Holme-next-the-Sea. Herry Notingham, civ. & w., *c.* 1405. Inscr., 1582, (P).
Honing. Nich. Parker, arm., 1496.
Honingham. Inscr., 1544, (P), 1556, (P).
Horstead. Arms, etc., Ward, 1645, and many inscriptions.
Hunstanton. Edm. Grene, civ. & w., *c.* 1480. Sir Roger le Strange, arm., canopied, 1506. Arms, etc., 1485, 1654.
Ingham. Fragments of two fine canopied brasses, Stapilton, 1438 & 1466, (P).
Ingoldisthorpe. Thos. Rogerson, eccles., wife & dau., 1608.
Kenninghall. Group of daughters, *c.* 1500.
Ketteringham. Lady, *c.* 1470. Thos. Hevenyngham, arm. & w., heraldic, kng., 1499. Child in shroud, *c.* 1530.
Kimberley. John Wodehows, arm. & w., *c.* 1530.
Kirby Bedon. Heart & scrolls, *c.* 1450. Dussyng & w., in shrouds, 1505.
Langley. Robt. Berney, civilian, 1628.

Loddon. Heart, hands, etc., 1462. 2 shrouds, 1546. Arm. in tab., 1561. Civ. & w., 1609.

Ludham. Inscr., Honyngg, *c.* 1350, and many others.

Lynn, St Margt. Adam de Walsokne & w., Flemish, 1349. Robt. Brauche & 2 ws., ditto, 1364, both very large qd. pl.

Lynn, West. Adam Owtlawe, priest, 1503.

Martham. Inscribed heart for Robt. Alen, priest, copy only, 1487.

Mattishall. Civ., *c.* 1480. Ditto, *c.* 1510, and many inscrs.

Melton, Little. Arms & inscr., Angwish, 1604.

Merton. Wm. de Grey, arm. in tab. & 2 ws., 1520. Arm., 1562, (P). Arms, etc., 1474, 1548, 1556, 1562, (P) and 1644.

Methwold. Sir Adam de Clyfton, arm., canopied, 1367.

Metton. Robt. Doughty, civ. & w., demi, 1493.

Mileham. Xpofer Crowe, civ. & w., 1526.

Morston. Rich. Makynges, rector, 1596.

Morton-on-the-Hill. Kath. Awdley, 1611.

Moulton. Lady, kng., 1544, (P).

Mundham. Arms & inscr., Harborne, 1617.

Narburgh. Civ. & w., 1496. Arm., 1545. Judge & w., her., kng., 1545. Arm. & w., kng., 1561. Arm., 1581, (P). Inscr., 1556, (P).

Necton. Lady, 1372, 1596. Vowess, 1383. Civ., 1528. Civ. & w., 1532.

Newton Flotman. 3 men in armour, Blondevile, kng., 1571.

Northwold. Arms & inscr., Scott, 1616.

Norwich—

St *Andrew.* Canopy, etc., 1467. Civ. & w., *c.* 1500. Mark, etc., 1527. Arms, etc., for John Underwood, Bp. of Chalcedon, 1541.

St *Clement.* Margt. Pettwode, 1514.

St. *Etheldred.* Priest, 1487, and inscrs. from St Peter Southgate.

St *George Colegate.* Wm. Norwiche, civ. & w., on a bracket, 1472. Mark & inscr., Warryn, 1514.

St *George Tombland.* A civilian, *c.* 1450.

St *Giles.* Civ. & w., 1432. Ditto, 1436. Chalice for priest, 1499.

St *John Maddermarket.* Civ. & w., 1412, 1472, 1476, 1525. Ditto on brackets, 1524, 1558, (P). Lady, 1506. Inscr., 1540, (P) and many others.

St *John de Sepulchre.* Civ. & w., *c.* 1535, (P). Arm. & w., 1597.

St *Laurence.* Civ., 1436. A prior, on bracket, 1437. Skeleton, 1452. Priest, 1483, and many inscrs.

St *Margaret.* Anne Rede, 1577, (P).

St *Martin at Palace.* Arms, etc., 1588. Inscr., 1550, (P) and others.

St *Mary Coslany.* Arms & inscr., Claxton, 1605.

St *Michael at Plea.* Skeleton, etc., 1588. Arms & inscr., Ferrer, 1616.

St *Michael Coslany.* Man & w. in shrouds, 1515, and several inscrs.

St *Peter Mancroft.* Arm., 1568, (P) and sev. inscrs.

St *Stephen.* A prioress, 1546, (P). Civ., 1460. Civ. & w., *c.* 1513. 2 civs., 1513. Priest in cope, 1545.

St Swithin. Civ. & w., 1495. Inscr., 1514, (P) and others.
Ormesby, Great. Lady, demi, w. heart, 1538, (P). Scrolls, etc., 1446. Sir Robt. Clere, arm.,
    1529.
Outwell. Rich. Qwadryng, arm., 1511.
Oxnead. Arms & inscr., Lambert, 1608. Ditto, Paston, 1608.
Paston. Erasmus Paston, civ. & w., shields, *c.* 1582, (P).
Pentney. Arms & inscr., Wyndham, 1620.
Plumstead, Little. Civ. & w., *c.* 1480. Sir Edw. Warner, arm., 1565.
Potter Heigham. Arms & inscr., Baispoole, 1613.
Rainham, East. Civ., *c.* 1500. Priest in acad., w. scarf, 1522. Labels.
Ranworth. Inscr., *c.* 1540, (P).
Raveningham. Margt. Wyllughby, 1483. Arms & inscr., Castle, 1614.
Reedham. Elizth. Berney, 1474. Inscr., 1502, (P). Arms, etc., Berney, 1536.
Reepham. Sir Wm. de Kérdeston, arm. & w., can., mutil., 1391. Inscr., 1577, (P).
Ringstead, Great. Rich. Kegell, priest, 1482.
*Rougham. Judge & w., 1472. Arm. & w., *c.* 1510. 2 chrysoms, 1510. Civ. & 2 ws., 1586.
Sall. Civ., *c.* 1420. Civ. & w., 1440. Ditto, on bracket, 1441. 2 ladies, 1453. Shroud, 1454.
    Inscr., *c.* 1480, (P).
Salhouse. Inscr., *c.* 1540, (P).
Salthouse. Chalice for Robt. Sevyr, priest, 1519.
Sandringham. Arms & inscr., Cobbis, 1546.
Scottow. Chalice for Nich. Wethyrley, priest, *c.* 1520.
Sculthorpe. Henry Unton, arm., kng., 1470. Civ. & w., 1521. Mark & inscr., Stebyrd, *c.* 1480.
Sharington. Arm., *c.* 1445. Priest, 1486. Lady, *c.* 1520. Arm. & w., kng., 1593.
Shelton. Inscr., 1456, (P).
*Shernbourne. Thos. Shernborne, arm. & w., 1458.
Sheringham. John Hook, civ. & w., 1513.
Shimpling. Inscription, 1692, (P).
Shotesham St Mary. Edw. Whyte, arm. & w., 1528.
Snettisham. Lady, *c.* 1560, (P). Civ. & w., 1610. Arms & inscr., Gurlin, 1644.
Snoring, Gt. Sir Ralph Shelton, mutil., & w., heraldic, 1424.
Southacre. Sir John Harsick, arm. & w., her., 1384. Thos. Leman, pr. in acad., kng., 1584.
    Frag., 1454, (P).
Sparham. Wm. Mustarder, priest, *c.* 1490.
Sprowston. John Corbet, mutil., & w., kng., 1559.
Stalham. A civilian & wife, *c.* 1460.
Stokesby. Arm. & w., 1488. Pr. in acad., 1506. Lady, 1570, (P), 1614.
Stradsett. Thos. Lathe, arm., 1418.
Surlingham. Alnwik, priest in acad., 1460. Chalice for priest, 1513.
Sustead. Arms & inscr., Damme, *c.* 1500.
Swaffham. Man in armour, *c.* 1480.
Swainsthorpe. Arms & inscr., Havers, 1628.
Swanton Abbott. Stephen Multon, priest, 1477.
Swardeston. Inscr., 1550, (P).

Tasburgh. Arms & inscr., Baxter, 1586. Ditto, Burman, 1642.
Themelthorpe. Wm. Pescod, civ., 1505.
Thornham. Label, *c.* 1460. Initial on shield & inscr., 1464
Thwaite. John Puttock, civ. & w., 1469.
Tottington. Margt. Unger, kng., 1598.
Trowse. Wife of Roger Dalyson, 1585.
Trunch. Heart & scrolls, *c.* 1530.
Tuddenham, E. A civilian & 2 wives, *c.* 1500.
*Upwell. Priest in cope, canopied, *c.* 1430. Henry Martyn, pr. in cope, with crossed stole, 1435. Civ., 1621.
Wacton. Arms & inscr., Sedly, 1623.
Walpole St Peter. Arms & inscr., Butler, 1630. Ditto, Frenchan, 1652.
Walsham, N. Chalice for priest, 1519. Ditto, *c.* 1520. Arms, etc., Grocers', 1625.
Walsingham, Little. Civ. & w., 1485, (P), 1509, *c.* 1540, (P). Chalice and hands, *c.* 1520. Inscr., 1539, (P).
Warham All Saints. Wm. Rokewod, arm, 1474.
Weston. Elizth. Rokewoode, 1533.
Whissonsett. Wm. Bozon, arm., *c.* 1485. Thos. Gybon, arm., 1484.
Wiggenhall St Mary. Heart & scrolls, Kervile, *c.* 1450.
Wighton. Arms & inscr., Bedingfeild, 1629.
Witchingham, Gt. Arms & inscr., Meares, 1626.
Witton. Dame Juliana Anyell, vowess, *c.* 1500.
Wiveton. Priest w. chal., 1512. Skeleton in shr., *c.* 1540. Arms, etc., 1558. Civ. & w., 1597.
Wood Dalling. Priest, 1465. Civ., 1504, and 1507. Chalice, 1510. 2 civs., 1518.
Woodrising. Arms & inscr., Sowthwell, 1586. Arms & Garter, Crane, 1636.
Woodton. Cristiana Bacon, kng., 1532. Inscr., 1678, (P).
Worstead. Priest, demi, 1404. Civ., *c.* 1500, 1520, and several inscrs.
Yelverton. Margt. Aldriche, 1525, and several inscrs.

NORTHAMPTONSHIRE

Addington, Gt. John Bloxham, priest w. chalice, 1519.
Aldwinkle. Wm. Aldewyncle, civ., 1463. Arms & inscr., Pickering, 1659.
Ashby, Canons. John Dryden, civ., 1584.
Ashby, Castle. Wm. Ermyn, priest in cope, w. saints, 1401.
Ashby St Leger. Civ. & w., canopied, 1416. Arm. & w., heraldic, can., 1494. Arm. in tab., kng., *c.* 1500, 1553. Priest in acad., 1510.
Ashton. Robt. Mariott, civ. & w., 1584.
Aston-le-Walls. Alban Butler, civ. & 2 ws., 1609.
Barnwell, St Andrew. Christopher Freeman, civ. & w., qd. pl., 1610.
Barton, Earl's. John Muscote, prothonotary, & w., 1512.
Barton Segrave. Jane Floyde, qd. pl., 1616.
Blakesly. Matth. Swetenham, arm., 1416.
Blatherwyck. Sir Humphrey Stafford, arm. & w., 1548.

Blisworth. Roger Wake, arm. & w., 1503.

Boddington. Wm. Procter, rector, 1627.

Brampton, Church. Jone Furnace, skeleton, qd. pl., 1585.

Brampton-by-Dingley. Arm. & w., can., *c.* 1420. Simon Norwiche, arm. with B.V.M., 1476.

Brington, Gt. Priest, demi, on a bracket, *c.*1340 and many inscrs.

Burton Latimer. Lady in shroud, *c.* 1510. Margt. Bacon, 1626.

Chacomb. Arms, mark, monogram, etc., Myghell Fox, *c.* 1545.

Charwelton. Andrewe, civ. & w., can., 1490. Ditto, *c.* 1490. Arm. & w., *c.* 1541, (P). Inscr., *c.* 1520, (P).

Chipping Warden. Wm. Smart, priest, 1468. Civ. & w., 1584.

Cotterstock. Robt. Wyntryngham, priest in cope, on bracket, can., 1420.

Cranford. Fossebrok, arm. & w., 1418. Ditto, civ. & 2 ws., 1602.

Cransley. Edw. Dalyson, arm. & w., 1515.

Deene. Sir Edm. Brudenell, arm. & 2 ws., qd. pl., 1584. Civ. & w., 1586. Arm. & w., 1606.

Doddington. French inscr. to Wm. de Pateshull, 1359.

Dodford. Cressy, arm. & w., 1414. Wylde, ditto, 1422. Lady, 1637.

Easton Neston. Rich. Fermer, arm. & w., 1552, (P).

Fawsley. Knyghtley, arm. in tab. & w., 1516. Arm. & w., 1557.

Floore. Arm. & w., 1498. Ditto, 1510. Small cross & inscr., 1537.

Geddington. Henry Jarmon, civ. & w., *c.* 1480. Mark & inscr., Maydwell, 1628.

★Greens Norton. Sir Thos. Grene, arm. & w., 1462. Lady, *c.* 1490.

Grendon. 2 men in armour & w., *c.* 1480.

Harrowden, Gt. Wm. Harwedon, arm. & w., 1433.

Hemington. Thos. Mountagu, civ. & w., 1517.

Heyford, Lower. Arms & inscr., Mauntel, *c.* 1400, (P). Arm. & w., 1487.

★Higham Ferrers. Priest, can., 1337. Cross, etc., Chichele, 1400. Civ. & w., can., 1425. Lady, *c.* 1435. Pr. w. chal., 1498. Civ. & w., 1504. Heart, *c.* 1500. Civ., 1518. Pr. in cope, 1523. Civ., *c.* 1540. Ditto, *c.* 1540.

Horton. Roger Salusbury, arm. & 2 ws., 1491.

Irchester. Lady, 1506.

Kelmarsh. Morrys Osberne, civ., 1534.

Kettering. Edm. Sawyer, arm. & w., qd. pl., 1630.

Lowick. Hen. Grene, arm. in tabard & w., 1467.

Marholm. Sir Wm. Fytzwilliams, arm. & w., heraldic, 1534.

Naseby. John Olyver, civ. & w., 1446. Arms & inscr., Shakbrugh, 1576.

Newbottle. Peter Dormer, civ. & 2 ws., 1555.

Newnham. Letticè Catesby, 1467.

★Newton-by-Geddington. John Mulsho, civ. & w., kng. to cross, 1400. Lady, qd. pl., 1604.

Newton Bromshold. Wm. Hewet, priest, sm., 1426. Rog. Hewet, pr., 1487.

Northampton, St Sepulchre. Geo. Coles, civ. & 2 ws., 1640.

Norton. Wm. Knyght, civ. & w., 1504.

Orlingbury. Wm. Lane, civ. & w., sm., 1502.

Potterspury. Agnes Ogle, sm., 1616.

Preston Deanery. Sir Clement Edmonds, arm. & w., sm., 1622.

Raunds. John Tawyer, civ. & w., *c.* 1510. Lady, *c.* 1510.
*Rothwell. Wm. de Rothewelle, priest in cope, 1361. Civ. & w., 1514.
Spratton. Robt. Parnell, civ. & w., 1474 (under organ).
Staverton. Thos. Wylmer, civ. & w., 1590.
Stoke Bruerne. Rich. Lightfoot, rector, qd. pl., 1625.
Sudborough. Wm. West, civ. & w. and others, 1415.
Tansor. John Colt, priest, 1440.
Wappenham. Arm., mutil., *c.* 1460. Judge & w., mutil., 1479. L., 1499. Arm. & w., *c.* 1500.
　　Ditto, *c.* 1500.
Warkworth. Arm., 1412, 1420 and 1454. Lady, 1420. Ditto, 1430.
Welford. Francis Saunders, arm. & 3 ws., qd. pl., 1585.
Woodford-by-Thrapston. Simon Malory, arm., *c.* 1580.
Woodford-cum-Membris. Nich. Stafford, priest, *c.* 1420.

NORTHUMBERLAND

*Newcastle-upon-Tyne, All Saints. Roger Thornton, merchant, & w., foreign, large, qd. pl.,
　　1411.

NOTTINGHAMSHIRE

Annesley. Wm. Breton, civ., 1595.
Clifton. Clyfton, arm., 1478. Ditto, 1491. Arm. & w., 1587.
Darlton. Man in armour & w., *c.* 1510.
Hickling. Rad. Babyngton, priest w. chalice, 1521.
Holme Pierrepont. Lady, *c.* 1390.
Markham, E. Millicent Meryng, 1419.
*Newark. Alan Fleming, civ., Flemish, large qd. pl., 1361. Arms, etc., 1532. Civ., *c.* 1540,
　　1557, and many inscrs.
Ossington. Reynolde Peckham, arm. & w., 1551, (P).
Radcliffe. Anne Ballard, qd. pl., 1626.
Stanford-on-Soar. Priest w. chalice, *c.* 1400.
Strelley. Sir Robt. Strelly, arm. & w., 1487.
Wheatley, N. Inscr., Sheffeld, 1445, (P).
Wollaton. Rich. Wylloughby, arm. & w., 1471.

OXFORDSHIRE

Adderbury. Man in arm. & w., *c.* 1460. Jane Smyth, 1508.
Aston Rowant. Civilian & w., sm., 1445. Lady, mutil., *c.* 1470. Elynor Eggerley, 1508.
Bampton. Priest in almuce, demi, *c.* 1420. Pr. in cope, sm., 1500. Frances Hord, 1633.
Barford, Great. Wm. Foxe, civ. & w., sm., 1495.
*Brightwell Baldwin. Eng. inscr. to John the Smith, *c.* 1370. Judge & w., sm., kng., and again,
　　large, canopied, 1439.

Brightwell Salome. Mores John, priest, sm., 1492. Rich. Crook, civ., 1549.
Broughton. Philippe Byschoppesdon, large, 1414.
Burford. Civ. & w., kng. to bracket, 1437. Civ. & w., qd. pl., 1614.
Cassington. Cross fleury, 1414. Man in shroud, qd. pl., 1590.
Chalgrove. French inscr., *c.* 1370. Arm., 1441. Arm. & w., 1453.
Charlton-on-Otmoor. Thos. Key, priest in cōpe, 1476, (P).
Chastleton. Kath. Throkmorton, sm., 1592. Edm. Ansley, civ. & w., sm., 1613.
Checkendon. John Rede, civ., canopied, 1404, (P). Soul & angels, *c.* 1430. Inscr., Rede, 1435, (P).
Chesterton. Wm. Mawnde, civ. & w., 1612.
Chinnor. Flor. cross & head of pr., *c.* 1320. Pr. in acad., demi, 1361. Arm. & 2 ws., *c.* 1385. Arm. & w., demi, 1386. Pr. w. chal., demi, 1388, and 6 others, mutil., *c.* 1390–1514.
Chipping Norton. Civ. & w., 1450, 1451, 1484. Civ. & w., *c.* 1467. Lady, *c.* 1503, 1507 and 1530.
Cottisford. Man in armour & w., *c.* 1500.
Crowell, John Payne, priest, demi, 1469, (P).
Cuxham. John Gregory, civ. & 2 wives, sm., 1506.
Deddington. A civilian, demi, *c.* 1370.
Dorchester. Arm., mutil., 1417. Abbot Bewfforeste, *c.* 1510. Lady, *c.* 1490. Civ. & w., 1513.
Ewelme. Thos. Chaucer, arm. & w., 1436. Pr., demi, 1458, 1467, *c.* 1470, Pr. in acad., 1517. Arm. & w., 1518. Civ. & w., 1599. Inscr., 1494, (P).
Garsington. Thos. Radley, arm. & w., sm., 1484.
Glympton. Thos. Tesdale, civ., 1610.
Goring. Lady, canopied, 1401. Civ. & w., *c.* 1600, (P).
Hampton Poyle. John Poyle, arm. & w., 1424.
Handborough. Alex. Belsyre, in shroud, qd. pl., 1567.
Harpsden. Lady, *c.* 1460. Arm. & w., *c.* 1480. Walter Elmes, priest, 1511. Sara Webb, 1620.
Haseley, Gt. Pr. in almuce, 1494. Shroud, 1497. Lady, 1581.
Heythorpe. John Aschefeld, arm. & w., 1521.
Holton. Wm. Brome, arm., 1461. Wm. Brome, child, 1599.
Ipsden. Thos. Englysche, arm. & w., sm., 1525, (P).
Islip. Robt. Banks, Hen. Norrys & w., qd. pl., 1637.
Kingham. Catherine James, 1588.
Langford. Walter Prunes, civ. & w., 1609.
Lewknor. John Alberbourne, priest, demi, *c.* 1380.
Mapledurham. Sir Robt. Bardolf, arm., canopied, 1395.
Nettlebed. Arms & inscr., Tavener, 1637.
Newnham Murren. Letticé Barnarde, kng., 1593.
Noke. Wm. Manwayringe, Hen. Bradshawe, judge, & w., qd. pl., 1598.
Northleigh. Man in armour, 1431.
Nuffield. Beneit Engliss, civ., demi, *c.* 1360.
Oddington. Ralph Hamsterley, pr., skeleton, *c.* 1510.
Oxford—
    St Aldate. 2 civs., kng., qd. pl., 1607. Civ., qd. pl., 1612. Civ. in hood, qd. pl., 1637.
    St Cross, Holywell. Lady in childbed, qd. pl., 1622. Lady, kng., qd. pl., 1625.

St Mary Magd. Physician, in gown & hood, kng., 1580. Inscr., 1574, (P).
St Mary-the-Virgin. Pr. in almuce, 1507. Civ., qd. pl., 1581. Lady, 1584.
St Michael. Flexney, civ. & w., 1578. Pendarves, commoner, 1617.
St Peter-in-the-East. Civ. & w., sm., 1487. Civ. & w., qd. pl., 1572, 1599. Civ. & 2 ws., 1574, (P).
St Peter-le-Bailey. Civ., 1419. Lady, *c.* 1420. Civ. & w., kng., *c.* 1650, (P).
All Souls' Coll. Pr. in cope, kng., sm., 1461. Pr. in acad., 1490. 2 acad., demi, 1510.
Christ Church Cath. Civ., sm., *c.* 1450, 1452. Pr. in almuce, 1557, (P). Students in acad., 1578, (P), 1584, 1587, 1588, 1602 and 1613.
Corpus Christi Coll. John Claimond, President, in shroud, *c.* 1530.
Magdalen Coll. 10 academics, some demi, 1478–1523. Pr. in cope, 1480 & *c.* 1480. Pr. in almuce, 1515. Canon of Windsor, 1558, (P). Inscr., 1516, (P).
*Merton Coll. Pr., demi, in head of cross, 1322. Pr. in tunic, in cross, 1351. 2 acad. on bracket, can., *c.* 1400. Acad., demi, 1445. Pr. in cope, can., 1471. Pr. in acad., w. chal., demi, 1519.
*New Coll. Archbp., 1417. Bishop, 1526. 4 pr. in cope and 8 in acad., 1403–1521. Pr. in shroud, 1472. Pr. in euch., demi, 1507. Notary, *c.* 1510. Physician, 1592, and 1619. Acad., 1601.
Queen's Coll. Acad., 1477. Pr. in cope, 1518. Bishop, qd. pl., sm., 1616. Eccles., ditto, 1616.
St John's Coll. Acad., 1571, 1578. Ditto, kng., 1573. Acad., 1577. Inscr., 1600, (P).
Rollright, Gt. Jas. Batersby, pr. w. chalice, 1522.
Rotherfield Greys. Sir Robt. de Grey, arm., canopied, 1387.
Shiplake. John Symondes, civ. & w., *c.* 1540.
Shipton-under-Wychwood. Elizth. Horne, in shroud, qd. pl., 1548, (P).
Shirburn. Rich. Chamburleyn, arm. & w., 1496.
Somerton. Wm. Fermoure, arm. & w., 1552, (P).
Souldern. Thos. Warner, priest, 1514. A child, *c.* 1620.
Stadhampton. John Wylmot, civ. & w., 1498. Ditto, 1508.
Stanton Harcourt. 2 civilians, sm., 1460. Lady, 1516. Priest, 1519.
Stanton St John. Inscr., 1524, (P).
Stoke Lyne. Edw. Love, civ. & w., 1535. Civ. & w., kng., 1582.
Stoke, North. Roger Parkers, Canon of Windsor, demi, 1363(?).
Stoke Talmage. John Adene, civ. & w., 1504. John Pettie, arm. & w., 1589.
Swinbrook. John Croston, arm. & 3 ws., *c.* 1470. Anthony Fetyplace, arm. in tab., 1510.
Tew, Gt. Arm. & w., can., 1410. Fragments, 1487. Civ. & w., 1513.
Thame. 2 arm. & ws. on bracket, *c.* 1420. Arm., *c.* 1460. Civ. & w., *c.* 1500, 1502, 1503, 1508. Arm. in tab., kng., 1539. Civ., 1543, (P) and 1597.
Waterperry. Lady, sm., *c.* 1370. Curson, arm. & w., *c.* 1540, (P).
Watlington. Civ. & w., 1485. Ditto, in shrouds, 1501. Civ., 1588.
Whitchurch. Thos. Walysch, arm. & w., *c.* 1420. Roger Gery, pr. w. chal., *c.* 1455. Peter Winder, curate, 1610.
Witney. Wenman, civ. & 2 ws., 1500. Ayshcome, civ., 1606.
Woodstock. Bailly, civ., 1441. Keyt, in gown & hood, kng., qd. pl., 1631.

RUTLAND

Braunston. Kenelme Cheseldyn, civ. & w., 1596.
*Casterton, Little. Sir Thos. Burton, arm. & w., *c.* 1410.
Lyddington. Lady, 1486. Edw. Watson, civ. & w., 1530.

SHROPSHIRE

*Acton Burnell. Sir Nich. Burnell, arm., canopied, 1382.
Acton Scott. Thos. Mytton, civ. & w., kng., 1571.
Adderley. Prelate in pontif., mutil., *c.* 1390. Sir Robt. Nedeham, arm. & w., 1560, (P).
Burford. Elizth. de Cornewaylle, *c.* 1370.
Drayton. Rowland Corbet, boy, kng., qd. pl., *c.* 1580.
Edgmond. Francis Yonge, in shroud, & w., 1533.
Glazeley. Thos. Wylde, civ. & w., 1599.
Harley. A man in armour & wife, *c.* 1475.
Ightfield. Margery Calveley, can., mutil., *c.* 1495. Civ., 1497.
Middle. Arthur Chambre, civ. & w., 1564.
Newport. Forty-one inscrs., mostly 18th cent.
St Alkmund, Shrewsbury. Lady, *c.* 1500.
Tong. Sir Wm. Vernon, arm. & w., 1467. Priest in alm., 1510. Pr. in tippet, w. chalice, 1517.
Upton Cressett. Rich. Cresset, civ. & w., kng., qd. pl., 1640.
Wenlock, Much. Rich. Ridley, civ. & w., 1592.
Withington. John Onley, arm. & w., kng., 1512. Priest in cope, 1530.

SOMERSETSHIRE

Axbridge. Roger Harper, civ. & w., kng., 1493.
Backwell. Rice Davies, civ. & w., qd. pl., 1638.
Banwell. Civ. & w., sm., *c.* 1480, 1554. Priest in cope, 1503.
Batcombe. Priest in acad., 1613.
Bath Abbey. Sir Geo. Ivy, civ. & w., 1639.
Beckington. Seyntmour, arm. & w., 1485. Compton, civ. & w., 1505.
Broomfield. Priest, *c.* 1450.
Burnett. John Cutte, civ. & w., qd. pl., 1575.
Cheddar. Sir Thos. Cheddar, arm., 1442. Isabel Cheddar, *c.* 1475.
Chedzoy. A man in armour, large, *c.* 1490.
Churchill. Raphe Jenyns, arm. & w., 1572.
Cossington. John Brent, arm. & wife, 1524.
Crewkerne. Thos. Golde, arm., kng., sm., 1525. Inscr., 1723, (P).
Croscombe. Wm. Bisse, civ. & wife, 1625.
Dunster. John Wyther, civ. & wife, *c.* 1520.
Fivehead. A lady, *c.* 1565, (P).

Hinton St George. Adam Martin, civ. & wife, *c.* 1590.
Hutton. John Payne, arm. & w., 1496. Thos. Payne, arm. & w., 1528.
★Ilminster. Sir Wm. Wadham, arm. & w., canopied, *c.* 1440. Nich. Wadham, arm. & w., 1618.
Ilton. Nich. Wadham, in shroud, 1508.
Langridge. Elizth. Walsshe, 1441.
Luccombe. Wm. Harrison, civ., 1615.
Lydiard, Bishop's. Nich. Grobham, civ. & w., 1594.
Minehead. Lady, canopied, mutilated, 1440.
Monkton, West. Demi priest in acad., *c.* 1440.
Petherton, North. Priest in acad., kng., *c.* 1525.
Petherton, South. Arm. & w., canopied, *c.* 1430. Lady, 1442.
Portbury. Sara Kemish, sm., 1621.
St Decumans. Wyndham, arm. & w., 1571. Ditto, arm. & w., 1596. Arm., 1676.
Shepton Mallet. Wm. Strode, arm. & w., qd. pl., 1649 and late inscrs.
Stogumber. Margery Windham, 1585.
Swainswick. Edm. Forde, civ., 1439.
Tintinhull. John Heth, priest in cope, 1464.
Weare. John Bedbere, civ., *c.* 1500.
Wedmore. Geo. Hodges, military, qd. pl., *c.* 1630.
Wells Cathedral. Priest in cope, demi, *c.* 1460. Willis, civ., qd. pl., 1618. Mitre for Bp. Lake,
    1626.
Wells, St Cuthbert. Francis Hayes, civ., sm., 1623.
Yeovil. A monk, demi, on lectern, *c.* 1460. Civ. & w., 1519.

STAFFORDSHIRE

Abbots Bromley. John Draycote, civ., 1463.
★Audley. Sir Thos. de Audley, arm., large, 1385. Wm. Abnet, 1628.
Biddulph. Wm. Bowyer, civ. & w., qd. pl., 1603.
Blore. Wm. Basset, civ. & wife, 1498.
★Clifton Campville. A lady, demi, on a bracket, can., *c.* 1360, (P).
Elford. John Hille, ecclesiastic, 1621 (modern restoration).
Hanbury. Priest in cope, *c.* 1480.
Horton. John Wedgwood, civ. & w., qd. pl., 1589.
Kinver. Sir Edw. Grey, arm. & 2 wives, 1528.
Leek, St. Edw. John Ashenhurst & 4 wives, qd. pl., 1597.
Madeley. John Egerton, civ. & w., 1518. Hawkins, boy, 1586.
Norbury. Hawys Botiller, can., 1360. Arms, etc., Skrymshire, 1667.
★Okeover. Oker, arm. & w., 1538, (P).
Rugeley. John Weston, civ., 1566.
Standon. Cross brass, *c.* 1420.
Stone. Thos. Crompton, arm. & w., qd. pl., 1619.
Trentham. Sir Rich. Leveson, arm. & w., 1591.

Acton. Sir Robt. de Bures, arm., *c.* 1315. Lady, can., 1435. Arm., 1528. Civ. & w., 1589. Civ., 1598.

Aldeburgh. Civ., 1519. Lady, *c.* 1520, *c.* 1570. Civ. & w., 1601, 1606, 1612, 1635.

Ampton. Civ. & w., kng., *c.* 1480. Lady, *c.* 1480. Ditto, *c.* 1490, (P). Children, *c.* 1490. Arms & inscr., Coket, *c.* 1500.

Ashbocking. Edm. Bockinge, arm. & 2 ws., 1585.

Assington. Man in armour & wife, *c.* 1500.

Badley. Arms & inscr., Poley, 1613.

Barham. Robt. Southwell, civ. & w., 1514.

Barningham. Wm. Goche, priest in acad., 1499.

Barrow. Sir Clement Heigham, arm. & 2 ws., kng., 1570.

Barsham. A man in armour, *c.* 1415.

Belstead. A man in armour & 2 ws., 1518.

Benhall. Edw. Duke, civ. & w., 1598. Ambr. Duke, arm. & w., 1611.

Bergolt, E. Robt. Alfounder, civ., 1639.

Bildeston. Alice Wade, 1599.

Blundeston. Arms & inscr., Sydnor, 1613.

Boxford. David Birde, child in cot, 1606. Arms & inscr., Doggett, 1610.

Bradley, Little. Civ. & w., *c.* 1510, 1584, 1605. Arm., 1530. Arm. & w., qd. pl., 1612.

Braiseworth. Alex. Newton, arm., 1569.

Bredfield. Leonard Farrington, civ. & w., 1611.

Bruisyard. Two wives of Michael Hare, 1611.

Brundish. Priest, *c.* 1360. Arm., 1599. Arm. & w., 1560. Lady, *c.* 1570. Youth, kng., *c.* 1570.

Bungay. Arms & inscr., Throckmorton, 1599.

Burgate. Sir Wm. de Burgate & w., canopied, 1409.

Bury St Edmunds, St Mary. Civ. & w., kng., *c.* 1480. Pr. in almuce, 1514. Many arms and inscrs. Inscr., 1600, (P).

Campsey Ash. Alex. Inglisshe, priest w. chalice, 1504.

Carlton. A civilian, *c.* 1480, *c.* 1490.

Cavendish. Arms, Cavendish, *c.* 1530.

Chattisham. Mary Revers, 1592.

Cookley. Wm. Browne, civ. & w., 1595, (P).

Cove, N. Arms, etc., Sengylton, 1498. Inscr., 1548, (P).

Cowlinge. Robt. Higham, civ. & w., 1599.

Cratfield. Arms & inscr., Warner, 1654.

Darsham. Ann Bedingfield, 1641.

Debenham. Arm. & w., demi, *c.* 1425. Arms, etc., Gawdy, 1650.

Denham. Anth. Bedingfeld, civ., 1574, (P).

Denstone. Henry Everard, arm. & w., heraldic, 1524. Lady, *c.* 1530.

Depden. 2 arm. & ws., kng, Waldegrave & Jermyn, 1572.

Easton. Arm, *c.* 1425. John Wingfeld, arm., 1584. Lady, 1601.

Edwardstone. Benj. Brand, civ. & w., 1636. Arms, etc., Brand, 1642.

Ellough. Arms, *c.* 1480. Lady, *c.* 1520, 1607. Arms, etc., 1612.

Elmham, S. Civilian & wife, *c.* 1500.

Euston. Civ. & w., *c.* 1480. Ditto, *c.* 1520. Lady, *c.* 1520. Arm. & w., *c.* 1530.

Eyke. Judge Staverton & w., *c.* 1430. Hen. Mason, eccles., 1619.

Flixton St Mary. Arms & inscr., Tasburgh, 1583.

Fornham All Saints. Thos. Barwick, physician, 1599. Sev. inscriptions.

Fressingfield. Wm. Brewes, arm. & wife, 1489.

Gazeley. Chalice, *c.* 1530. Arms, Heigham, *c.* 1500, Blennerhasset, *c.* 1560.

Gisleham. Arms & inscr., Bland, 1593.

Glemham, Little. Arms & inscr., Glemham, 1571.

Gorleston. Man in armour, of Bacon family, *c.* 1320.

Hadleigh. Lady, 1593. Civ., kng., 1637. Civ. & w., qd. pl., 1637. Inscr., *c.* 1560, (P).

Halesworth. Civ., demi, 1476. Lady & inscr., 1581, (P).

Hawkedon. Civilian and wife, *c.* 1510.

Hawstead. Boy, *c.* 1500. Girl, *c.* 1530. Lady, *c.* 1530. Sir Wm. Drury, arm. & 2 ws., 1557.

Holbrook. A man in armour, *c.* 1480.

Honington. Geo. Duke, civ., 1594.

Hoxne. Arms & inscr., Thruston, 1606. Ditto, 1613.

Huntingfield. Arms & inscr., Paston, 1595.

Ipswich—

    St Clement. John Tye, civ. & 2 ws., 1583. Wm. Cocke, civ. & w., 1607.

    St. Lawrence. Arms & inscr., Moor, *c.* 1580.

    St Mary Quay. Henry Toolye, civ. & w., kng., 1565. Lady, 1583.

    St Mary Tower. Notary, *c.* 1475. Civ. & 2 ws., *c.* 1500. Civ., notary & w., 1506. Civ. & 2 ws., on bracket, *c.* 1525. Arms, etc., 1697.

    St Nicholas. Civ. & w., 1475, *c.* 1500, *c.* 1600. Arms, etc., 1604.

    St Peter. John Knapp, civ. & w., 1604.

Ixworth. Rich. Codington, civ. & w., kng., 1567.

Kenton. John Garneys, arm. & w., kng., heraldic, 1524.

Kettleburgh. Arthur Pennyng, civ. & 2 ws., 1593.

Knodishall. John Jenney, arm. & w., 1460.

Lakenheath. Civilian & wife, *c.* 1530.

Lavenham. Civ. & w., shrouds, etc., 1486. Civ. & w., kng., qd. pl., *c.* 1560. Chrysom, 1631.

Letheringham. Sir John de Wyngefeld, arm., heraldic, 1389.

Lidgate. Priest, once in head of cross, *c.* 1380.

Livermere, Gt. Arms, Clarke, *c.* 1520.

Long Melford. L., *c.* 1420. Civ., *c.* 1420. 2 ladies, heraldic, canopied, *c.* 1480. Arm., 1577. Civ. & 2 ws., 1615. Civ. & 3 ws., 1624.

Lowestoft. 2 skeletons, *c.* 1500. Civ. & w., *c.* 1540, and sev. inscrs.

Melton. Pr. in acad., civ. & lady, canopied, *c.* 1430.

Mendham. Lady, 1615. Civ., 1616. Ditto, 1634. Arms & inscr., 1641.

Mendlesham. John Knyvet, arm., 1417.

Metfield. Arms & inscr., Jermy, 1504.

Mickfield. Peter Preston, civ. & w., qd. pl., 1617.

Middleton. Civ. & w., *c.* 1500. Anth. Pettow, civ., 1610.
Mildenhall. Sir Hen. Warner, arm., qd. pl., 1617. His son, ditto, 1618.
Monewden. Thos. Reve, acad., in gown, kng., 1595. Arms, etc., 1587.
Nacton. Arms & inscr., Fastolf, 1479.
Nayland. Lady, can., mutil., *c.* 1485. Civ. & w., *c.* 1500. Civ. & w., 1516.
Nettlestead. A man in armour, *c.* 1500.
Occold. Wm. Corbald, civ. & w., *c.* 1490.
Orford. Twelve civilian brasses, with ladies, *c.* 1480–1640. Civ., 1580, (P).
Pakefield. John Bowf, civ. & w., 1417. Pr. in acad., 1451.
Petistree. Francis Bacon, civ. & 2 wives, 1580.
Pettaugh. A civilian and wife, *c.* 1530, (P).
*Playford. Sir Geo. Felbrigg, arm., heraldic, 1400.
Polstead. Priest, *c.* 1430. Civilian and wife, *c.* 1490.
Preston. Arms & inscr., Ryece, 1629. Ditto, 1638.
Raydon. Elizth. Reydon, 1479.
Redgrave. Anne Butts, 1609.
Rendham. Chalice, etc., to Thos. Kyng, vicar, 1523.
Ringsfield. Nich. Garneys, arm. & w., kng., qd. pl., *c.* 1595.
Rishangles. Arms & inscr., Grimeston, 1599. Ditto, 1610.
*Rougham. Sir Roger Drury, arm. & wife, 1405.
Rushbrook. Arms & inscr., Badby, 1583.
Saxham, Gt. John Eldred, civ., 1632.
Sibton. Civ. & w., kng., 1574. Civ. & w., 1582. Ditto, qd. pl., 1626.
Sotterley. Arm., *c.* 1480, 1572 and *c.* 1630. Arm. & w., 1479. Lady, 1578, & inscrs.
Southolt. Margt. Armiger, 1585.
Spexhall. Arms, Baynard, *c.* 1460. Silvester Brown, 1593.
Stoke by Clare. Lady, *c.* 1530. Civ., 1597. Alice Talkarne, 1605.
*Stoke by Nayland. Lady, *c.* 1400. Sir Wm. Tendring, arm., 1408. Lady, heraldic, *c.* 1535. Arms, etc., 1590. Lady, 1632.
Stonham Aspall. John Metcalfe, eccles, in gown, 1606.
Stowlangtoft. Arms, Wingfield, *c.* 1500. Ditto, Ashfield, 1546.
Stratford St Mary. Edw. Crane, civ. & w., 1558.
Stowmarket. Ann Tyrell, child in shroud, 1638.
Tannington. Ann Dade, 1612. Arms & inscr., Dade, 1619. Ditto, 1624.
Thrandeston. Arms & inscrs., Cuppledicke, 1619.
Thurlow, Gt. Arm. & w., 1460. Lady, *c.* 1460. Arm. & w., *c.* 1530.
Thurlow, Little. Man in armour & wife, *c.* 1520.
Ufford. Civ. & 3 ws., 1483. Skeleton, etc., qd. pl., 1598. Arms, 1684.
Waldingfield, Little. Civ. & w., 1506. Arm. & w., 1526. Lady, *c.* 1530. Civ., 1544.
Walsham le Willows. Arms & inscr., Smalpece, 1602.
Walton. Wm. Tabard, civ. & w., 1459. Boy, kng, qd. pl., 1612.
Wangford by Southwold. Arms & inscr., Rous, 1635.
Wenham, Little. Thos. Brewse, arm. & w., canopied, 1514.
Westhorpe. Arms & inscr., Elcocke, 1630.

Wetherden. Arms & inscr., Daniell, 1584.
Wickham Brook. Thos. Burrough, civ. & 2 ws., qd. pl., 1597. Inscr., *c.* 1540, (P).
Wickham-Skeith. A lady, kneeling, *c.* 1530.
Wilby. Civ., *c.* 1530. Arms & inscr., Bayles, 1588, 1620, 1638, 1639.
Withersfield. Arms & inscr., Bury, 1579.
Wiston. Arms & inscr., Le Gris, 1630.
Woodbridge. John Shorlond, child, 1601.
Worlingham. Nich. Wrenne, civ. & w., 1511. Arms & inscr., Duke, 1615.
Worlingworth. Children, *c.* 1520. Arms, Barker, 1622.
Wrentham. Ele Bowet, 1400. Humphr. Brewster, arm., 1593.
Yaxley. Andrew Felgate, civ., 1598.
Yoxford. John Norwiche, arm. & w., 1428. Lady, in shroud, 1485. Civ., 1613. Lady, 1618, &
  inscrs.

SURREY

Addington. Thos. Hatteclyff, arm., 1540. Leigh, civ. & w., 1544.
Albury, Old Church. John Weston, arm., 1440.
Beddington, L., 1414. Cross, 1425. Civ. & w., *c.* 1430. 1432. Arm., 1437. L., 1507. All under
  stalls except 1432 and 1507.
Betchworth. Wm. Wardysworth, priest w. chalice, 1533.
Bletchingley. Lady, *c.* 1470. Priest, 1510. Civ. & w., 1541.
Bookham, Gt. Lady, 1433, 1597. Civ. & w., 1598. Civ., 1668.
Byfleet. Thos. Teylar, priest in almuce, *c.* 1480.
Carshalton. Nich. Gaynesford, arm. & w., *c.* 1490 (copper). Pr. w. chalice, mutil., 1493. Arm.,
  1497. Lady, 1524.
Charlwood. Nich. Saunder, arm. & w., 1553.
Cheam. Civ., mutil., *c.* 1390. Civ., demi, *c.* 1390, 1459. Civ. & w., 1458. Arm., *c.* 1480, (P).
  Civ. & w., 1542, (P). Inscr. & arms 1579, (P).
Chipstead. Lucy Roper, 1614.
Cobham. Adoration, *c.* 1500. Arm., *c.* 1560, (P).
Compton. Thos. Genyn, civ. & w., 1508.
Cranleigh. Resurrection, 1503. Priest, demi, 1507.
Crowhurst. John Gaynesford, arm., 1450. Ditto, 1460.
Croydon. Priest in cope, 1512. Wm. Heron, arm. & w., 1562.
Ditton, Long. Castelton, civ. & w., 1527. Hatton, civ. & w., 1616.
Ditton, Thames. Arm. & w., 1599. 2 civs. & w., 1580, (P). Civ. & w., 1582, 1587, *c.* 1587 and
  1590.
Egham. Anth. Bond, civ. & 2 wives, qd. pl., 1576.
Ewell. Lady, heraldic, kng., 1519. Lady, 1521. 2 ladies & civ., 1577.
Farley. John Brook, civ. & w., 1495.
Farnham. Benedict Jay, civ. & w., qd. pl., 1594. Lady, qd. pl., 1597.
Godalming. Civ. & w., 1509. John Barker, arm., 1595.
Guildford, Holy Trin. Civ., *c.* 1500. Maurice Abbot, civ. & w., qd. pl., 1606.

Guildford, St Mary. Civilian and wife, *c.* 1500.
Guildford, St Nicholas. Civ., 1677, (portrait medallion).
Horley. Lady, 1516, (P). Civ., *c.* 1510.
Horsell. John Sutton, civ., 1603. Thos. Sutton, civ., 1603. Thos. Edmonds, civ. & w., 1619.
★Horsley, E. Civ., demi, *c.* 1390. Bishop Bowthe, kng., 1478. Civ. & w., 1498.
Kingston-on-Thames. Robt. Skern, civ. & w., 1437. John Hertcombe, civ. & w., 1488.
Leatherhead. A civilian, *c.* 1470.
Leigh. John Arderne, civ. & w., 1449. Susanna Arderne, *c.* 1450. Trinity, 1499.
★Lingfield. Lady Cobham, 1375, 1420. Sir Reg. de Cobh., 1403. Arm., 1417. Lady, demi,
    c. 1420. L., *c.* 1450. Priest, demi, 1445, 1458. Priest, 1469, 1503.
Merstham. Civ. & w., 1463. 2 ladies, 1473. Arm., 1498. Arm. & w., 1507. Children, 1587.
Mickleham. Wm. Wyddowsoun, civ. & w., 1513.
Molesey, W. Arms & inscr., Brende, 1598.
Nutfield. Wm. Graffton, civ. & w., *c.* 1465.
Oakwood. Edw. de la Hale, arm., 1431.
Ockham. Walt. Frilende, pr., demi, 1376. Arm. & w., 1483.
Oxted. Priest, mutil., 1428. Lady, 1480. Child, 1611, and 1613.
Peper-Harow. Joan Brokes, 1487. Cross, 1487. Elizth. Woodes, 1621.
Puttenham. Edw. Cranford, priest, 1431.
Richmond. Robt. Cotton, civ. & w., 1591.
Sanderstead. John Awodde, civ. & w., 1525, (P). Inscr., 1586, (P).
Send. Laur. Slyffeld, civ. & w., sm., 1521.
Shere. Priest, 1412. Civ., 1512. Civ. & w., 1516. Lady, *c.* 1520. Sir John Towchet, arm.,
    c. 1525.
★Stoke d'Abernon. Sir John Daubernoun, sen., 1277. Ditto, jun., 1327. Lady, 1464. Chrysom,
    1516. Civ. & w., qd. p., 1592.
Thorpe. Bonde, civ. & w., 1578, (P). Denham, civ. & w., qd. pl., 1583, (P).
Titsey. Wm. Gresham, civ. & w., 1579.
Walton-on-Thames. John Selwyn, park-keeper, & w., 1587, (P).
Weybridge. 3 skeletons, *c.* 1520. Civ. & 3 ws., 1586. Civ. & 2 ws., 1598.
Witley. Thos. Jonys, civ. & w., *c.* 1530.
Woking. Joan Purdan, 1523. John Shadhet, civ. & w., 1527.
Wonersh. Elyot, civ. & w., 1467. Ditto, 1503. Inscr., 1578, (P).

SUSSEX

Amberley. John Wantele, arm. in tabard, 1424.
Angmering. Eden or Ellen Baker, 1598.
Ardingly. Wakeherst, civ. & w., can., *c.* 1500. Culpepyr, arm. & w., can., 1504. Ditto, 1510.
    Lady, 1633. Children, 1634.
Arundel. Pr. in cope, demi, 1382. Pr. in almuce, 1419. Arm., mutil. & w., can., 1430. Pr.,
    demi, *c.* 1450, 1474. Pr., 1455. Arm., 1465.
Battle. Arm., 1426. Pr., *c.* 1430. Arm., demi, 1435. L., 1590. John Wythines, vice-chancellor
    of Oxford, 1615.

Billinghurst. Thos. Bartlett, civ. & w., 1499.

Bodiam. Arm., mutil., heraldic, *c*. 1360. Pr. in shroud, 1513.

Brede. Robt. Oxenbrigg, arm., mutil. & w., 1493.

Brightling. Civ. & w., *c*. 1510, (P). Thos. Pye, child, kng., 1592.

Broadwater. Priest in cope, can., 1432. Inscribed cross, 1445.

Burton. Arm., 1520. Lady in a man's tabard, 1558.

Buxted. Pr. in head of cross, 1408, and several fragments.

Chichester Cath. Heart, *c*. 1500. Arms, Bp. Day, 1556. Wm. Bradbridge, civ. & w., qd. pl., 1592.

Clapham. John Shelley, arm. & w., her., 1526. Arm. & w., 1550. Ditto, qd. pl., 1592.

Clayton. Rich. Idon, priest w. chalice, 1523.

Cowfold. Prior Nelond, triple canopy, 1433. Civ., *c*. 1500.

Crawley. Lady, *c*. 1520.

Cuckfield. Arms & inscr., 1509. Arm., 1589. Henry Bowyer, arm. & w., qd. pl., 1601.

Etchingham. Sir Wm. de Echingham, arm., mutil., 1388. Arm., w. & son, canopied, 1444. Two ladies, 1480, (P).

Ewhurst. Wm. Crysford, civ., kng., *c*. 1520.

Firle, W. Arm & w., 1476. Arms, etc., Gage, 1557. 3 Gage brasses, *c*. 1595. Lady in shroud, 1638.

Fletching. Sir Edw. Dallingridge, arm. & w., heraldic, canopied, *c*. 1380. Gloves & inscr. to Peter Denot, *c*. 1400.

Framfield. Edw. Gage, civ. & w., qd. pl., 1595.

Friston. Thos. Selwyn, civ. & w., sm., 1542, (P).

Goring. Arm. & w., *c*. 1490. Arms, etc., Cooke, 1693, 1707.

Grinstead, E. 2 men in armour, 1505. Civ., sm. (misplaced), *c*. 1520.

Grinstead, W. Philippa Halsham, can., *c*. 1440. Arm. & w., can., 1441.

Hastings, All Saints. Thos Goodenouth, civ. & w., *c*. 1520.

Hastings, St Clement. Thos. Wekes, civ., 1563. John Barley, civ., 1601.

Hellingly. A lady, *c*. 1440.

Henfield. Thos. Bysshopp, civ., 1559. Ann Kenwellmersh, 1633.

Horsham. Thos. Clerke, priest in cope, 1411. Lady, 1513.

Hurstmonceux. Sir Wm. Fienlez, arm., canopied, 1402.

Iden. Walter Seller, priest, 1427.

Isfield. John Shurley, arm., kng., 1527. Shurley, arm. & w., 1558. Ditto, 1579.

Lewes, St. Mich. Arm., mutil., *c*. 1430. Braydforde, priest, demi, 1457.

Lewes, St Anne. Arms & inscr., Twyne, 1613.

Mundham, N. Arms & inscr., Nowell, 1580 (in old altar slab); Bowyer, 1594, 1610; Birche, 1627.

Northiam. Robt. Beuford, priest, 1518. Nich. Tufton, civ., 1538. Inscrs., 1553, (P), 1583, (P).

Ore, St. Helen. Civilian & wife, *c*. 1400.

Poling. Walter Davy, priest, demi, *c*. 1460.

Pulborough. Thos. Harlyng, pr. in cope, can., 1423. Civ. & w., 1452. Civ., 1478.

Ringmer. Arms & inscr., Mascall, 1631.

Rodmell. Inscr. to John de la Chambre, 1673, (P).

Rusper. John de Kyggesfolde, civ. & w., demi, *c.* 1370. Thos. Challoner, civ. & w., 1532.
Rye. Arms, *c.* 1600. Thos. Hamon, civ., 1607.
Shoreham, New. Civilian & wife, *c.* 1450. Arms & inscr., West, 1648.
Slaugham. John Covert, arm., can., 1503, (P). Rich. Covert, arm. & 3 ws., 1547. Jane Fety-
place, 1586.
Slinfold. Rich. Bradbryge, civ. & w., 1533. Lady, *c.* 1600. Arms, etc., Cowper, 1678.
Stopham. Bartelot, civ. & w., *c.* 1460, 1601. Arm. & w., *c.* 1460, civ. & w., 1462. Arm & 2 ws.,
c. 1630. Civ., kng., *c.* 1630.
Storrington. Henry Wilsha, ecclesiastic, 1591.
Thakeham. Beatrix Apsley, 1515. Thos. Apsley, civ., 1517.
Ticehurst. Man in arm. & 2 ladies, 1503, (P).
Tillington. Arms & inscr., Cox, 1697.
Trotton. Margt. de Camoys, *c.* 1310. Thos., Lord Camoys, K.G., & w., can., 1421.
Uckfield. John Fuller, civ., qd. pl., 1610.
Waldron. Arms. & inscr., Dyke, 1632.
Warbleton. Wm. Prestwyk, priest in cope, 1436.
Warminghurst. Edw. Shelley, civ. & w., 1554.
Willingdon. John Parker, arm. & w., 1558. Inscr., 1618, (P).
Winchelsea. Civilian, mutilated, *c.* 1440.
Wiston. Sir John de Brewys, arm., 1426.

WARWICKSHIRE

Astley. A lady, mutilated, *c.* 1400.
Aston. Thos. Holte, in judicial robes, and wife, 1545.
Baginton. Sir Wm. Bagot, arm., heraldic, & wife, 1407.
Barcheston. Hugh Humfray, priest in acad., 1530.
Barton. Edm. Bury, civilian, 1608.
Chadshunt. Wm. Askell, civilian, 1613.
Clifford Chambers. Hercules Raynsford, arm. & w., 1583. Lady, 1601.
Coleshill. Priest w. chalice, 1500. Lady, 1506. Eccles. in gown, 1566. Arms & inscr., Beresford,
1651.
Compton Verney. Anne Odyngsale, 1523. Rich. Verney, arm. & w., 1526. Arm., *c.* 1630.
Coughton. Sir Geo. Throkmerton, arm. & w., *c.* 1535. Arms & inscr., 1547 and 1580.
Coventry, Holy Trin. John Whithead, civ. & 2 ws., qd. pl., *c.* 1600.
Exhall. John Walsingham, arm. & wife, *c.* 1590.
Hampton-in-Arden. A civilian, *c.* 1500.
Harbury. Arms & inscr., Wright, 1685.
Haseley. Clement Throkmorton, arm. & w., 1573, (P).
Hillmorton. A lady, under floor, *c.* 1410.
Itchington, Long. John Bosworth, civ. & 2 ws., qd. pl., 1674.
Merevale. Robt., Lord Ferrers, & w., 1413.
Meriden. Elizth. Rotton, 1633.
Middleton. Sir Rich. Byngham, in judicial robes, & w., 1476. Arms & inscr., Fitzherbert, 1507.

Preston Bagot. Elizth. Randoll, 1637.
Quinton. Joan Clopton. Vowess, can., *c.* 1430.
Shuckburgh, Upper. Shukburgh, lady, *c.* 1500. Arm. & w., 1549. Ditto, 1594.
Solihull. Wm. Hyll, civ. & 2 ws., 1549. Wm. Hawes, civ. & w., kng., qd. pl., 1610.
Stratford-on-Avon. Inscr. to Anne, wife of Wm. Shakespeare, 1623.
Sutton Coldfield. Barbara Eliot, 1606. Josias Bull, civ., 1621.
Tanworth. Margt. Archer, kng., qd. pl., 1614. Arms & inscr., Chambers, 1650.
Tysoe. Priest w. chalice, 1463. Lady, demi, 1598. Arms & inscr., 1611.
Ufton. Rich. Woddomes, eccles. & w., kng., qd. pl., 1587.
*Warwick, St Mary. Thos. de Beauchamp, Earl of Warw., arm. & w., heraldic, 1406. Civ. & w., 1573.
Warwick, St Nich. Robt. Willardsey, priest, 1424.
Wellesbourne Hastings. Sir Thos. le Strange, arm., sm., 1426.
Weston-under-Weatherley. Arms & inscr., Saunders, 1563.
Weston-upon-Avon. Greville, arm. in tab., 1546. Ditto, 1557.
Weston-sub-Edge. Wm. Hodges, civ., 1590.
Whatcote. Wm. Auldington, priest, 1511.
Whichford. Nich. Asheton, eccles. in gown, 1582, (P).
Whitnash. Civilian & w., *c.* 1500. Priest w. chalice, 1531.
Withybrook. A civilian, *c.* 1500.
*Wixford. Thos. de Cruwe, arm. & w., canopied, 1411. Child, qd. pl., 1597.
Wootton-Wawen. John Harewell, arm. & w., 1505.

WESTMORELAND

Kendal. Alan Bellingham, civ., 1577.
Morland. Inscr. to John Blythe, pr., 1562, (P).
Musgrave, Gt. Thos. Ouds, priest, *c.* 1500.

WILTSHIRE

Aldbourne. Hen. Frekylton, priest, and chalice, 1508.
Alton Priors. Agnes Button, 1528. Wm. Button, from tomb, *c.* 1620.
Barford St Martin. Alis Walker, 1584.
Bedwyn, Gt. John Seymoure, civ., 1510.
Berwick Basset. Wm. Bayly, civ., demi, 1427.
Bradford-on-Avon. Thos. Horton, civ. & w., *c.* 1520. Lady, 1601.
Broad Blunsden. A lady, 1608.
Bromham. Lady, *c.* 1490. Baynton, arm., 1516. Arm. & 2 ws., 1578.
Broughton Gifford. Robt. Longe, tomb w. death, etc., 1620.
Charlton. Wm. Chaucey, arm. & w., 1524.
Chisledon. Francis Rutland, civ. & w., 1592.
Cliffe-Pypard. A man in armour, *c.* 1380.
Collingbourne Ducis. Edw. Saintmaur, child, 1631.

Collingbourne Kingston. Joan Darell, 1495.
Dauntsey. Sir John Danvers, arm. & w., 1514. Lady, qd. pl., 1539.
Dean, W. Geo. Evelyn, child, sm., 1641.
Devizes, St John. John Kent, civ. & wife, 1630.
Draycot Cerne. Sir Edw. Cerne, arm. & w., 1393.
Durnford, Gt. Edw. Younge, civ. & w., qd. pl., 1607.
Fovant. Geo. Rede, priest in acad., qd. pl., *c.* 1500.
Lavington, W. John Dauntesay, arm., 1559, (P). Inscr., 1571, (P).
Lacock. Robt. Baynard, arm. & wife, heraldic, 1501.
Melksham. Inscr. & arms, 1612, (P).
Mere. John Bettesthorne, arm., 1398. Arm., mutil., *c.* 1425.
Minety. Nich. Poulett, arm. & w., qd. pl., 1609.
Newnton, Long. John Erton, priest, 1503.
Ogbourne St George. Thos. Goddard, civ. & wife, 1517.
Preshute. John Barley, civ. & w., 1518.
Salisbury Cath. Bishop Wyvil, demi, in castle, 1375. Bp. Geste, 1576.
Salisbury, St Thos. John Webbe, civ. & wife, 1570, (P).
Seend. John Stokys, civ. & wife, sm., 1498.
Steeple Ashton. Inscr., (copper), 1730, (P).
Stockton. Elizth. Poticary, qd. pl., 1590. Potecary, civ. & w., 1596.
Tisbury. Civ. & wife, *c.* 1520. Laur. Hyde, civ. & w., qd. pl., 1590.
Upton Lovell. A priest, demi, *c.* 1460.
Wanborough. Thos. Polton, civ. & w., demi, 1418.
Westbury. Thos. Bennet, civ. & wife, 1605.
Wilton. John Coffer, civ. & wife, 1585.
Woodford. Gerrard Erington, civ., 1596.

WORCESTERSHIRE

Alvechurch. Philip Chatwyn, arm., 1524.
Birlingham. Thos. Harewell, civ. & wife, qd. pl., 1617.
Blockley. Priest in academicals, kng., 1488. Priest, kng., 1510.
Bredon. Arms, mitre, etc., for John Prideux, Bp. of Worcester, 1650.
Broadway. Anth. Daston, arm., 1572, (P).
Bushley. Thos. Payne, civ. & wife, 1500.
Chaddesley Corbet. Thos. Forest, civ. & wife, 1511.
Daylesford. Wm. Gardiner, civ., 1632.
Fladbury. Arm. & w., 1445. Priest in cope, demi, 1458. Arm., 1488. Priest, sm., 1504.
Kidderminster. Sir John Phelip, Walt Cookesey, arm. & w., canopied, 1415.
Longdon. Wm. Brugge, arm. & wife, 1523.
Mamble. John Blount, arm. & wife, *c.* 1510.
Stockton. Wm. Parker, civilian, 1508.
Stoke Prior. Hen. Smith, civ., 1606. Robt. Smith, civ. & 2 ws., 1609.
Strensham. Russel, arm., *c.* 1390. Ditto, can., 1405. Ditto & w., heraldic, 1562.

Tredington. Priest in cope, 1427. Priest in almuce, kng., 1482. Lady, 1561.
Yardley. Wm. Astell, Simon Wheler, civs. & wife, qd. pl., 1598.

YORKSHIRE

*Aldborough, near Boroughbridge. Wm. de Aldeburgh, arm., heraldic, on a bracket, *c.* 1360.
Allerton Mauleverer. Mauleverere, arm., her., & wife, sm., qd. pl., 1400.
Almondbury. Arms & inscr., Netleton, 1621, and other inscrs.
Anston. Arms & inscr., Hutton, 1662.
Aston. Arms & inscr., Melton, 1510.
Aughton. Rich. Ask, arm. & wife, 1466.
Bainton. Roger Godeale, priest w. chalice, 1429.
Bedale. Arms & inscr., Wilson, 1681, Samwaies, 1694.
Beeford. Thos. Tonge, pr. in amice, alb & cope, w. book, 1472.
Bentham. Arms & inscr., Fetherstone, 1653.
Birstall. Elizth. Popeley, in shroud, qd. pl., 1632.
Bolton-by-Bowland. Hen. Pudsey, arm. & w., heraldic, kng., 1520.
Bradfield. John Morewood, civ. & wife, qd. pl., 1647.
*Brandsburton. Priest, demi, on bracket, 1364. Sir John de St Quintin, arm. & wife, 1397.
Burgh Wallis. Thos. Gascoign, arm., 1566.
Burton, Bishop. Chalice, 1460. Lady, 1521. Estoft, civ. & w., 1579.
Catterick. Wm. Burgh, arm. & son, 1465. Wm. Burgh, arm. & w., 1492.
Cottingham. Nich. de Louth, pr. in cope, canopied, 1383. Civ. & w., 1504.
Cowthorpe. Brian Rouclyff, judicial, and fragments, 1494.
Coxwold. Arms & inscr., Manston, 1464.
Crathorne. Arms & inscr., Crathorn, *c.* 1410.
Darfield. Arms & inscr., Rodes, 1666.
Darrington. Arms & inscr., Farrer, 1684.
Doncaster. Arms, etc., Flower, 1662, Braylsford, 1683, Gibson, 1699.
Easby. Arms & inscr., Bowes, 1623.
Escrick. Arms & inscr., Robinson, 1636.
Fishlake. Arms & inscr., Perkins, 1673.
Forcett. Anne Underhill, recumbent, qd. pl., 1637.
Halifax. Arms & inscr., Barraclough, 1668, and other inscrs.
Hampsthwaite. A civilian, mutilated, *c.* 1360, (P).
Harpham. Sir Thos. de St Quintin, arm. & w., canopied, 1418. Thos. St Quintin, arm., 1445.
Hauxwell. Wm. Thoresby, civ. & w., kng., qd. pl., 1611.
Helmsley. Arm. & wife, *c.* 1480 and inscrs.
Hornby. Thos. Mountford, arm. & w., 1489. Fragments, 1443.
Howden. Arm., canopied, *c.* 1480. Inscr., 1621, (P).
Hull, Holy Trin. Rich. Byll, civ. & w., demi, 1451.
Hull, St Mary Lowgate. John Haryson, civ. & 2 ws., qd. pl., 1525.

Ilkley. Inscrs. 1562, (P). Arms, etc. Heber, 1649, Lawson, 1671.

Kirby Knowle. Arms, etc., 9 brasses, 1676–1770.

Kirby Malzeard. Civ. & w., kng., sm., 1604. Arms, etc., Dawson, 1640, 1735.

Kirby Moorside. Lady Brooke, kng., 1600.

Kirkby Wharfe. Wm. Gisborne, pr. in cope, *c.* 1480. Arms, etc., Ledes, 1564.

Kirkheaton. Adam Beaumont, arm. & wife, 1655.

Kirkleatham. Robt. Coulthirst, civ., 1631.

Laughton-en-le-Morthen. John Mallevorer, arm., *c.* 1620.

Leake. John Watson, civ. & wife, *c.* 1530.

Ledsham. Arms & inscr., Foljambe, 1658.

Leeds, St Peter. Sir John Langton, arm. & w., 1459. Arm., 1467. Chalice for Thos. Clarell, priest, 1469. Civ., 1709. Inscr., 1792, (P).

Londesborough. Margt. Threlkeld, 1493.

Lowthorpe. Man in armour, sm., 1417. Arms & inscr., 1665.

Malton, New. St Leonard. Arthur Gibson, kng., qd. pl., 1837.

Marr. John Lewis, civ. & wife, 1589.

Masham. Arms & acrostic inscr., Kay, 1690.

Middleham. Arms & inscr., Colby, 1727.

Moor Monkton. Arms & inscr., Hesketh, 1665.

Otley. Francis Palmes, civ., recumbent, qd. pl., 1593.

Owston. Robt. de Haitfield, civ. & w., 1409. Arms, etc., Adams, 1667.

Rawmarsh. John Darley, civ. & w., 1616.

Ripley. Chalice for Rich. Kendale, priest, 1429. Arms, etc., Ingilby, 1682.

Ripon Cath. Arms & inscr., Crosland, 1670, and other inscrs.

Rotherham. Robt. Swifte, civ. & w., qd. pl., 1561. Inscr., 1637, (P), 1688, (P).

Rothwell. Arms & inscr., Collings, 1682.

Routh. Sir John Routh, arm. & w., canopied, *c.* 1420.

Roxby Chapel. Thos. Boynton, arm., 1523.

Ryther. Arms & inscr., Robinson, 1619 & 1636.

Seamer. Arms & inscr., Lisle, 1694, and inscrs.

Sessay. Archdeacon Magnus, in cope, 1550, (P).

Sheffield, St Peter. Arms & inscr., Talbot, 1541, Lister, 1663.

Sheriff Hutton. Mary Hall, 1657. Arms & inscr., Wytham, *c.* 1480.

Skipton-in-Craven. A Holy Trin., 1570. Arm. in tab., kng., 1570. Arms, 1588.

Sprotborough. Wm. Fitz William, arm. & w., 1474.

Tanfield, West. Thos. Sutton, priest in cope, *c.* 1490.

Thirsk. Robt. Thresk, priest, demi, 1419.

Thornhill. Arms & inscr., Waterhouse, 1614.

Thronton-le-Street. Arms & inscr., Laton, 1664, Talbot, 1680.

Thornton Watlass. Geo. Ferrars, rector, in shroud, 1669.

Thwing. Arms & inscr., Stafford, 1671.

Todwick. Thos Garland, civ., kng., qd. pl., 1609.

*Topcliffe. Thos. de Topclyff, civ. & w., Flemish, qd. pl., (P), 1391.

Waddington. Arms & inscr., Parker, 1673.

Wadworth. Arms & inscr., Pierrepont, 1653.
Wath. Rich. Norton, judicial, & w., 1420. Arm., *c.* 1490.
Wellwick. Wm. Wryght, civ. & w., 1621.
⋆Wensley. Simon de Wensley, priest, Flemish, large, *c.* 1375.
Wentworth. Mich. Darcy, arm. & w., qd. pl., 1588.
Wilberfosse. Robt. Hoton, arm. & wife, sm., 1447.
Winestead. Arm. & wife, mutil., *c.* 1540, (P).
Wycliffe. Arms, etc., Wyclif, *c.* 1380. Wicklif, kng., qd. pl., 1606.
York—
　　⋆Minster. Archbp. Grenefeld, 1315. Elizth. Eynns, demi, 1585. Jas. Cotrel, civ., demi,
　　　　1595. Weathercock cut from inscr. of 1597.
　　All Saints, North Street. Thos. Atkinson, civ., demi, 1642. Symbols, etc., 1482. Arms,
　　　　etc., 1609.
　　St Martin, Coney Street. Christopher Harington, civ., demi, 1614. Arms, etc., Colt-
　　　　hurst, 1588.
　　St Michael, Spurriergate. Chalice for priest, 1466, and inscrs.
York City. Many inscrs. in 16 churches.

IRELAND

Dublin, St Patrick's Cath. Dean Sutton, in almuce, qd. pl., 1528. Dean Fynche, ditto, 1537.
　　Sir Edw. Fiton & w., qd. pl., 1579.
　　Christchurch Cath. 2 chil., 1 a chrysom, *c.* 1580.

SCOTLAND

Aberdeen, St Nich. Dr Duncan Liddel, large, Flemish, qd. pl., 1613.
Edinburgh, St Giles. Arms & inscr., Jas. Stewart, Earl of Murray, Regent of Scotland, 1569,
　　(P).
Glasgow Cath. Man in arm., Mynto fam., qd. pl., 1605.

WALES

Anglesey

Beaumaris. Rich. Bulkley, civ. & w., *c.* 1530.
Llanwenllwyfo. Civ. & w., kng., 1609.

Carnarvonshire

Clynnog. Wm. Glynne, child, sm., 1633.
Dolwyddelan. Meredith ap Ivan ap Robert, arm., kng., 1525.
Llanbeblig. Rich. Foxwist, in a bed, qd. pl., 1500.

Denbighshire
Llanfwrog, nr. Ruthin. Inscr. in path to church, 1867, (P).
Llanrwst. 6 lozenge-shaped plates, w. busts, Wynne fam., 1626–1671.
Holt. Skel., 1666.
Ruthin. Edw. Goodman, civ., 1560. Edw. Goodman, civ. & w., 1583.
Whitchurch. Rich. Middleton, civ. & w., 1575.
Wrexham. Skeleton, 1673.

Flint

Hawarden. Inscr., 1683, (P).
Mold. Civ., kng., 1602.

Glamorganshire

Llandough. Wenllan Walsche, lady, 1427.
Llangafelach. Qd. pl., 1631.
Swansea. Sir Hugh Johnys & wife, w. Resurrection, *c.* 1500.

Montgomeryshire

Bettws, Newtown. John ap Meredyth de Powys, priest w. chalice, 1531.

Pembrokeshire

Haverfordwest. John Davids, civ. & wife, qd. pl., 1654.

Index

Aachen, 15
abbesses, 54
abbots, 54
academic dress, 56
Acton, 25, 62, 69, 100
Acton Burnell, 38
Adderley, 98
ailettes, 67
aketon, 62, 65
alb, 52
Albury, 100
Aldborough, 45, 104
Aldershot, 100
Alington, Sir Rich., 42
almuce, 53–4
amice, 51
anchorite, 54, 55
Anglesey, 28
Antoing, 17, 33
Antwerp, 33, 109
apparel, 52
Appleton, 56
Ardingly, 44
armelausa, 56, 57
armour, fashions in, 61–74
Arundel, 75
Ashford, 27, 104
Ash-next-Sandwich, 75
Ashton, Henry, 49
Ask, Rich., 45
Askwith, 46
Aston Rowant, 25
Aughton, 45
Augmentations, Court of, 84
Aunsell, Susan, 49
Aveley, 33

aventail, 39, 62, 69
Aylesbury, 44

Bache, Simon, 51
Bacon, Sir - de, 25,   Adam de, 28
Baginton, 104
Balsham, 106
barristers-at-law, 58
bascinet, 64, 66, 69
Basingstoke, 19
Battle, 54
beards, 48, 58, 59
Beaufort, 80
Beaumont, Bishop Louis de, 18, 19
Beauner, Robt., 54, 56
Beeston Regis, 77
bevor, 64, 66
Beckenham, 105
Beddington, 101
Beeford, 51
Bekingham, Sir Elyas de, 27
bell founders, 46
Belvoir Household Accounts, 42
Benedictines, 54
Bergen-op-Zoom, 86
Berkhampstead, Great, 46
Berkhamstede, Abbot John, 28
Bibury, 82
Bierenghiers, Jehan, 17
Bigby, 40, 51
Bindon Abbey, 28
Bitton, 54
bitumen, 23, 37, 111
Black Death, 29, 37, 49
black letters, 97, 98
Blatherwyck, 40

Blickling, 75
Blount, Sir Hugh le, 25, Sir Michael, 41,
    Sir Rich., 42
Bodiam, 29
Bohun, Alianor de, 80
Bondues, Sebelain de, 17
Bookham Great, 58
boots, 61, 72
Boston, Lincs, 19, 58
Bottesford, 42
Bottisham, 27
Bowers Gifford, 25
bracket brasses, 24
Bramley, 77
Brandesburton, 45
Brasses, manufacture of, 15
        recasting of, 16, 42
        import of, 37
        losses of, 83–88
        rubbing of, 108–116
        density of, 125–6
Brasyer, 46
Braunton, 40, 90
Bray, 111
breastplate, 69, 70
Brightwell Baldwin, 98, 99
Brigitine, 56
Brington, Great, 27
Bristol, 43, 58, 84
British Museum, 79, 80, 110
Bromham, 90
Brook, John, 58
Broughton Malherbe, 81
Broxbourne, 104
Bruges, 29, 33, 79, 80, 86, 92
Bryene, Sir Wm. de, 38
Bul, Joos de, 79, 80
Bures, Sir Robt de, 25, 62, 100
Burgh, Lady Maud de, 28
Burnell, Sir Nich., 38
Burwell, 27, 45
Buslingthorpe, 25, 67
'butterfly' headdress, 75, 76
byrnie, 67

Cadbury, North, 101
calamine, 15, 42
Calvinists, 84
Camden's Annals, 86
Cambridge, Arch & Eth. Museum, 23, 93
Cameron, H. K., 16
Camoys, Lady Margt de, 28, 74
canopies, 24
Canterbury Cathedral, 24, 25
Canteys, Nich., 60
Cantilupe, Bishop St Thos. de, 28
cappa clausa, 55, 56
Cardiff, 78
Cardington, 105
Cary, Wilmot, 43
cassock, 53, 56
Castle Ashby, 51
Cellini, Benvenuto, 80
cementation process, 15
Chalfont St Peter, 90
chalice, 49
Chanterelle, Sir Pierre de, 26
chaperon, 56, 59
chapewe, 71
Chartham, 24, 25, 67, 69, 74, 104
Charwelton, 27, 40
Chaucer, 7
chasuble, 52
Chercq, 17
Chevening, 54
Chigwell, 44
Childrey, 104
Chinnor, 27
Chipping Campden, 111
chrysoms, 81–2
civilian dress, 58–61
Clayden, Charlis, 28
Clifton Campville, 24, 29
clock faces, 84
Cluny Museum, 26
Cobham, Kent, 28, 74
Cockburn, Alex, 46
coif, 57, 58
Cologne, 15, 17

Constantine, 76
copes, 49, 54, 55
Cople, 101
copperplate, 99
cork heels, 61
Corringham, 27
Coryton, 70
Cosmati, 21
Côte hardi, 76
Cotrel, Jas, 46, 101
Coues, Jacques, 17
'crackowes', 61
Crecy, 69
Creeny, 17, 44
Creke, Sir John de, 25, 62
'crespine' hair style, 76
crests, 73, 105
Crockford's directory, 112
Croft, 25
Cromfliet, 86
cross brasses, 24
cross staff, 53
Crowan, 25, 40
Croxden Abbey, 28
Croyden, 51
Croyland, Abbot Godfrey de, 28
crozier, 53
cuir bouilli, 69
cuirie, 67
cuisses, 64, 71
Culpeper, Eliz., 44
Cumnor, 43
Cumpton, Sir Robt de, 25
Cure, Wm, 41, 42
cyclas, 65

dabbing, 115
Dagenham, 58
daggers, 64, 66, 71
dalmatic, 52
'Daston' style, 38, 42
David, Gerard, 86, 87
Dean, Beds., 23
Deerhurst, 57, 58

Delamare, Rich., 66
Delamere, Abbot, 33
D'Elboux, 81
Dean, 98
Delft, 108, 109
Denham, 56, 89
Deynes, John, 60
Digswell, 79, 80
Dinant, 17
Dissolution, 84, 100
dowels, 37, 111
Draper, John, 65
Dunche, Wm, 41
Dundrennan Abbey, 18, 19
Dunstable, 79, 80
Durham Cathedral, 18, 19
Dymoke, Sir Lionel, 46

Easton Neston, 40, 81, 90, 93
Edinburgh, 46
Edlesborough, 25, 40
Edward IV, 80
Edward, John, 58
Egan, Brian, 111
Ellesborough, 92, 93
Elsing, 25, 64, 69
Elstow, 54
Ely Cathedral, 19, 27, 54
Emneth, 25
Emptage, Ann, 101
enamel, 25
Enfield, 105
engravers mark, 26
Eschallers, Thos d', 25
Esdaile, Mrs, 42
Evesham, Epiphany, 43
Evron, Abbey of, 20
Evyngar, 88
Ewell, 89
Ewelme, 7

farthingales, 78
Felbrigg, 39, 104, 112
Felbrigge Psalter, 49

'Fermour' style, 38, 40, 42, 70, 73, 81, 93
Filmer, Sir Ed., 44, 72
Fingeringhoe, 98
fireback, 84
Firle Place, 42, 48, 70
Firle, West, 42, 48, 77
fishmonger, 29
Fitzralph, Sir, Wm, 25, 37
Flemish brasses, 32–36, 60
Fliit, Thos, 59
Fontaine Daniel, Abbey of, 20
footscraper, 84
Fowler, Robt, 30
Foxle, Sir John, 111
Fransham, Geoffrey, 66
Fransham, Great, 66
Freshwater, 88
Fulham, 33, 36
Fulke, Dr William, 49

Gage, 42, 48, 70, 77
Gagnières, 19, 20, 31
gambeson, 65
garters, 61
gauntlets, 64, 68, 71
Gawthorpe & Sons, 44
Ghent, 17, 29, 33, 36
Gifford, Sir John, 25
Gloucester Cathedral, 44
gloves, 53
goldsmiths, 46
Gore, Nichol de, 27
Goring, 108
Gorleston, 25
Gosfield, 58
Gozlar, 15
greave, 71
Greenford, Great, 88
Greenhill, Thos, 101
Grenefeld, Wm de, 27, 49, 50
Grey, Jas, 46
Grofhurst, John de, 19
guige, 69
Gunby, 92

Gundrada, 19
Gurnay, John de, 28

habits, monks, 54
Haines, 44
Hainton, 90
hair styles, 58, 75, 77
Hakebech, 25
Hakebourne, Richard de, 23, 27
Halvergate, 46
Hampden Court, 42
Hanseatic League, 32
Hanson, Robt, 90
Hargreave, Geoffrey, 56
Harling, East, 74
Harlington, 92, 93
Harlow, 86
Harpham, 45
Harper, 101
Harpley, 28
Harsnett, Archbishop, 44
Hartshorne, 110
Hartz mountains, 15, 16, 32
Harward, Rich., 55
Hastings, Sir Hugh, 25, 64, Lady Magdalen, 101
Hatfield, 43
hats, 59, 75, 77, 81
hauberk, 62, 67
Hautryve, Dr, 56
Hawton, 25
helm, 69
Henry III, 21
heraldry, 103–5
Hereford Cathedral, 28, 66, Museum, 43
Herne, 75
Heselshaw, Bishop Walter de, 28
Hever, 28
Higham Ferrers, 19, 30, 49, 107
Hine, Reginald, 49
Hitchin, 49
Holme Pierrepont, 75
Honingham, 46
hoods, 54, 55, 60

Hook Norton, 23
Horncastle, 46
Hornebolt, 36
'horned' headdress, 75, 76
Horsmonden, 19
Humfre, Thos, 46
Hunstanton, 104
Hutton, 68, 80
Hylle, 56

Iden, Thos, 81
Impington, 105
incised slabs, 16, 17, 21
infulae, 53
Ingeborg, Queen, 32
Ingham, 27
inscriptions, 97–102, reading of, 102
Ipswich, 33, 35, 59, 60
Iseni, Sir Wm d', 25
Isleham, 86
Isleworth, 29
Islington, 29, 30

jamber, 71
jewellery, 78, 79
Johnson, Gerard, 42, 43, 48, 70, 86
            Cornelius, 42
            Nicholas, 43
judges, 56, 57
jupon, 64, 65, 69, 104

Kemsing, 27
Kendrick, A. F., 49
kettlehat, 71
Kimpton, 49
Kings Lynn, 33, 34, 107, 112
Knebworth, 51
Knifeton, Thos, 85
Kyllingworth, John, 56

Lambourne, 92, 93
lance rest, 68, 71
Latoners, Mystery of, 39
Laver, James, 78

Laycestr', Walter, 65
Lee, St Margt, 43
Leicester, 46
Leigh, Roger, 100
Lenham, 101
Lerinne, Perone de, 17
Limoges enamels, 19, 20
Lincoln Cathedral, 24, 88
Littlebury, 43
Llanfaes, 28
Lombardic inscriptions, 21, 23, 25, 26, 31, 97,
            letters, 78, 98
London, 25, 33, 40, 48, 65, 86, 88, 90
Long Acre, 43
longbows, 69
Long Melford, 105
lost brasses, 83
Louis XIV, 31
Lowther, John, 56
Luda, Bishop Wm, de, 27
Lydd, 43
Lytchett Matravers, 29
'Lytkott style', 38

Macclesfield, 100
Magnus, Albertus, 15
mail, 38, 39, 67
Maners, Abbot Rich, de, 28
maniple, 52
mantle, 58
Marblers, 39
Marden, 76, 77, 81
Margate, 59, 60, 61
mariner, 60
Marshall, Ed, 39, 44
Marsworth, 43
Masons, 39, 84
mass vestments, 48–53
Matiu le fondeur, 17
Matravers, Sir John, 29
Mayenne, 20
Mechlin, 86
Mentmore, Abbot, 33
Menved, King Eric, 32

merchants' marks, 105
Merstham, 81, 82
Merton College, 23, 27
Milan, 59
Milton, 58
Milton Abbey, 27
Mineral and Battery Works, 42
Minster-in-Sheppey, 25, 26
mitre, 53
monastic dress, 54–6, 92, 93
Moore, John, 85
Moreton, 40
Mortival, Bishop, 23
mosaic, 21
Mur, Canon Jean du, 17
Mymms, North, 33, 36

Nayler, Ed, 51
'nebuly' headdress, 74, 75
Newport, Wm, de, 28
Newark, 33
Newcastle-on-Tyne, 33
Newcombe, Thos, 46
Norbury, 26, 28
Norfolk school, 46, 55, 98
Norris, Malcolm, 39, Tobie, 46
Northbrook, Lord, 7, 108
Northwoode, Sir John de, 25
Norton Disney, 25, 91
Norwich, 27, 37, 44
notary, 59
numerals, 99
nuns, 54

Oddington, 82
Oise, 20
Okeover, 83
opus anglicanum, 49
Ord, Craven, 108, 110, 111
Ormiston, 46
orphrey, 51, 52
Oulton, 28, 102
Ourscamp, Abbey of, 20
Oxford, 56, 86, 98

palimpsests, 27, 29, 36, 40, 49, 59, 83–95
100
pall, 53
pardons, 100
Paris, 15, 26, 43, 'Paris' cap, 76, 77
Paston, 43, 84
pauldrons, 65, 66, 70
Payne, John, 68, 80
Pearson, R. H., 91
peascod, 65, 70, 72, 73
Pebmarsh, 25, 37
'pedimental' headdress, 76, 77
Penn, 72
Pershore Abbey, 67
Perth, St Johns, 19
Peryent, 79, 80
Peterborough Cathedral, 28
Pettaugh, 24
Peytone, Sir John de, 25
Phillips and Page Ltd, 110
picadils, 70, 73
pileus, 56
Pitstone, 22, 24
placate, 70, 73
poetry, 101
poleyn, 62, 65, 71
Polsted, Ann, 47
pomanders, 81
portcullis, 68, 80
pourpoint, 59, 65
Pownder, Thomas, 35
priors, 54
processional vestments, 53–4
puns, 101
Purbeck marble, 25, 26

Ramsbury, 22, 23
Redenhall, 28
rerebrace, 62, 71
rings, 53, 78
Ripon Cathedral, 34, 36
Rodmarston, 58
Roger of Sarum, bishop, 19
Rolf, Thos, 58

INDEX

Roman letters, 98, 99, 101
rosary, 59, 80
Rothwell, 29, 30
Royston, 84
ruffs, 70, 78

sabatons, 62, 64, 66, 68, 71, 73
saints, 106–7
St Albans Abbey, 28, 33
St Bartholomew, 31
St Catherine, 86, 87
St Cross, Winchester, 55
St Decumans, 43
St George, 26
St James of Compostella, 89
St Jerome, 46
St John the Baptist, 57
St John of Jerusalem, 92, 93
St John, William de, 22, 23
St Leger, Ralph, 68
St Maur, Lawrence de, 19, 30, 49
St Mellion, 42, 70, 77
St Michael, 19
St Quentin, Sir John de, 45
St Simon, 30
St Thomas of Canterbury, 53
Salisbury Cathedral, 19, 23
Sall, 36
Saltwood, 28
sandals, 53
Sandys, Sir William, 17
Santarem, Portugal, 23
Saunders, Dorothy, 44
Scheldt, river, 33
Scotland, 19
Sea Beggars, 86
Seal, 38
Sedgefield, 22, 24
Selwyn, Thos, 92
sergeants-at-law, 58
set square, 84
Setvans, 24, 25, 74, 104
Sheldwich, 82
Shepherdswell, 98

shield, 64, 69
Shiers, Robt, 58
shoes, 61
shrouds, 82
skeletons, 82
Society of Antiquaries, London, 40, 77, 85, 90, 93
Society, Monumental Brass, 84, 90, 91, 110
Somerton, 40
Southacre, 104
Southover, 19
Southwark, 41, 42, 43, 44
Spilsby, 45
spurs, 67
SS collar, 79–80
'Stafford' style, 38, 40, 93
Stamford St George, 46
starch, 78
'steeple' headdress, 76
Stephenson, Mill, 91, 112
Steventon, 43
Stewart, Jas., 46
Steyning, Philip, 101
Stoke, Kent, 81
Stoke by Nayland, 25, 44, 48, 64
Stoke d'Abernon, 24, 25, 67, 69, 71, 81, 104
Stoke-in-Teignhead, 27
Stokesby, 98
stole, 52
Stone, Nicholas, 43
Strethall, 40
Stubbs, Frances, 44
sundial, 43, 84, 86
surcoat, 62, 64, 67, 69, 104
surplice, 53
Sutton, East, 44
Swanton Abbot, 100
Swardeston, 101
sword, 69
Sydling, Abbot Walter de, 27
Syon, 56

tabard, 55, 56, of arms, 104
Taplow, 29

tasse, 65, 66, 68, 70, 73
Tendring, Sir Wm, 48, 64
Terling, 98
Terri, 57
Tewkesbury Abbey, 28
Thame, 83
Thames Ditton, 47
Thorneton, Rich., 88
Thornton Abbey, 19
Thorpe, 86, 92
Tor Mohun, 43
Topcliffe, 32, 33, 98
Tournai, 16, 17, 19, 29, 32, 33, 34, 36, 42
Tower of London, 41, 42
Treswell, R., 43
Trinity, Holy, 24, 100, 107
Trotton, 24, 74
Trumpington, 24, 69, 104
tunicle, 52
Twyford, 27, 28

Ulcombe, 68
Ullathorne, 110
unicorn, 7

Valence, Aymer de, 26
          John de, 21
          Margaret de, 21, 22
          William de, 21
vambrace, 71
Vavasour, Dame Anneys, 28
Verden, 16
Verdun, Theobaud de, 28
vexillum, 53
Victoria & Albert Museum, 49, 53, 79, 93
Visch, Rich., 86, 87, 92
Vliet, Hendrik van, 7, 108, 109

Wade, St Nicholas, 101
Wallingford, Abbot Rich., 28
Walsingham, Little, 28
Walsokne, Adam de, 34, Margt, 36

Walton-on-Thames, 91, 92
wambais, 65
Warenne, William de, 19
Warwick, St Mary's, 43
Washfield, 101
Wautone, Sir John de, 25
weathercock, 84–5
Weekley, 28
Wegeschede, Jacob, 89
Wells Cathedral, 28
Wenemaer, Wm, 36
Wensley, 33, 36
West, Edmund, 43
Westley Waterless, 25, 26, 28, 62, 67
Westminster Abbey, 21, 22, 23, 26, 80
Weston, Wm of, 100
Weybridge, 82
Whaddon, 25
whistle, ship's, 60
Whithorn Priory, 19
widows, 54, 56
wigs, 58
Wilpe, Bishop Yso, 16
Wimbish, 25, 26
wimples, 74, 76
Winchelsea, 19
Wittenham, Little, 41
Woodchurch, 27
Woodford by Thrapston, 43
workshops, 25, 37–46, 82
Wotton, R. de, 24
Wotton-under-Edge, 24
Wrotham, 105
Wyddiall, 27

Yateley, 43
Yealmpton, 89
York, 27, 37, 45, 46, Minster, 46, 50, 84, 85, 101
Yorkshire school, 46

zinc, 15, 16